MORE
THAN
WORDS

MORE THAN WORDS

Contemporary Writers on the Works That Shaped Them

Compiled and Introduced by

PHILIP YANCEY

Edited by

JAMES CALVIN SCHAAP

Baker Books

A Division of Baker Book House Co
Grand Rapids, Michigan 49516

Copyright © 2002 by The Chrysostom Society

Published by Baker Books
a division of Baker Book House Company
P. O. Box 6287, Grand Rapids, MI 49516-6287

Printed in the United States of America

Some of the material in this book was previously published by Word Publishing under the
title *Reality and the Vision*.

Library of Congress Cataloging in Publication Data

More than words : contemporary writers on the works that shaped them / com-
piled and introduced by Philip Yancey ; edited by James Calvin Schaap.
     p.   cm.
   Includes bibliographical references.
   ISBN 0-8010-6404-X (pbk.)
    1. Christian literature—Authorship. I. Yancey, Philip. II. Schaap,
James C., 1948–
  BR44 .M67 2002
  809′.93382—dc21   2002009127

For current information about all releases available from Baker Book House, visit our web
site:
                   http://www.bakerbooks.com

When he, the Spirit of truth, comes,
he will guide you into all truth.

JOHN 16:13a

CONTENTS

Contents

PREFACE

T he students I teach are overly fond, I believe, of a phrase they use with such frequency that it sometimes seems more of a mantra than a simple cliché. The entire phrase is just two words, but I see it in one of its various forms every time I ask them to write about a character or a relationship. The wording goes like this: "My grandfather's death was a very emotional moment for me because throughout my childhood he always took great pains to *be there* for me," or "Adam is a great guy because he makes a practice of *being there* for me."

My frustration rises with every usage, so I red-pencil the phrase and demand they unpack its meaning for the reader, rather than simply drop it in the sentence, where it often sounds altogether too much like some breakfast cereal jingle. With luck, I can, through a semester, successfully suppress its incidence. But with a new roll of students, I start all over again.

Those demographers who study my students' generation have long ago suggested that what is most endearing to their hearts is a desire to belong. More than any generation, they are, after all, children of broken marriages, latchkey kids, an entire generation lugged off to day care before they were capable of saying they'd rather not leave the family room. Their almost habitual use of "be there" as a testimony to their desire for deep and abiding loyalties is something they've earned, I suppose.

I'm not trying to be trendy or someone younger than I am when I suggest, as I'd like to now, that perhaps my students' most beloved phrase fittingly describes and defines the relationships which exist between the writers of the essays in this book and those writers the essayists cite as their own literary mentors; for if there is an attribute that links all of the contributions to this collection, it is their autobiographical soul. Each writer locates a moment or series of moments in his or her life when some literary master seemed, without a doubt, to *be there* for them—counseling, guiding, edifying. For most, the work of the masters was the

9

source of their own literary endeavors and continues today as a resource during those sometimes difficult long hours of lonely composition.

William Griffin remembers how one Shakespearean play per day brought healing when, as a young man, he was hospitalized. Jeanne Murray Walker recollects how the sights and smells and the simple day-to-day-ness of Alice Munro's fiction seemed to save her from her own lofty ambitions at a time when she was finishing her doctoral dissertation. "In Paul Tournier," says J. Keith Miller, "I met at last a living model of the kind of communication I was trying in a stumbling, uncertain way to find." When Madeleine L'Engle needed a certain kind of nourishment, George MacDonald would *be there* for her, widening her world, she says.

Being there is a phrase that is effusive with empathy, selflessness, and servanthood. And what you will discover in the essays in this collection, as well as the range of literary masters whose work is here defined—Milton, Dostoevsky, Donne, Kierkegaard, among them—is that these classic writers became, entirely without their own knowledge, a true blessing to the writers, who testify by way of their contributions to this volume. People feel called to a vocation for a variety of reasons, but it is interesting to note in the nature of these tributes, specifically, how often writers like Hans Christian Andersen and J. R. R. Tolkien create writers out of readers. The wonderful writers honored here were often instrumental in ordaining beginning writers into the life of letters, sources of inspiration and commitment and truth.

In my students' language, the literary masters here described—many of them long since deceased—performed a great kindness when their work, providentially, seemed to *be there* for those writers who needed them.

Maybe it's time I temper that red pencil.

JAMES CALVIN SCHAAP

INTRODUCTION

In an address delivered at Harvard University, Annie Dillard told of a visit to China in which she met with sixteen members of the Chinese Writers Association. The Chinese host leaned forward eagerly and asked, "Which are the best fiction writers in the United States? Whose fiction should we translate for China?" Dillard and her American colleagues weighed their response:

> The room in which a Chinese reader lives may, or may not, have a single 25-watt bulb. China has little paper, for printing books or anything else. How many trees should they fell to print what, and why? Doctorow? Mailer? Roth? Chinese peasants stack hay in the fields, for there are no building materials for barns. Still, we all know why books are worth it. But our books? Today's books? . . .
>
> The woman pours tea again, and we gain some time. We look around. Through the windows of the meeting room, we can see the street outside. Some men in the street are working with astonishing concentration at an astonishing task: they are lifting twelve-foot slabs of concrete. Each slab is fifteen inches across and four inches thick. The four men raise the slab without breathing; they carry it by ropes slung between bamboo poles on their bare shoulders.
>
> What novels have we got that will encourage these people not to throw in the towel?
>
> ". . . Which works should we translate for China?" We are struck dumb. Our six person delegation of U.S. scholars, publishers, and writers cannot think of a blessed thing to say. One man suggests *Lolita*. He receives a light, surreptitious kick. We appear never to have heard of any American writers in our lives.[1]

Each year The Chrysostom Society, a group of writers of faith, gathers together to consider a variation of Dillard's question—not works to translate for China, specifically, but works that will inspire us to reach higher and farther. Works that endure. As colleagues, we are seeking to raise each other's sights beyond the books of pure pragmatism and entertainment that fill most bookstores, and toward those which express what T. S. Eliot called "the permanent things."

In a nation that publishes over fifty thousand new titles a year, it is easy to lose sight of the almost sacred aura that once surrounded books. John Updike has written of the products of the *samizdat* press in Eastern Europe in the 1970s: blue carbon typing on onionskin paper, bound in leather, their titles stamped in hand-punched silver letters. The sight of such fragile books, so lovingly assembled, restored for him the archetypal sense of what a book was, "an elemental sheaf, bound together by love and daring, to be passed with excitement from hand to hand."[2] Across time and generations, books carry the thoughts and feelings, the essence, of the human spirit.

Great books do, at least. And in this collection we wish to pay tribute to those authors who have pointed the way for us. What books are worth passing on? Which ones should be read in the next century, and beyond? Which have influenced us as writers?

We offer here no "canon" of acceptable literature. No one coaxed us to agree upon a list of literary mentors. You will find that the constellation of people written *about* is as odd and diverse a group as the constellation of people writing. You will encounter the classics (Shakespeare, Milton, Dostoevsky), and also contemporaries (Bradbury, Waugh, Tournier). Some excel because of style, others because of content. The writers of these chapters selected their subjects on one criterion alone: Who has helped form you as a writer of faith?

※

For all their diversity, the authors discussed in this book nevertheless share a certain perspective on this planet and the people who populate it. In striking and varied ways, all these authors acknowledge the sober reality of the human condition, and they also offer at least a glimpse of vision that inspires hope.

Some of the authors focus on the grim reality. Solzhenitsyn and Dostoevsky, for example, both learned about human nature while serving time in a Russian labor camp. Dostoevsky, thrust into close quarters with peasants and prisoners of the lower classes, emerged with his nobleman's idealism profoundly shaken. Nearly a century later Solzhenitsyn entered prison with a different kind of idealism. A committed Marxist, he truly believed that his revolutionary government was serving the welfare of "the people" by punishing enemies of the state. Solzhenitsyn later reflected back on his change in perspective:

It was only when I lay there on rotting prison straw that I sensed within myself the first stirrings of good. Gradually, it was disclosed to me that the line separating good and evil passes, not through states, nor between classes, nor between political parties either, but right through every human heart, and through all human hearts. This line shifts. Inside us, it oscillates with the years. And even within hearts overwhelmed by evil, one small bridgehead of good is retained. And even in the best of all hearts, there remains . . . an unuprooted small corner of evil.[3]

A dawning awareness of humanity's essential helplessness—theologians would call it fallenness—helped nudge Solzhenitsyn toward Christian conversion. At roughly the same time, a young dandy named Thomas Merton was learning a similar truth, but in nearly opposite surroundings: the decadence of Manhattan. Three centuries before, John Donne had arrived at a remarkably similar "doctrine of man" while lying in a London parsonage, believing himself to be dying of plague. From such disparate training grounds, each of these writers went on to excel at portraying the reality of the human condition.

There are subtle pressures today—in the church, especially—for writers to alter the truth, to "touch up" reality, to avoid an obsession with the dark side of humanity. Shouldn't we rather focus on brighter things, and strive to elevate our readers with a lofty vision of what a human being should be? Shouldn't the heroes and heroines of our fiction more resemble Mother Teresa, and not the motley crew who populate the novels of Flannery O'Connor?

Art that endures, not to mention the Bible itself, teaches us otherwise. Some of the authors discussed in this book—O'Connor, Waugh, Kierkegaard—turn their gaze on the church. Redeemed people are still proud, cantankerous, selfish, and sometimes intolerant. Their one distinction is that their lives have been invaded by grace. They are not sanitized but forgiven.

Novelist Frederick Buechner defines faith as a form of "homesickness,"[4] and sometimes the church succeeds best of all in making us homesick for a better reality. But homesickness would be a cruel joke unless there is, in fact, a home. A brilliant depiction of reality will lead to despair unless the artist can also offer up a new vision. In some way, all the authors discussed in this book see beyond the reality of this world to a vision of a better one.

The fantasists, such as Tolkien, Bradbury, and MacDonald, create a new reality that sends echo waves back to this one. The reader who lives through fifteen hundred pages of suspense and tension and darkness in Tolkien's great trilogy may well feel, at the moment when the spell of evil breaks and the darkness of Mordor lifts, a gust of glory and freedom and light: an encounter with "joy beyond the walls of the world more poignant than grief," in Tolkien's own words.[5]

Milton took a more literalistic approach, adopting the outline of Christian theology and transforming it into a shining revelation of paradise, fall, and redemption. In a very different way, the poets and devotional masters discussed in this book also summon up a vision that carries a reader beyond nature, and toward God himself.

In fact, every author represented here renders both reality and a vision of a new, re-created reality. Perhaps that, more than anything, helps explain why they have endured, and why they have affected us contemporary writers so deeply. They proclaim to us the unembellished truth about the nature of the universe, and of ourselves; and they follow with a gentle hint of what the world could be, of what *we* could be.

Ironically, great literature, using a wide brush to paint the universals that apply to all humanity, inevitably leaves behind a fine trail of particularity. As you read the chapters in this book, you will observe deeply personal changes at work in the individual writers. Walt Wangerin tells how a weaver of fairy tales prepared him for everyday life in a troubled family. Steve Lawhead explains how the fantastic world of Tolkien disclosed to him the trade secrets of "Sub-creation." Virginia Stem Owens confesses that a Danish philosopher famous for his melancholy helped her cope with a family crisis. Richard Foster learned from the ancients how to manage a frenetic modern schedule; Emilie Griffin learned uncomfortable truths about her own vanity. Eugene Peterson became a better pastor by scheduling regular appointments with a long-dead Russian libertine; John Leax decided *against* a vocation in ministry by studying the life of a monk; Greg Wolfe felt drawn to the church by the writings of a novelist who often chided it.

We offer, then, a record of some of the ways we have been shaped and changed by literature. Popular culture, including popular religious culture, sometimes encourages what Dorothy Sayers called "the snobbery of the banal": people who look down on classical music as highbrow, who prefer lazy worship, who would choose television over a book any evening, who want art mainly as decoration for religious calendars and fiction mainly as another weapon in the arsenal of propaganda.

Those of us who make our living by writing feel such temptations too. South Africa, abortion, racism, the inner cities—these urgent problems need solutions, and they tempt us away from the quiet reflection that gives us strength to look at our world with the long view, the half-millennium view. We are tempted to write "how to" books on coping in this world, substituting the easier task of telling people what to *do* for the far more important task of telling them how to *be*. James Elroy Flecker once said, "It is not the business of the poet to save men's souls, but to make them worth saving." In the end, that is what art can do for all of us.[6]

In 1962 Alexander Tvardovsky, editor-in-chief of the Russian literary magazine *Novy Mir,* took some manuscripts home to read in bed. He thumbed through them at a high rate of speed, making snap judgments and tossing most of them into a mounting pile of rejects. He came to a manuscript by an author unknown to him, with the simple title *One Day in the Life of Ivan Denisovich*. He read ten lines. And then, as he later told a friend, "Suddenly I felt that I couldn't read it like this. I had to do something appropriate to the occasion. So I got up. I put on my best black suit, a white shirt with a starched collar, a tie and my good shoes. Then I sat at my desk and read a new classic."[7]

We don't expect you to change clothes every time you pick up a book by one of the authors represented in this book. But we do hope to awaken a thirst for nourishment of the spirit, the same thirst that Tvardovsky sensed after just ten lines of Solzhenitsyn's novel. We have collaborated on this book with one goal in mind: to spread the virus of good reading. May it prove contagious.

PHILIP YANCEY

1

THE DEVOTIONAL MASTERS
A Love Affair

Richard J. Foster

Desperation led me to the Devotional Masters. I was pastoring a little church in southern California that would rank as a marginal failure on the ecclesiastical scoreboards. I gave them everything I knew, but it was making little difference in their lives—or in mine. On any given Sunday few could remember what I had preached the Sunday before; worse yet, I couldn't remember.

Mind you, these were good people, and I was preaching solid, biblical sermons. The problem was that I was seeing Scripture from the vantage point of my impoverished twentieth-century experience of Christian life and faith. Although we had had all the charismatic experiences that abound in our day, and were using the best church growth techniques, and relied on the finest Bible study aids and small group programs, it all was an inch deep and a mile wide. Nothing seemed to lead us into experiencing the depths of Jesus Christ. So you can understand that the first

Richard J. Foster founded The Chrysostom Society; the Academy of Christian Editors; The Milton Center, which is housed at Newman University, Wichita, Kansas; and RENOVARE. He has written six full-length books including *Celebration of Discipline, Prayer: Finding the Heart's True Home,* and *Streams of Living Water,* in addition to numerous articles and forewords.

sentence I penned for *Celebration of Discipline* was an anguished cry from my heart: "Superficiality is the curse of our age."

I knew we needed more: more of God, more of his love, more of his presence, more of his power. And that led me to the Devotional Masters. To be sure, I had read them in times past. But then it was primarily an academic exercise; now I yearned for their intimate walk with God and firmness of life orientation. Oh, they had plenty of human frailties—harebrained ideas, strange choices, even inadequate theology—but in the midst of all their weaknesses somehow they had learned to know God profoundly. And so I turned to my neglected friends, "the communion of saints."

Bonhoeffer: Call to Commitment

As I sat in my shoebox of an office poring over these writings so ancient yet so modern, I thought back to my first real encounter with the Devotional Masters. I was a high school sophomore and a new Christian, zealous like all new converts. I had begun an in-depth study of St. Paul's Epistle to the Romans and was greatly moved by the theological depth and profound experience of the great apostle.

I was also discouraged when I looked around me. In my youthful naivete I had expected Christians to obey the call to discipleship. The biblical imperative is clear enough: "Offer your bodies as living sacrifices" (Rom. 12:1). But who was living it? In my youthful idealism, I could see no one walking in this way. I nearly despaired that perhaps the faith was a fraud. Maybe it didn't result in transformed lives after all.

In the midst of my quandary I discovered the writings of Dietrich Bonhoeffer. I clung to them like a drowning person does to a life preserver. Even now I look at my dog-eared copy of *The Cost of Discipleship,* its cover torn and held together with library tape, marked and underlined almost beyond readability, and I remember again my debt to this man martyred by Hitler's Third Reich. How many times as an idealistic adolescent did I ponder Bonhoeffer's words, "When Christ calls a man, he bids him come and die"?[1]

I cheered his invectives against "cheap grace," his term for "grace without discipleship, grace without the cross, grace without Jesus Christ, living and incarnate."[2] He spoke to my condition and the condition of so many I knew when he declared, "Costly grace is the gospel which must be *sought* again and again, the gift which must be *asked* for, the door at which a man must *knock.*"[3] These words and many like them kept me from abandoning the Christian faith.

Ironically, this man who affirmed my yearnings for Christian disci- pleship also released me from my clenched-teeth moralism. While urg- ing me to take the gospel seriously, Bonhoeffer freed me from taking myself so seriously. I remember one incident during an especially hectic time. I received a phone call from a friend who wondered if I could take him on a number of errands. Trapped, I consented, inwardly cursing my luck. As I ran out the door, I grabbed Bonhoeffer's *Life Together,* think- ing I might have an opportunity to read in it. Through each errand I fret- ted and fumed at the loss of precious time. Finally, at the final stop, a supermarket, I waved my friend on, saying I would wait in the car. I picked up my book, opened it to the marker, and read these words: "The second service that one should perform for another in a Christian com- munity is that of active helpfulness. This means, initially, simple assis- tance in trifling, external matters. There is a multitude of these things wherever people live together. Nobody is too good for the meanest ser- vice. One who worries about the loss of time that such petty, outward acts of helpfulness entail is usually taking the importance of his own career too solemnly."[4] I chuckle even now at that event. It taught me an important lesson: these "trifling, external matters" that seem so disrup- tive may actually be the voice of God seeking to free me a little more from a stifling preoccupation with myself. It is a lesson I must relearn daily.

I found a similar process at work when I returned to Bonhoeffer years later, in the midst of my spiritual doldrums with the church in south- ern California. That first congregation was good to me in many ways. But they were also ordinary folk, and fought as ordinary folk are prone to do. The conservatives would get mad at the liberals, and the liberals would get mad at the radicals, and the radicals (bless their hearts) just always seemed mad.

With such a cantankerous flock, I had abundant reason to grumble and complain, I thought. But Bonhoeffer showed me another way: the way of gratitude for the most trivial of things. His *Letters and Papers from Prison* are peppered with thanksgiving for the small gifts of life. Listen: "In the prison courtyard here there is a thrush which sings beau- tifully every morning, and now he has started in the evening too. One is grateful for little things, and that also is a gain. Goodbye for now!"[5]

Most moving of all was the way Bonhoeffer came to value his friend- ships while in prison. Following a visit by some friends on 26 Novem- ber 1943, he wrote:

So it really came off! True, it was all too brief, but that does not matter. Even an hour or two wouldn't be enough. After we have been cut off from the world here for so long, we become so receptive that even a few minutes gives us food for thought for a long time after. I shall often think of how the four people who are my nearest and dearest were here with me. When I got back to my cell afterwards I paced up and down for a whole hour, while my dinner lay waiting for me on the table until it got quite cold, and in the end it made me laugh when I caught myself saying from time to time, "How wonderful it was!"

I never like calling anything "indescribable," for it is a word you hardly ever need use if you take the trouble to express yourself clearly, but at the moment that's just what this morning seems to be. Karl [Barth's] cigar is on the table before me, and that's something really indescribable!

. . . It would be quite wrong to think that prison life is just uninter-rupted torture. Far from it. And visits like yours relieve it for days on end, even if they do stir up long forgotten memories. But that doesn't do any harm either. It reminds me once more how many blessings I had, and gives me new hope and resolution. Many thanks, both to yourself and all the others.[6]

These were words of life and freedom to me. Slowly, almost imper-ceptibly, I found myself growing in thankfulness for those dear, frus-trating folk in that first church. Bonhoeffer reminded me that disciple-ship, while it may be "costly," need not be sober or heavy. Discipleship, after all, means growing in grace and peace and gratitude.

St. Augustine: The Knottiness of Sin

Bonhoeffer, the first of the Devotional Masters I encountered, pro-vided a foretaste of what was to come in the years that followed. I remem-ber my discovery of the fifth-century Bishop of Hippo, St. Augustine. In his *Confessions* I found many familiar statements, the most famous being his prayer, "You made us for yourself, and our heart is restless until it rests in you."[7] I reveled in his famous conversion in a Milan garden: on hearing a child say, *"Tolle lege"* ("Take and read") and he "snatched up" the Book of Romans and found his "heart filled with a light of confidence and all the shadows of doubt were swept away."[8] I thrilled at his intel-lectual search from Cicero to "the Academics" to Plato.

But more than all these I was drawn to his story of the pear tree and his protracted musings about what, on the surface, appeared to be a rather trivial event. At age sixteen, Augustine, along with several friends, had stolen some pears—not for food, for they threw the pears away, but apparently for the sheer joy of thievery. After recalling this adolescent prank, Augustine launches into a brilliant meditation upon pride, ambition, sensuality, laziness, prodigality, emulation, fear, and vengeance. Like Adam and Eve before him, he recognized that the tree represented a lot more than fruit.

Perhaps I identified with Augustine's story because my very first awareness of willful disobedience to the ways of God involved a tree and its fruit. I was about nine years old (sin comes earlier nowadays!) and was walking through an orange grove on my way home from school. Suddenly I realized that no one would know if I picked some oranges—no one, that is, except God. Knowing that God knew, I picked them anyway. Like Augustine, I didn't eat the fruit, and, like Augustine, I too was driven to consider the sinfulness of sin. Out of this "trivial" incident I came to see that willful disobedience leads to a whole multiplicity of other evils, each building on the other and each necessary to hide the previous. I needed deceit to cover up the original act, and lying to make the deceit plausible, and so on—a process Augustine called "the whirlpools of vice."[9]

What I had learned from Augustine proved very helpful as I struggled with the problems of my first parish. That tiny church contained a microcosm of the tangled issues of life. Family feuds, rape, incest, alcohol, drugs—we had them all. People had such twisted and complicated histories, and I as their pastor—what was I to do? Well, Augustine refused to let me give easy, glib answers to what he called the "knottiness" of sin. He understood better than most how personal disobedience, institutional evil, and social corruption all have a way of working into the very warp and woof of our lives. Pondering the complexity of sin, Augustine cries out, "Who can disentangle this most twisted and most inextricable knottiness? It is revolting; I hate to think of it; I hate to look at it."[10]

But—and here is the good news—Augustine's life and writings make it clear that the Gordian knots of sin can be severed. The journey was arduous for Augustine and, make no mistake, it will be arduous for us as well. While the wonderful grace of God is free, it is not cheap. But it is grace and it does come to those who seek it. The word of the Lord through Jeremiah the prophet can be ours: "You will seek me and find me when you seek me with all your heart" (Jer. 29:13). This I taught to that little group in my first parish and the results were often startling.

Juliana: Enfolded in Love

The impact of those first encounters with the Devotional Masters led me into a lifelong journey of discovery. If I learned about sin from St. Augustine, I later learned about the depths of love from Juliana of Norwich. I was teaching a university class in which we were reading the writings of many of the great Christians: Bernard of Clairvaux, Thomas à Kempis, Martin Luther, John Calvin, John Wesley, and more. For one particular session I innocently assigned Juliana's *Revelations of Divine Love,* thinking only that it was appropriate for us to read this first book

21

written by a woman in English. When we gathered the next week, however, I found students in an uproar. We had discussed many great writings with intelligence, reason, even good humor. But this was different. No one sat back in proper academic detachment. Everyone was speaking, debating, even shouting. Some loved the book, others hated it, but all were passionately engaged.

As I sought to referee the discussion, I searched for a reason for this turn of events. How could a book whose only concern is the love of God cause such intensity? It espouses no political or social agenda. It embraces no questionable doctrine. It makes no practical applications to daily life. It was, I thought, an unlikely book to engender controversy, and yet there I was watching twentieth-century students spiritedly debating its contents.

The *Revelations of Divine Love* (sometimes titled simply *Showings*) is the mature reflection upon sixteen visions that were given to Juliana on 8 May 1373 when she was thirty years of age. Our classroom controversy centered around her passionate language of love. These students were not unfamiliar with such language—contemporary movies, books, and television shows have an abundance of it—but they clearly were unaccustomed to hearing it used in Christian devotion. Juliana writes, "The Trinity is our everlasting lover, our joy and our bliss, through our Lord Jesus Christ."[11] On another occasion she speaks of Jesus as "our clothing. In his love he wraps and holds us. He enfolds us for love, and he will never let us go."[12] Meditating upon the passion of Christ, she writes earnestly, "I desired to suffer with him."

Well, you can begin to understand the debate that was going on in the class—and in me. Is such language (and experience) appropriate for the life of Christian devotion? If not, why not? If it is appropriate, what difference should it make in the walk of faith? Our class began to realize that contemporary culture had conditioned us to think of passionate love exclusively in erotic and sexual terms. We all found Juliana illuminating many biblical passages such as the story of John—"the one whom Jesus loved"—laying his head on Jesus' breast at the Last Supper. At the same time, we found it hard to believe that this relationship of deep, holy intimacy could be right, could be true, could be ours.

Finally, one wise student asked for a show of hands. Who loved Juliana's writings, and who thought her worse than the Gnostics? As hands were lifted, I got my first clue to what was happening. Overwhelmingly, the women resonated with Juliana's work and the men found it problematic at best. *Aha!* I thought. The men, for whom contemporary culture seldom gives permission to express passionate love outside of an erotic context, found words such as these nearly incomprehensible: "Our lover desires that our soul should cling to him with all its might, and that we should ever hold fast to his goodness."[13] Conversely, the women, who are encouraged—no, urged—by society to express tenderness, could appreciate her words of intimacy: "As the body is clad in clothes, and the flesh in the skin, and the bones in the flesh, and the heart in the whole, so are we clothed, body and soul, in the goodness of God and enfolded in it."[14]

That day in that classroom Juliana was freeing us to look at God's love for us and our response of love with new eyes. No longer could we view the crucifixion in detachment and endlessly debate theories of the atonement. No, she drew us near to see "the body plenteously bleeding . . . the fair skin . . . broken full deep into the tender flesh with sharp smiting all about the sweet body. So plenteously the hot blood ran out that there was neither seen skin nor wound, but as it were all blood."[15]

No longer could we recite the Apostles' Creed as an intellectual affirmation only. Instead, those words of faith drew us close to the heart of Jesus where "praising him, thanking him, loving him and blessing him forever" became our preoccupations. These were some of the lessons Juliana taught us that day—lessons I am only beginning to learn.[16]

St. Francis: Buoyant Joy

I have found that one obstacle above all keeps people from the old writers—namely, that they are old. That obstacle never hindered me, for I had long since rejected the modern heresy of contemporaneity (i.e., if it is newer, it must be better). I reveled in the wisdom of the ancients. But I did fear one thing: I was concerned that they might corner me into a cold, heartless religion devoid of laughter and good sense. It was this very fear that led to my most unexpected and delightful discovery, and no one corrects that misconception better than the poor little monk of Assisi, St. Francis. I was simply not prepared for his buoyant joy and radiant life.

Paul Sabatier, perhaps the most authoritative biographer of St. Francis, wrote of Francis's missionary zeal, "Perfectly happy, he felt himself more and more impelled to bring others to share his happiness and to proclaim in the four corners of the world how he had attained it."[17] Francis sent out his Brothers Minor—Little Brothers—all over Europe with the task to "revive the hearts of men and lead them into spiritual joy." He called this humble band "God's Jugglers."[18]

These thirteenth-century Friars Minor not only preached but also sang. With the soul of a poet, Francis would improvise their hymns. Best known is his "Canticle of the Sun" with its celebration of Brother Sun and Sister Moon, Brother Wind and Sister Water—a joyous adoration of God as the Creator of all things. In *The Little Flowers of St. Francis* stories abound of how these early Franciscans lived inebriated with the love of God. Exuberant and joyful, they were often caught up in ecstasy as they worshiped.

A love for the creation certainly marked these simple Friars, who lived close to the earth and took special joy in it. On one occasion Francis and Brother Masseo went begging bread in a small village. Returning with a few dried crusts, they searched until they found a spring for drinking and a flat rock for a table. As they ate their meager lunch, Francis exclaimed several times, "Oh Brother Masseo, we do not deserve such a great treasure as this!" Finally, Brother Masseo protested that such poverty could hardly be called a treasure. They had no cloth, no knife, no dish, no bowl, no house, no table. Elated, Francis replied, "That is what I consider a great treasure—where nothing has been prepared by human labor. But everything here has been supplied by Divine Providence, as is evidenced in the baked bread, fine stone table, and the clear spring." They finished their meal and then journeyed on toward France, "rejoicing and praising the Lord in song."[19]

A joyous trust characterized their lives. At one time Francis gathered some five thousand Friars in an open plain for something akin to a camp meeting among the Brothers. St. Dominic and several other prominent people had come to watch the event. At one point Francis rose and delivered a moving sermon, concluding with the command that they not have "any care or anxiety concerning anything to eat or drink or the other things necessary for the body, but to concentrate only on praying and praising God. And leave all your worries about your body to Christ, because He takes special care of you."

Hearing this, Dominic was distressed at the seemingly imprudent order. However, within a short period of time people from all the surrounding towns began arriving, bringing with them generous supplies of food. A great celebrative feast followed as the monks rejoiced in this gracious provision of God. Dominic was so moved by the scene that he meekly knelt before Francis and said, "God is truly taking care of these holy little poor men, and I did not realize it. Therefore I promise henceforth to observe the holy poverty of the Gospel."[20]

How refreshing these stories were to me, and what a contrast they made to the modern stereotype of these people as morbid ascetics. St. Francis and many like him have permanently marked my understanding of true spirituality, teaching me that joy, not grit, is the hallmark of holy obedience. I found that the walk of faith is a merry abandonment to divine providence. Often I find myself chuckling or laughing in the most unorthodox settings, while preaching, for example. People often comment on my laughter when I'm preaching. It's even a bit embarrassing at times. God, you see, shares a little joke or points to the comical way in people and allows me to share in the humor. So I laugh.

I hope you understand that I am not referring to the silly, superficial "joy" flaunted in modern society, which produces laughter at the expense of others. No, through St. Francis and others like him we learn of a deep, resonant joy that has been shaped and tempered by the fires of suffering and sorrow—joy through the cross, joy because of the cross. Blaise Pascal once wrote in his journal, "Joy, joy, joy, tears of joy."[21] It was the experience of Pascal and St. Francis; it can be ours as well.

Woolman: Compassionate Prophet

But personal joy is not the whole story. As I continued my journey with the Devotional Masters, they kept pushing me to expand my horizons beyond a preoccupation with myself and my own spiritual state to a concern for the bruised and broken of humanity. In an odd twist, I found that these old writers brought new insight into my understanding of contemporary social issues. And no one did this more than John Woolman. I do not know when I first read *The Journal of John Woolman,* nor how many times I have read it, nor how many editions of it I have read. I do know that no writing outside of the Bible has meant more to me than Woolman's *Journal.* This simple Quaker tailor from New Jersey in the eighteenth century penned a journal that remains the most contemporary of all the religious journals. The issues Woolman pinpointed are the issues we wrestle with today: racism, consumerism, militarism. He dealt with these issues in a striking combination of both compassion and courage, tenderness and firmness.

I gained many things from John Woolman, but by far the most important was an understanding of the profound social implications of the Christian walk. After reading his *Journal,* I could never again separate love of God from love of neighbor, for Woolman rightly saw them as one commandment and not two. A faith that does not drive me to the hurting and bleeding of humanity is a false faith.

Woolman was at the head of a groundswell of antislavery conviction that was to assail and eventually abolish the practice of slaveholding among Quakers. This strong social action took place nearly 150 years before the American Civil War! John Woolman had perceived the dire consequences of America's bondage to the powers of racism and oppression. "I saw a dark gloominess hanging over the Land," he wrote. If people were not willing to "break the yoke of oppression," he saw that "the Consequence will be grievous to posterity."[22] It is a genuine tragedy that the rest of the nation was unwilling to heed his prophetic discernment.

As G.M. Trevelyan has said, "Close your ears to John Woolman one century, and you will get John Brown the next, with Grant to follow."[23]

The combination of a gentle spirit and a tough nature permeates Woolman's *Journal*. Out of toughness, he refused to use the products of slave labor, including sugar, and dye for clothing. Out of tenderness, he experienced "inward sufferings," knowing that his actions would distress and anger those who opposed him. One story from the *Journal* illustrates the kind of impact he had. On 18 November 1758 Woolman preached a powerful sermon against slavery, and afterward was taken to the home of one Thomas Woodward for dinner. Upon entering the house he saw black servants and inquired as to their status. Upon learning that they were slaves, he quietly got up and left the home without a word. The effect of this silent testimony upon Thomas Woodward was enormous. The next morning he freed all his slaves—in spite of his wife's objections.

Woolman's prophetic but compassionate ministry was immensely helpful to me and those with whom I worked in that tiny first pastorate. He gave us a model of an all-inclusive community of loving persons. He also helped us by his example of mighty wrestling over the issue of consumerism. We were struggling with our responsibilities, obligations, and privileges as part of a highly affluent culture. Woolman dealt with very similar issues on a personal level. A businessman, a tailor, and a nurseryman, he soon found that his trade "increased every way, and the way to large business appeared open, but I felt a stop in my mind."

Woolman was not tempted by an affluent lifestyle. Long ago he had, as he says, "learned to be content with a plain way of living."[24] Rather, for him the problem was twofold. First, there was the issue of marketing items that catered to people's vanity more than they served real needs. When he sold such a product, he felt it weakened him as a Christian. The second and deciding issue was the need to be free from "cumbers" in order to give full attention to the Lord's call upon him. In the end, he decided to cut back his business, which freed him to engage in a remarkable traveling ministry.

Woolman's *Plea for the Poor* is a tract for our times. Addressed to affluent Americans, it asks us to tender our hearts to the needs of the poor. It includes many practical suggestions on how we can identify with the poor and needy of the earth, especially those who "labor for us out of our sight."[25] Woolman even recommends that we take up the work of the poor for a time in order to feel their burdens.

All through those years of struggle, our little fellowship gained help from Woolman's insights. We too wrestled with our creeping materialism. We too were concerned about institutional structures that dehumanized those for whom Christ died. We too debated issues of war and peace. But Woolman not only warned us of the large idolatries; he also nurtured us in the small fidelities, whether we were dealing with the problem of overcommitments, or the ethics of business conduct. In all these matters Woolman taught us to have our hearts "enlarged in love."[26]

De Caussade: The Sacrament of the Present Moment

There is a tendency today to think of the great Devotional Masters almost as people from another planet, certainly as folk unconcerned with life in our hectic workaday world. And yet so often I have discovered just the opposite: these were people who sought to redeem and "hallow" the common ventures of life. Jean-Pierre de Caussade was one such person and his book, *The Sacrament of the Present Moment,* has changed forever the way I look at "ordinary" life.

I covet for you an experience akin to my first encounter with *The Sacrament of the Present Moment.* I was aboard one of modern technology's finest inventions for solitude—the airplane. Traveling from Santa Barbara, California, to Providence, Rhode Island, I had ample time to read through the entire book slowly, thoughtfully. Released from all interruptions—no telephone to answer, no meetings to attend, no letters to write—I was able to concentrate for the entire day on a single task. Quietly, I pondered each sentence and invited God's Spirit to interpret it into my experience.

The journey from Pacific Coast to Atlantic was long, but the inward journey I entered into that day was far greater. It seemed that I was reaching back across the centuries (or was I being reached?) to feel the pulse of this humble disciple of Christ whose heart throbbed with divine yearnings. I felt caught up into the communion of saints that day, and sensed that Jean-Pierre de Caussade had become my teacher in the life of the Spirit. It seemed that de Caussade had joined the cloud of witnesses of Hebrews 12 and was urging me to experience each moment—this very moment—as a holy sacrament. I felt a gracious invitation to cease my frantic striving for holiness and rest in the Light of Christ. That airplane trip became a hallowed time, a holy day, a sacramental moment.

This wonderful experience was followed by many more. None was quite so radiant as the initial encounter, surely, but taken together these "sacramental" encounters proved even more substantial and lasting in transforming the inner personality. Because of my readings in de Caussade, these persistent questions had begun to intrude upon the ordinary events of my day. "In what sense can this experience be a divine sacrament?" "How is Christ mediated to me through this task?" "How can the fulfillment of this present duty be a participation in the life and death of Christ?"

Please understand, I am not referring to "religious" tasks, such as prayer or Holy Communion. I could quite readily understand and experience their sacramental character. Rather, I was examining much more ordinary activities, the "stuff" that made up the bulk of my days—teaching students, answering correspondence, playing with my boys, repairing broken window panes, paying bills, washing dishes. How could these events take on sacramental significance?

This reality is perhaps the most common theme found in the writings of all the Devotional Masters. And yet, although not a new idea, it broke into my life with new force. Slowly, and without my conscious effort, a greater sense of wonder and spiritual wholeness began to make its way into my daily activities. Quiet worship and adoration began to flow out of (rather than in spite of) common tasks. Inward strength and spiritual graces began to slip into my heart as mysteriously as the life of God steals into us through the Eucharist.

I cannot witness that this has been, or is, universally true. More times than I care to remember I have endured my tasks without any thought for, or concern about, God's life being mediated to me. Often the present moment is not a sacrament but a burden. Some acts, such as my attempts to discipline the children (complete with angry shouts), still feel decidedly unsacramental. Yet in a strange, almost imperceptible way, even these events are not immune to this heightened awareness of the sacrament of the present moment.

De Caussade understood that our obedience to "the duty to the present moment"[27] is the path to holiness. If for us the duty of the moment is to fix the screen door or rake the leaves, then to engage in prayer and meditation instead would be "harmful and useless."[28] "No moment is trivial," observes de Caussade, "since each one contains a divine Kingdom, and heavenly sustenance."[29]

De Caussade beckons us to a way of living that eschews all sacred/secular dichotomies. For him nothing is secular since God's activity permeates all things, even the most trivial. He urges us never to look "for the holiness of things but only the holiness within things."[30] Even time itself is a sacrament for "time is but the history of divine action!"[31]

This duty to the present moment as the place where I find God is not always a welcome word to me. Perhaps you too find it difficult. Often I want to bypass this moment, this duty, in favor of some future moment—one that is more challenging, more stimulating, more rewarding. That, I assume, is the place where God will bless me, not here, not in this task. The simple truth, of course, is that the only place God can bless me is where I am, because that is the only place I am.

Take this writing assignment for example: there are many tasks that feel more important, more urgent, more honoring to God than putting these words on paper. And yet it is in fulfilling this task that I will discover God; for me this small work is "the sacrament of the present moment."[32]

As I mentioned earlier, this notion that the ordinary stuff of life is filled with spiritual significance is a theme that reverberates throughout all the Devotional Masters. They take our days and our hours and invest them with sacramental value. And they invite you, they invite me to discover that right where we are is holy ground, in the families we have been given, in the tasks we are assigned, among our neighbors and friends. It is this that makes living in our modern world bearable, even enjoyable. Indeed, it enables us, as George Fox put it, to "walk cheerfully over the earth."[33]

I began my journey among the Devotional Masters out of desperation, but it has not ended there. Over the years desperation has turned to delight and delight has turned to a deep and abiding friendship—a love affair with the Masters. I invite you to join me.

GETTING STARTED
WITH THE DEVOTIONAL MASTERS

DIETRICH BONHOEFFER. I would begin with *The Cost of Discipleship,* the best known of Bonhoeffer's writings. Based upon the Sermon on the Mount, it is a clarion call to "costly grace." Then, proceed to *Life Together,* which tells of a small, clandestine seminary at Finkenwald under the shadow of Hitler's Third Reich. Finally, sample *Letters and Papers from Prison.* Because it consists of material smuggled out of prison, the book has no orderly progression; you can dip in at any point and savor Bonhoeffer's insights.

SAINT AUGUSTINE. His *Confessions,* the granddaddy of all journal writing, is available in several translations (I use E. M. Blaiklock's). Some of the language will be strange to your ears, but you will be amply rewarded if you persist.

JULIANA OF NORWICH. Her classic work is *Showings.* Again, don't be put off by the language. These folk come from a different culture and a different century. Her visions are fascinating; add to them her reflections, and you will have plenty to chew on.

BROTHER UGOLINO DI MONTE SANTA MARIA. Don't try to reconcile every theological jot and tittle in his book, *The Little Flowers of St. Francis*. Just relish the delightful stories of these early "Friars Minor." The well-known stories of Francis's life are there, along with many lesser-known ones (my favorite is the account of how Francis freed Brother Rufino from a temptation of the Devil). Don't miss the stories about Brother Juniper or the sayings of Brother Giles.

JOHN WOOLMAN. A Library of Protestant Thought publishes *The Journal and Major Essays of John Woolman*. Enjoy the tenderness in Woolman's rather archaic words.

JEAN-PIERRE DE CAUSSADE. Kitty Muggeridge translated *The Sacrament of the Present Moment* from de Caussade's *Self-Abandonment to Divine Providence*. Please do not try to speed-read this book—it won't work. It is best to take a single paragraph or short section and live with those words for a week. And most of all, read with the heart.

2

SØREN KIERKEGAARD
Desperate Measures

Virginia Stem Owens

L et me give you fair warning. If you are a confirmed optimist, a Pollyanna by persuasion, someone who insists on looking on the bright side, you can forget about reading Kierkegaard. Nowhere within the considerable number of his published pages will you find a single silver lining. Only a brief gleam of gold here and there, or a point of crimson embedded in shadows, in the manner of a Rembrandt painting: a single speck of light set amid deep and brooding gloom.

It takes a certain temperament, I suppose, to appreciate the kind of writer or painter who sees the world that way. I suspect a predilection for gloom may be a product of physiology and weather. My husband, for example, says I like Kierkegaard because my favorite color is black. Still,

Virginia Stem Owens has written fifteen books on subjects as diverse as families and the new physics. Her newest work, *Living Next Door to the Death House,* profiles people connected in various ways to Texas's death row. She also served for five years as director of The Milton Center, an institute devoted to developing the talent of young writers of faith.

on several occasions in my life I have been relieved to find someone who has articulated the truth about the dark side of life. Every generation needs a writer who insists on stripping away the veneer of false security we so carefully protect and who tells us certain bare and bony truths about ourselves.

This dark, distorted Dane has been haunting the murky recesses of my life for at least a quarter of a century now. Some writers you grow into and others you grow out of. Few seem to move along beside you through life, revealing new facets of themselves as your own perspective changes. Kierkegaard is one of these. He has appeared in different guises as the conditions of my own life change.

My first brush with Kierkegaard came in the 1960s when I was a college student minoring in philosophy. What time or place could have been more propitious for our meeting? The civil rights movement was just beginning to heat up in Texas, and I was enrolled in the only integrated university in the state. President Kennedy was assassinated just thirty miles down the road. The world seemed to be turning upside down. Søren Kierkegaard, who is summed up in one literary encyclopedia as "rebel against secure bourgeois morality," would have felt right at home.

Students, many of them the first in their families to go to college, haunted Voertman's bookstore across from the campus, hungry for books like *Notes of a Native Son, The Plague,* and *Catch-22.* The very scent of freshly printed paper, the crack of a book's virgin spine, the physical heft of a volume fitting snugly between the thumb and the palm—these were the sacraments of books, words that could change the world, that could rip through the callused skin of hypocrisy and deceit to reveal the living heart of reality.

One searched for writers then whose encounter with the world seemed as desperate as one's own and who saw that its true reporting was a matter of life and death. That's what I found in Kierkegaard. Here was an iconoclast as passionate as James Baldwin, as stark as Camus, as ironic as Joseph Heller. But Kierkegaard also did something none of those other writers did. He ran, lance fixed, full tilt at the church.

Few of the voices we heard in the sixties wasted their breath on the church; to them she was just a dead horse they didn't stop to beat on their way to the barricades. But for someone like me, who had spent two decades of Sundays on oak pews, who had committed hymns indelibly to memory and rocked on the ebb and flow of a vast sermonic ocean, for someone who had learned most of her early aesthetics and all her rhetoric from the church, there was no avoiding that particular confrontation. For it was the church by whom I felt betrayed. This very mother, who had given me to understand that Jesus wanted me for a sunbeam, who had taught me to feel simultaneously guilty and safe—this same mother now appeared to be no better than Hosea's harlot-wife, a mouther of truths she daily betrayed.

She had taught me, for example, to sing about the little children, red and yellow, black and white, all precious in Jesus' sight. But by design and explicit policy there were no multicolored rows of faces in the Sunday school where I went as a college student. And furthermore, one was not allowed to call this rather glaring discrepancy to anyone else's attention. I knew because I had been personally requested by the deacons not to mention the matter.

There had been earlier altercations also, over "sword drills" with the Bible, Pack the Pew night during revivals, and other attempts to reduce spirituality to the level of a softball game. And once an adolescent sinks her sharp and implacable teeth into a betrayed ideal, nothing can assuage the hunger for vindication. By the time I got to college, both the time and I were ripe for rebellion. And Kierkegaard provided the manifesto for the revolution.

Kierkegaard had been brought up in an oppressively religious household. His father, whom he described as "the most melancholy man I have ever known," required him to wear dowdy old men's clothes instead of dressing like the other children at school. Though Kierkegeard and his father were exceptionally close, this youngest child recognized later in life that his father's religious understanding was exceedingly morbid. Thus, when Kierkegaard went off to the university—and found himself liberated from the gloom at home—he began to castigate in his journal "the strange, stuffy atmosphere which we encounter in Christianity" and "its narrowbreasted asthmatic conceptions."

From there he went on to criticize the "many people who reach their conclusions about life like schoolboys. They cheat their master by copying the answer out of a book without having worked out the sum for themselves."[1] Amen to that, I thought, as I looked around at the somnolent deacons in my church. Still, neither his quarrel with Christianity nor mine sprung from the rationale of atheism, which I had already dismissed as even more asthmatic and narrow breasted than religion. His rebellion was necessary in order to wrench what he had been taught into line with what he had experienced. In April of 1838, at the age of twenty-five, he wrote in his journal, "If Christ is to come and take up his abode in me, it must happen according to the title of today's Gospel in the Almanac: Christ came in through locked doors."[2] I understood in my bones that belligerent response to salvation.

And I also understood his extreme uneasiness, even after Christ had penetrated those locked doors, about taking up a false position in the world, his fear of being sucked into what he called "bourgeois mediocrity canonized by parsons." Being a Christian is an extreme position, not a safe one. One doesn't follow Christ down the middle of the road toward respectability.

Kierkegaard felt existence as keenly as a paper cut, and he expected that same intensity from others, especially those who claimed to be witnesses to the truth. Falling short of the glory of God was no mere theological formula for him. It was the image—no, more than that—it was the reality of man's impossible and paradoxical position in the world. And when, inevitably, he found the very institution set up to glorify God settling instead for mere respectability, he proposed desperate measures:

> Let us collect all the New Testaments there are in existence, let us carry them out to an open place or up upon a mountain, and then, while we all kneel down, let someone address God in this fashion: Take this book back again; we men, such as we are now, are no good at dealing with a thing like this, it only makes us unhappy. My proposal is that like the inhabitants of Gadara we beseech Christ to "depart out of our coasts." This is an honest and human way of talking, quite different from that disgusting, hypocritical, mealy mouthed trash about life being of no value to us apart from the inestimable blessing of Christianity.[3]

When I projected this scene into my own time, I envisioned the deacons from my church kneeling by the water tower on the only hill in town, along with the minister, fresh from blessing the noon meeting of the Chamber of Commerce.

Kierkegaard's refusal to let social decorum soft-pedal his painful witness to truth made him something of a hero among student radicals during his own lifetime. And when he died, his notoriety created a problem as to how the funeral should be conducted. His father had been close friends with the Bishop of Copenhagen; his brother was himself a bishop in the established Danish church. Yet Kierkegaard had refused on his deathbed to receive Communion even from his lifelong friend Pastor Boelen because, he said, "the parsons are royal functionaries, and royal functionaries are not related to Christianity." On the other hand, his popularity, especially among dissident students, was so great that his death could not safely be ignored. Finally, his brother, from whom Kierkegaard had been estranged for years, agreed to perform the funeral service in the main church in Copenhagen.

One of Kierkegaard's nephews, however, led a contingent of students into the church, a contingent who formed a phalanx around the body as a protest. The funeral service ground to a halt, and the brother who was presiding stormed from the church. Later at the cemetery, the student-nephew insisted on speaking about Kierkegaard's radical religious beliefs, over the dean's protest. When the young man persisted, reading aloud pointed passages from the Revelation about the Laodiceans who were neither hot nor cold, the dean left the cemetery in a huff. Kierkegaard was quickly lowered, unceremoniously and before he could cause any more offense, into the frozen earth.

I still get a good deal of enjoyment from that story. Today, when revolt is so easily dismissed as only a young person's prerogative, a passing phase, it encourages me that Kierkegaard remained on the barricades to the end of his life. His sharp edges never got ground down; he never accommodated. Even now that I am a teacher instead of a student, I lean on this frail and sickly Dane when I need shoring up.

Like one fall when I was approached about contributing to a Christmas ad to be run in the university newspaper. The ad copy proclaimed "Jesus is the reason for the season," which sentiment was to be followed by the names of "faculty friends" willing to talk to students about how "Jesus offers the solutions to life's questions." Harmless enough. Exactly. A catchy jingle, a promise of relief from mental confusion. But, as I tried to explain to the young solicitor on the phone, I cannot honestly tell students that Jesus will uncomplicate their lives. If anything, he will make them, depending on the person's temperament, either knottier or more interesting. And are "solutions" what life needs anyway? How does one "solve" life?

That is the story of how and why I was originally attracted to Kierkegaard, the unlikely, ungainly rebel who thumbed his large nose at the ecclesiastical establishment. A second and deeper level of attachment came not because he was a rebel but because he was a spy.

As a writer, Kierkegaard was consumed with the problem of how adequately to represent life as we live it. Like many other writers, he knew the uneasy sense of forging a fabrication, of perpetrating a fraud, when one makes abstract generalizations about life. Abstractions are necessary to analysis, certainly. But to represent man as no more than "a rational animal" is to falsify his total reality. People respond to life with more than just their minds. And not unless that other part, which Kierkegaard called passion, is taken into account, is one dealing with a true human being.[4]

The philosophers and theologians of his day had "forgotten what it means to exist," Kierkegaard wrote. And it showed in their writing. To reclaim the essential passion of human life, Kierkegaard felt there had to be a new way of writing, what he called "indirect communication." Reason can be explicit and overt. Passion, however, does not yield to logic. To capture passion, one needs the "cunning and craftiness" of a spy.

When I worked on my first book, I felt this same split between reason and passion slicing me in two. As soon as I started propounding abstractions, the life itself seemed to drain away from the words. A tinny

35

note of falsity crept in. And somewhere in the back of my head, a thin, impatient voice kept repeating, "You're only saying that because it sounds like it ought to be so. It makes sense. But is that the way life is? What does it feel like to be inside life?" I knew that as long as I wrote from that remote plateau of intellectual detachment, I would never get it right.

Once again it was Kierkegaard who provided me with a manifesto, not for a revolution this time but for writing. "I am like a spy in a higher service," he said in a book published after his death:

> I have nothing new to proclaim; I am without authority, being myself hidden in a deceit; I do not go to work straightforwardly but with indirect cunning; I am not a holy man; in short, I am a spy who in his spying, in learning to know all about questionable conduct and illusions and suspicious characters, all the while he is making inspection is himself under the closest inspection. Observe that this is the sort of people the police make use of. They will hardly select for their purposes the sort of people whose life was always highly honest; all that they take into account is that they are experienced, cunning, intriguing, shrewd people who can nose anything out, always follow a clue, and bring things to light.[5]

Getting it right, then, meant watching, observing—spying. One must pay attention to otherwise unregarded details—how a person's hair grows, the color of the skin between the eye and the bridge of the nose, the shape of the fingertips. The particulars that make a person himself and no one else. Such attention often involves a certain amount of pretense, even deception. You go to parties, you listen to conversations, smile at jokes, serve on committees—all those activities that comprise the ongoing human enterprise. But all the while you are attending to them for your own hidden purposes. You aren't what you appear to be. You are, in fact, a spy, seeking to discover what their life is like "from the inside."

I still have a letter from a reader outraged at a piece I wrote on patients in a V.A. hospital. I had worked as a volunteer there once a week, mostly pushing wheelchairs. "Vile ministrations" was the way the letter-writer described my activities. He felt I had only used the occasion of volunteer work to satisfy my writer's morbid curiosity about the grosser physical details of the patients' various conditions. Instead, he said, I should have been cultivating "a respect for persons."

Kierkegaard acknowledged the morally ambiguous position of the spy. He even imagined his own accusers saying, "your whole activity as an author is a sort of misanthropic treachery, a crime against humanity." But he also supplied me with my only defense against a charge of treason toward the human race:

I have not endeavored with the slightest fraction of the talents granted me to express the thought (which perhaps is what is meant by loving men) that the world is good, that it loves the truth or even is God. I have endeavored to express the thought that to employ the category "race" to indicate what it is to be a man is a misunderstanding. . . . Every single individual within the race (not merely distinguished individuals but every individual) is more than the race.[6]

In admonishing me to cultivate "a respect for persons," my own accuser, I felt, had reduced their reality to an abstraction like "human race." Persons in the abstract are slippery and elusive. How is one to have "respect"—or any other feeling—for them unless one first pays close attention to their individual incarnations? It was the particularity of each individual that Kierkegaard insisted was important, not some mathematical set called humanity. To preserve the particularity of an individual, that work calls for a spy. And only Kierkegaard's paradox— that each individual within the race is always more than the race itself— could justify such work.

My third engagement with Kierkegaard was occasioned by questions not about writing but about living. His answer—which is strictly speaking no answer at all—is the same as that of Paul and Jesus and Abraham: we live by faith. But "faith" has been bowdlerized, tamed, and packaged by the culture of which the church is a part, and when one in need of spiritual relief reaches for the faith-remedy, one often finds instead a cherry-flavored placebo.

No one, I'm convinced, should be allowed to claim faith who knows where his next meal is coming from or where he will sleep tonight. Faith is a word we should fear to have on our lips, lest it be defined for us in ways we cannot imagine. Kierkegaard would go further. You should not talk about faith, he would say, unless you are prepared to stand, like Abraham, with the knife raised over your child's body.

It was only this last year that I discovered what he meant. I know that I had read Kierkegaard's great book on faith, *Fear and Trembling,* long before, because when I went back to it a few months ago I found sections marked with a yellow highlighter. But I couldn't remember why I had once seen fit to mark those particular sections. The parts I marked now with a ballpoint pen were entirely different.

For Kierkegaard, Abraham was a pivotal figure. No one, not theologians, not philosophers, not ministers, had taken seriously enough the story of Abraham's willingness to sacrifice his son Isaac. He recounts the events of the story: the voice with the arbitrary, seemingly senseless instruction, the early morning march up Mount Moriah, building the pyre in preparation for the sacrifice, binding the child, raising the knife. Such a person, he points out, if we should encounter him as an actual man in the modern world, would either "be executed or sent to the lunatic asylum."

Even the effort to honestly imagine such a scene is immense. "I can think myself into the hero, but into Abraham I cannot think myself," Kierkegaard said. "Abraham I cannot understand, in a certain sense there is nothing I can learn from him but astonishment."[7] Why is it so hard for us to understand Abraham? Simply because he had faith and we don't. Not the kind of faith that can sacrifice the dearest thing in the world to a God we had believed was good. We had rather hate God first.

I know this. Not that I was put in quite the position Abraham was with Isaac upon Mount Moriah. God, being gracious, condescends to our weakness. It was not my own hand that held the knife over my child last year but another's. Nor was it death that the knife threatened, which would perhaps have been easier to bear. A clean end to a child in her twenties, full of energy and beauty, even that can be borne. But if the knife were used instead to disfigure and mutilate that life, what would become of faith then? I was to find out last summer.

In short, our daughter faced a custody suit for her two children, which, owing to no-fault divorce laws and the legal precedent that the sex of a parent or child cannot be a determining factor in assigning custody, she was by no means certain of winning. Money, however, is allowed as a determining factor, and money was something she didn't have much of. As the case developed over the course of the year, it turned, as these things tend to do, into a monstrous nightmare. Neither she nor her children could leave the state they were living in. Both her resources and ours were depleted. The knife, which would deliver such a blow as no mother could presume to survive, was poised to descend.

One prays, of course. There are, after all, those psalms about being delivered from one's enemies, rescued from those wanting to cause you harm. There are even psalms calling on God to do terrible, bloodthirsty things to your enemies. But after one has vented anger, grief, and vengeance, after one has implored, beseeched, raged, bargained, and threatened, after wearing out all the available emotions, what is left?

Faith, you might say. Don't kid yourself. The more accurate word, supplied by Kierkegaard, is resignation. At least that was the best I could muster. And there is a world, literally, of difference between resignation and faith.

What most of us aspire to when faced with some great reversal, some tragedy in our lives, is not faith at all but resignation. This in itself is a noble enough virtue; indeed, its nobility is beyond the reach of most of us. It requires a stoic acceptance of our fate at the hands of a God we do not and cannot understand. One who can call up this response to adversity Kierkegaard calls "the knight of infinite resignation."[8] He certainly does not scorn such a person. In fact, he admires the tragic hero, sketching for the reader how he imagines he would act in such a guise, had he, like Abraham, "been summoned to undertake such a royal progress to Mount Moriah":

> I would not have been cowardly enough to stay at home, neither would I have lain down or sauntered along the way, nor have forgotten the knife, so that there might be a little delay—I am pretty well convinced that I would have been there on the stroke of the clock and would have had everything in order, perhaps I would have arrived too early in order to get through with it sooner. But I also know what else I would have done. The very instant I mounted the horse I would have said to myself, "Now all is lost. God requires Isaac, I sacrifice him, and with him my joy—yet God is love and continues to be that for me; for in the temporal world God and I cannot talk together, we have no language in common."[9]

Kierkegaard knows that we may be tempted to find such a response even "more ideal and poetic than Abraham's narrow-mindedness."[10] Because what was required of Abraham is not reasonable. It is not even ethical. It flies in the face of all we think we know about God and his nature. To command a father to murder his own child doesn't accord with what we know either of truth or goodness.

Herein lies the difference, Kierkegaard points out, between resignation and faith, between the tragic hero and Abraham. "Faith begins," he says, "precisely where thinking leaves off." Only a paradox, radically disrupting our logical analysis, is capable of making murder into a "holy act well pleasing to God." The tragic hero remains within the bounds of ethics and can only gaze uncomprehendingly, in resignation, upon such a grisly scene.

I recognized all too well this figure of the knight of infinite resignation. All summer long, despite my prayers, despite my pillaging of the psalms, the best I could come up with was resignation. And I had only arrived at that point out of exhaustion. It takes enormous sums of energy to sustain anger. And I am one who, like Kierkegaard's hypothetical figure, arrives at a particularly painful emotional state ahead of time "in order to get through it sooner." I was trying to prepare myself for disaster. Yet every time I tried to think about the possibilities, my mind skittered spastically away from them. I could not bear to think about what might happen to my daughter if her children were taken away from her. This was the place where, as Kierkegaard said, "thinking leaves off." How does one think, maintain cool detachment, in such a situation? Yet faith did not begin there. Nothing began there. There was only a black abyss, filled with waiting terror.

I went to Houston to see a priest who had been my spiritual mentor for several years. He is a Dickensian character, with a red nose and a round paunch from too many cruise ship buffets. He is, in many ways, very childlike, and children don't make a virtue of resignation.

"Your problem is you've already decided on how this would turn out," he told me.

"Yes," I said. "The children won't be safe. My daughter will go crazy."

"You're not willing to accept any other answer?"

"No," I said.

"Well then?"

"Actually, I guess I've worked myself up to where I could accept another answer. But I'm afraid."

"I'm sure you are. But the Lord will protect those children."

"Maybe so. But what about my child? Rachel weeping for her children and refusing to be comforted? I'm afraid that I'll never be able to trust God again. I don't blame him, you understand. I know this isn't his fault. But I just don't know that I can trust him with my child."

He rubbed his chin. "You are in a pickle then, aren't you? Who will you trust?"

I didn't know. But that's when I found out what it felt like to be Kierkegaard's knight of infinite resignation, getting on his horse, heading for Mount Moriah, thinking, *Now all is lost. God and I cannot talk together; we have no language in common.* Life is a desperate thing and calls for desperate measures. And yet I now learned what Kierkegaard had known, that this "prodigious resignation" was only a "surrogate for faith."

The problem with resignation, as opposed to faith, is that it kills joy. The story might have the same ending in both cases, whether Abraham resigned himself to his fate or remained faithful. Either way, God might, at the last minute, have stayed the hand that held the knife. But if Abraham—or I—had merely resigned ourselves to whatever came, the last minute rescue could bring relief, but not joy. Resignation can only receive its children back again with pain. Only faith produces joy.

Kierkegaard made clear to me this distinction between resignation and faith. I could see that more was called for here than stoical acceptance, which is, after all, of one's own making. But how to come by Abraham's faith? How to offer up on the pyre of trust one's own child? Faith, like the world, must be created out of nothing, a feat beyond our powers.

The night before the trial date, I got grimly to my knees again and started to pray the same agonizing prayer I had prayed for months. I took a deep breath. But before I could even begin, it came: the lightness which Kierkegaard describes as the lightness of a dancer. The iron weight of resignation by which one subjects the unruly will—it suddenly lifted, fell away, evaporated.

Understand that the lightness was not of my own making. I was profoundly shocked, even a little embarrassed at first, to be feeling this way when disaster still loomed. I still had no sense of assurance about what exactly would happen the next day. I only knew that a hand was pulling me to my feet and offering to whirl me around like a feather. And though I had been weighed down for months, though my soul was as brittle and desiccated as a dry leaf, I still remembered what trust felt like. This was it.

"Most people," Kierkegaard said, "live dejectedly in worldly sorrow and joy; they are the ones who sit along the wall and do not join the dance."[11] I felt as though I had gotten an invitation to dance. I got up, dusted off my knees, and began to whistle.

GETTING STARTED WITH KIERKEGAARD

A small book called *A Kierkegaard Anthology* (Robert Bretall, editor) offers a sampling from many of Kierkegaard's works and makes a good place to start. The Harper Touchbook series used to put out the best editions of Kierkegaard's works, complete with illuminating introductions by the translators and helpful but unobtrusive notes. I have five different Kierkegaard Touchbooks; unfortunately, the only one still in print is *Purity of Heart*. If one has access to a used bookstore around a university, however, it's quite possible some may turn up there. On the other hand, it's probably best to start with the journals, now printed as a paperback under the title *The Diary of Søren Kierkegaard* by Citadel Press. And such classics as *Purity of Heart* and *Fear and Trembling* are constantly being reissued. The most marked up copy of Kierkegaard I have, though, is *The Point of View for My Work As an Author*.

3

THOMAS MERTON
Giving Up Everything

John Leax

The language of faith is dangerous. Most of us desire certainty but, like it or not, almost every statement about faith contains a contradiction. Yesterday, for example, Palm Sunday, I sat in church and listened to a sermon on self-denial. And as I listened, I grew gently angry. I thought, *I have lived my life trying to discover the self Christ is making of me, I will not deny what I have learned.* I wanted to stop the sermon. I didn't, of course. I sat silent, knowing that the sermon language was shorthand, that the audience knew what was meant, and that I, as usual, was being difficult. Perhaps the issue of self-denial was bringing back painful memories. "God writes straight with crooked lines," says a Spanish proverb, and it is true. The line he has traced across my life is all zigs and zags.

John Leax is professor of English and poet-in-residence at Houghton College. He writes poetry *(Reaching into Silence, The Task of Adam)*, as well as fiction *(Nightwatch, In Season and Out, Standing Ground)*, and essays *(Grace Is Where I Live)*. Most recently, he has published a collection of essays titled *Out Walking: Reflections on Our Place in the Natural World.* He has also contributed his work to several anthologies (*The Risk of Birth; Mindscapes; Wondrous Power, Wondrous Love;* and others).

At the age of twelve I was a runt of a boy with a soprano voice and a desire to please adults. This desire found its fullest expression in the life of Beulah Presbyterian Church. I remember one Saturday afternoon in particular. I was at the church office helping to fold bulletins for the next morning. The church secretary, making casual conversation, asked me what I wanted to be when I grew up. I answered, without ever having thought of it before that moment, "A minister." When she gushed in response, I knew I'd found my calling. Nothing else that I could imagine could possibly bring that depth of approval. And so I became, in my mind as well as in the minds of the adults, the good boy set apart to become a minister. It nearly ruined my life.

But let me jump to a later point of crisis. I did not become a minister; I became a writer and a teacher. For ten years I was an unsettled, apprehensive writer and teacher, unsure of my vocation. Had I missed my true calling? Desiring to settle the matter, I took a sabbatical. On it I would do two things; I (the potential preacher) would attend classes at Asbury Seminary, and I (the writer) would research a book on the Trappist monk and poet Thomas Merton. Both projects were directed at resolving my unease, for I knew that Merton had spent much of his adult life struggling with the conflicting demands of a contemplative and an artistic calling.

As part of my research, I scheduled a retreat at The Abbey of Gethsemani, where Merton lived out his vocation. And it was during that retreat that I encountered and accepted the self which Christ by his presence had been making and continues to make in me. I kept a journal, recording the events of the crucial day. From Matins, the predawn watch for the coming of Christ, to Compline, the evening yielding of the body to sleep and the care of Christ, I followed the canonical hours that had for twenty-seven years ordered Merton's life.

※

Oct. 12, 1977. I usually wear a small pewter cross. I couldn't find it when I was dressing this morning, so I called out, "Linda, I can't find my cross." She replied, only half ironically, "I'm sure you'll find it." I did, and I'm wearing it, but here in my tiny room in the Gethsemani guest house, I wonder about that other cross, the one I'm supposed to take up to follow Christ.

Nothing prepared me for this silence. I expected an absence of sound. I am overwhelmed by a positive presence.

The instruction sheet I was given tells me, "Retreats are made privately." The solitude I feel is a new thing, entirely unlike the solitude of the mountains or the river. It is a terrible confrontation with the noisiness of my own soul and mind. I want to make a noise, go introduce myself to the man down the hall. If I could talk about God, I wouldn't have to face Him. But here in this silence, all the talking is done by God.

Sext, 12:15 P.M. The long, narrow white church is filled with light. In the service, bells ring gloriously, and the monks begin to sing. In English. Because I sit, as inconspicuously as I can, in the back row of the balcony, I cannot see them. I only sit and listen. Sext, I have learned moments before, is a prayer to renew the fervor with which one begins the day. My lost cross, I discover, was waiting in the Scripture, "I have been crucified with Christ, and I live not with my own life but with the life of Christ who lives in me." Now, sitting before this notebook, finding my thoughts as I write them, I wonder. Have I the courage to pick it up?

None, 2:15. None is a petition for strength to persevere in the day's work. Like Sext, it begins, "O God, come to my assistance." The work that I am here to do, write about Thomas Merton, seems oddly unimportant in this place. Yesterday I felt as if I were coming to see Merton, I so identified Gethsemani with his life. Today he has fallen into the anonymity he desired. I am suddenly aware the only work worth doing is willing God's will. Marvelous paradox! To work at receiving grace, at becoming a person in whom God speaks to God.

Vespers, 5:30. I sit freezing in a wool sweater and flannel shirt, as the masculine strength of the monks' voices fills the church with praise. As the light fades the Light remains present. My imagination is stirred in a wholly natural way—but more than my imagination is at work.

Christ is present.

God in Christ has already done everything. I needn't worry about walking with Christ, as if it were something I could do. I need only sit down in His grace, be still, and listen. What will He tell me? The same thing He told Moses: I AM THAT I AM. He will reveal Himself, not things about Himself, and I will never want to move away.

Compline, 7:30. The twenty minutes of kneeling through the night office are minutes in which the Timeless inhabits time. Eternity is now. I am out of words. The Ineffable has taken them as He has taken the noise I have carried all my anxious, fretful life. "We will not fear the terrors by night, nor the arrow that flieth by noonday. . . . We have seen your salvation, O Lord!"

It is possible to live in Christ, in His peace and His grace. It is possible to be aware that in Him we live and move and have our being. And that in Him, through His perfected humanity which is continued in His Church, we are taken up into the life of the Trinity.

Epilogue, Oct. 14, 1977. My time here has been redemptive. My understanding of this place has deepened, as has my understanding of myself. I am called to images, to seeing through them the Christ who is the creator of all images. I am called to marriage, to living out the

metaphor of the incarnation in the realities of my daily tasks. I am
called to living among friends, to teaching students, to seeing in them
the Christ who redeems all. And I am called not to silence, but to the
silences between words that make the rhythms of poetry. I am called
to the way of Affirmation.

※

Nearly twenty-five years passed between that Saturday afternoon
when I was a twelve-year-old boy folding bulletins at Beulah Presbyterian Church and announcing my intention to be a minister, and that
bright evening at the Abbey of Gethsemani when I was freed to be what
God called me to be. Let me fill in some of the interval, tracing the crooked
line through time.

That line took its first twist at puberty. My voice did not change. It
cracked. Off and on for years. Always at the worst times. And I discovered I had a body that I had no imaginable use for. With that body came
guilt: no clear guilt related to any particular action, just a vague, ambiguous sense of confused identity. I had no idea who I was, and my self-defi-
nition as the boy who would be a minister failed to shore up the disin-
tegration. Peer pressure compounded the confusion.

When I left home to attend a prep school for boys, I learned I was good
at only one subject: English. I could write stories, but I could not do well
on exams, and I could not understand grammar. In my best subject I
muddled along at the rear of the advanced class.

Out of necessity I became an athlete. It was either that or suffer the
ignominy of being a reject. Since I was still a runt, I joined the wrestling
team. Over the next three years I grew from the lightest weight class to
a respectable middleweight class and earned a league championship. I
learned to wear my collar turned up, to walk with a swagger, and to sit
in the smoking section of the movie theater (though "in training" I didn't
smoke). I also learned to be a fake.

The most important thing I learned, I learned in the privacy of my
room the night I won my league championship. I wrote a poem describing the fear I'd felt as I stood alone on the mat, knowing I'd won the
championship, waiting for the referee to raise my arm signifying a victory that felt as empty and hollow as a defeat. For the first time in my
life, as I wrote that poem, I made contact with my deepest self. I learned
that words matter, that words are the way to truth, and I realized that
I wanted, needed, to follow the way of words.

But I did not understand, and had no one to tell me, that words are
tied by the incarnation of Christ to the Word. The two in my imagination became opposed. I could become a writer, or I could become a minister. I could serve myself or I could serve God.

In that state of mind I went off to college. My freshman year I was devout. In the atmosphere of a more-or-less secular institution, I held to faith. I participated in the life of a local church, and through the campus ministry program I did some lay preaching in small, rural churches. With a group of fellow Christians I edited a small literary magazine designed to serve as a witness. Whatever stories and poems I wrote were subordinate to our evangelistic cause, and it seemed to me that art fit easily into a life of Christian service. At the end of the year, convinced that my vocation was in the ministry, I transferred to an evangelical college.

There I quickly lost whatever sense of sureness I'd felt about my calling. I found myself within a community that defined commitment as conforming to the norms of a narrowly defined Christian life. Though devotional poetry fit within those norms, what I labored to write did not. Branded an outsider, I became an outsider. I began to attend, when I attended church at all, an Episcopal cathedral, and I began to read, simply because he was a Catholic and not an evangelical, Thomas Merton.

A few months later I discovered Merton's essay "Poetry and the Contemplative Life." Reading it, I thought I was reading about myself.

When Thomas Merton entered Our Lady of Gethsemani in December, 1941, he assumed that along with his name he would leave his poetry behind. For a time, he did. But in 1943, Robert Lax, an old friend from their undergraduate days at Columbia, visited him. When he left, he took with him the manuscript of *Thirty Poems,* which New Directions issued in late 1944.

Merton responded to the publication with indifference; as far as he was concerned more poems were out of the question. Lax returned for a Christmas visit, urging him to write. Merton records his reaction to Lax's enthusiasm in *The Seven Storey Mountain* and links it to an incident shortly after:

> I did not argue about it. But in my own heart I did not think it was God's will. And Dom Vital, my confessor, did not think so either.
> Then one day—the Feast of the Conversion of St. Paul, 1945—I went to Father Abbot for direction, and without my even thinking of the subject, or mentioning it, he suddenly said to me:
> "I want you to go on writing poems."[1]

To adequately comprehend the force of this direction, which struck Merton almost like a blow, one must understand that he was committed to what the early church called the *via negativa* or the Way of Rejection. This way, in Charles Williams's words, "consists in the renunciation of all images except the final one of God himself."[2] The order to continue writing poems meant to Merton the postponement of his deepest desire which he described as the desire "to pass through the center of his own soul and lose himself in the mystery and secrecy and infinite, transcendent reality of God."[3]

Nevertheless Merton accepted the direction and continued to write poems. His vow of obedience left him no other choice. Unfortunately, while the vow ensured the production of poems, it could not resolve the tension Merton felt between his religious and poetic selves. He revealed the seriousness of the tension in *The Seven Storey Mountain:*

> There was this shadow, this double, this writer who followed me into the cloister.
>
> He is still on my track. He rides on my shoulders, sometimes like the old man of the sea. I cannot lose him. He still wears the name of Thomas Merton. Is it the name of an enemy?
>
> He is supposed to be dead.
>
> But he stands and meets me in the doorway of all my prayers, and follows me into church. He kneels with me behind the pillar, the Judas, and talks to me all the time in my ear. . . .
>
> And the worst of it is, he has my superiors on his side. They won't kick him out. I can't get rid of him.
>
> Maybe in the end he will kill me, he will drink my blood.
>
> Nobody seems to understand that one of us has to die.[4]

Merton's conviction that writing would destroy his spiritual life, however, was a conviction that he eventually revised and then in practice rejected. What Merton's superiors recognized from the beginning, Merton learned slowly. In *No Man Is an Island* he effectively explains why he could not give up his poetry: "Nothing that we consider evil can be offered to God in sacrifice. We give him the best that we have, in order to declare that he is infinitely better. We give him all that we prize, in order to assure him that he is more to us than our 'all.'"[5]

Once Merton ceased to think of his poetry as an evil to be left behind, he began to understand it as a good not to be rejected but rather offered to the Lord. This led Merton to an appreciation of the Way of Affirmation. The Way of Affirmation, like the Way of Rejection, has as its end the loss of the believer in God. The means of achieving that end, however, involves looking closely at and then through the world, which, as the Psalms tell us, reveals the glory of God. That way is firmly established and made plain in the incarnation.

For most Christians, the Way of Affirmation is the dominant way. It is the way of marriage, the way of art, the way of politics, the way of economics. It is, in short, the way of doing all things to the glory of God. It is also a dangerous way, for the things of this world can become interesting in themselves, and the wise Christian usually tempers his affirmation with selected negations. The normal Christian way, then, can be viewed as a balancing of the two mystical ways.

But the life of Thomas Merton was not that of an ordinary Christian. Both his monastic vows and his priestly orders ruled out the simple balancing act of the layman. *The Seven Storey Mountain,* as well as the numerous recollections published since his death by his friends, shows Merton to have been incapable of doing anything halfway. Edward Rice in *The Man in the Sycamore Tree,* a popular biography he appropriately subtitles "An Entertainment," describes his first encounter with the pre-conversion Merton at Columbia University:

> One day, after I first began to submit drawings to *Jester,* amid all the confusion of the fourth floor, I heard an incredible, noisy, barrel-house blues piano drowning out everything else (my first impression of Merton was that he was the noisiest bastard I had ever met), like four men playing at once. "Who is that crowd playing the piano?" I asked. "Only Merton," said Gene Williams. Merton soon came bustling into *Jester.* He was always full of energy and seemed unchanged from day to day, cracking jokes, denouncing the Fascists, squares, being violently active, writing, drawing, involved in everything . . . Noisy. Authoritative. Sure of himself. But behind it all was that relentless, restless search to learn who he was.[6]

After his conversion, Merton carried this exuberance into his spiritual life, where it became a factor in his decision to enter Gethsemani rather than joining Catherine de Heuck Doherty in her work at Friendship House, Harlem. Interestingly, as he made his choice (recorded in the last entry of *The Secular Journal of Thomas Merton*), writing seemed to be on his mind:

> Today I think: should I be going to Harlem, or to the Trappists? Why doesn't this idea of the Trappists leave me? . . . I would have to renounce more in entering the Trappists. That would be one place where I would have to give up everything. . . . Perhaps I cling to my independence, to the chance to write. . . . It seems monstrous at the moment that I should consider my writing important enough to enter into the question. . . . I return to the idea again and again: "Give up everything, give up everything!"[7]

An appealing romanticism was involved, an excitement in going the whole route that his personality couldn't resist. But in seeing the Way of Rejection as a challenge worthy of his whole life, he also held on to a false self, an image of himself poor and sporting the tonsured haircut of a humble monk, and involved that false self in making his choice. He would assign the values to what he would give up, and he would give up what he considered worthless to gain the experience of God he wanted. As a result he contemptuously turned his back on the world.

Merton's early journals from the monastery are filled with references to giving up writing, and it is clear that, had his circumstances not been altered, Merton probably would have sacrificed his art. In 1948, however, his abbot died, and the order's vicar general traveled to Gethsemani for the funeral and the election of a new abbot. Merton served as his interpreter and secretary. Consequently, when Dom Gabriel Sortais was called to Louisville, Merton accompanied him, leaving the monastery for the first time in seven years. He recounts it in *The Sign of Jonas:*

> We drove into town with Senator Dawson, a neighbor of the monastery, and all the while I wondered how I would react at meeting once again face to face, the wicked world. I met the world and I found it no longer so wicked after all. Perhaps the things I had resented about the world when I left it were defects of my own that I had projected upon it. Now, on the contrary, I found that everything stirred me with a deep and mute sense of compassion. Perhaps some of the people we saw going about the streets were hard and tough . . . but I did not stop to observe it because I seemed to have lost an eye for the merely exterior detail and to have discovered, instead, a deep sense of respect and love and pity for the souls that such details never fully reveal. I went through the city, realizing for the first time in my life how good are all the people in the world and how much value they have in the sight of God.[8]

In the course of six hours, Merton's life had been turned around. He had left the monastery, committed to rejecting all images except the final one of God himself. He returned affirming, for the first time, the image called Man and seeing through that image the presence and grace of the Creator of all images. The possibility of a dual calling to poetry and to contemplation opened up to him. He responded by going forward. A year later he wrote: "And yet it seems to me that writing, far from being an obstacle to spiritual perfection in my own life, has become one of the conditions on which my perfection will depend."[9]

The conflict that had tormented Merton for seven years could not be laid aside in one dramatic affirmation. His doubts recurred, but he continued to write by choice. And as he gave up his largely selfish desire to be totally absorbed in contemplation, as he willed instead God's will, he found that the inner war between his religious and poetic vocations quieted, not because he had resolved them in theory but because God had willed them reconciled in practice.

When Merton struggled to comprehend the nature of his dual calling to contemplation and poetry, he had a spiritual tradition to frame the terms of his conflict, and he had superiors to whom he owed obedience to give him direction. When I faced a similar conflict between my desire to write and my perceived "calling" to ministry, I had neither a tradition that could comprehend an artistic vocation nor a spiritual leader to turn to. In confusion I dropped out of college and began to work as a laborer. I wanted to buy time and think. But in 1964 only failures left school, and I felt constant pressure to get my life back in order so that I could return to the straight and narrow road to Christian service I'd started out on.

I remember most clearly an encounter with the minister of the church my family was then attending. I idolized him. He was an eloquent and perceptive preacher. I typed out a group of my poems, sent them to him, and made an appointment to talk with him about vocation. We met one evening in his office. After about an hour of good talk, he rose to bring our session to a close. I resisted and asked about the poems. "Young man," he said, "it's time for you to put that nonsense behind you and get on with what's important in your life."

I went out in silence and closed behind me a door I never again went through. In the strangest possible way, writing the crookedest line imaginable, God had fixed my vocation, for when I closed that door, I closed it with a cold determination to go without approval, to be an artist and not a minister.

I was not, however, content. Though my act of rebellion could determine my vocation and set me on the right path, it could not form the basis for that vocation. I had to learn that another way.

I turned back to Merton. With greater intellectual maturity, I understood that the difficult struggle to accept a dual vocation he wrote about in "Poetry and the Contemplative Life" was nothing like my struggle. Merton was fighting against his past, a past in which poetry represented to him the false values of fame and ambition. My struggle, instead, was like the hidden struggle Merton's superiors had recognized lurking behind Merton's words: an inability to accept the worth of what my deepest self knew to be its need, the making of poems. Desperate for approval, my false self had latched onto the "ministry" course that had brought me the strongest and quickest approval I'd ever felt.

I did not understand these distinctions when I walked into the Abbey of Gethsemani that fall in 1977. But I learned them there. In *Conjec-tures of a Guilty Bystander,* one of his last books, Merton wrote, "A personal crisis occurs when one becomes aware of apparently irreconcilable opposites in oneself. . . . A personal crisis is creative and salutary if one can accept the conflict and restore unity on a higher level, incorporating the opposed elements in a higher unity."[10] What I learned was that the self I had to sacrifice was not the poem-making self that brought me disapproval but the praise-seeking self that would have used the ministry to gratify its basest desire.

GETTING STARTED WITH MERTON

I suggest three titles to a new reader of Merton, in the following order. First, *The Sign of Jonas,* Merton's journal of his early years in the monastery, gives insight into Merton's personality and also the nature of the religious life. Second, *New Seeds of Contemplation,* a devotional work of great sensitivity, reflects the ecumenical breadth of his mature thought. Third, *Raids on the Unspeakable* brings together essays and meditations that reveal the more unpredictable side of Merton's imagination.

If you care for poetry, you should, of course, dip into the *Selected Poems,* sampling both the devotional verse and the late experimental works (of these, *Cables to the Ace* is my favorite). Merton's autobiography *The Seven Storey Mountain* still attracts many followers, although Merton himself repudiated some of it as unloving. Michael Motts's 1984 biography *The Seven Mountains of Thomas Merton* is the definitive biography and is unlikely to be superseded. Henri Nouwen's *Pray to Live* offers a much briefer introduction to Merton.

4

HENRI NOUWEN
Climbing toward God

Luci Shaw

My senses are the five wide-open windows of my soul. Does this sound too "poetic," too self-consciously sentimental to be real? The sort of popular emotion one might expect to encounter in a Hallmark greeting card?

It is, nevertheless, a rational observation verified by my imagination. My senses—sight, smell, touch, hearing, taste—welcome the arrows of morning sunlight (and with that light comes not only sight but insight, in-*sight!*) into the room of fairly drab, functional furniture which is my logical mind. The sensuous connections flow naturally. Every day, when

Luci Shaw was born in 1928 in London, England, and has lived in Canada, Australia, and since 1953 in the U.S. Cofounder of Harold Shaw Publishers, she is author of twenty-three books and anthologies (ten of them poetry, the most recent of which is *The Green Earth: Poems of Creation*). She is writer-in-residence at Regent College and a frequent retreat leader and speaker in North America and abroad on topics such as the Christian imagination, art and spirituality, and journal writing as an aid to spiritual and artistic growth. She lives in Bellingham, Washington, with her husband, John Hoyte.

I watch the green ferns and Oregon grape growing, and finger the velvet moss in the verdant ravine under my study window, I think *grow - ing*. When I breathe into my lungs the spiced sharpness of morning mist moving across our Pacific Northwest lake, I am reminded of *the air of prayer*. When I look up at looming, capped-with-snow Mt. Baker, with its signature wisp of vapor, I wonder, "Is this a metaphor for *God-strength, God-presence?*" The thundering rattle of breakers on the pebbled shore of Puget Sound enters my ears like an echo of what God's voice might sound like. The surging tides pushing in and out of Bellingham Bay suggest to me the push and pull of my own journey, torn between faith and questioning.

You see, I have always been a natural skeptic, an investigator of the status quo, a sharp-eyed observer for whom the reality beneath the surface skin of things is of prime importance. Brought up in a family with a tight system of Christian belief, I desperately *wanted* to cling, like a rider on a runaway horse, to the biblical portrait of truth given me by my parents, who were ardent evangelical missionaries in the Solomon Islands. I was sent to Christian schools, a Christian college. I've had two husbands (one now in heaven) who never seemed to have doubts about their faith or the reality of God. And aunts and uncles and cousins and many friends—all of my life I've been surrounded by good people of simple, unquestioning, uncomplicated faith in the Almighty.

So why was *I* always the questioner, even the skeptic? Why was *I* afflicted, from time to time, with attacks of agnosticism (though I've been comforted during such attacks by Madeleine L'Engle's dictum that no true believer is without such assaults on faith)?

The truth is, I have never been satisfied with the platitudes and easy answers that seem to come from the pulpits and lecterns of evangelical churches and halls of learning. Somehow, although I tried long and earnestly to follow all the guidelines and approved procedures on the path to spiritual certainty and satisfaction, they never worked for me in any lasting way. At Christian conferences around the world, my father preached and practiced "the victorious life"; "Let go, and let God," was his slogan. He challenged Christian groups with the possibility of progressing from the unsatisfactory frustrations of Romans 7 into the triumph of Romans 8. Unfortunately, as the preacher's daughter, I wasn't one of his success stories.

Always a truth-seeker, a God-hungerer, in my search I have followed a fascinating track over mountains and valleys. The "ups" have been glorious, true epiphanies, showings, glimpses of God's face in which I've known his presence and help. Prayers answered. Truths demonstrated and received and acted on.

But some of the valleys have been abysses, places of grief and discouragement, disillusionment and despair.

> I really want to be
> drenched in God.
>
> Sometimes
> he lets down a small
>
> cloudburst, enough
> to leave me wet
>
> and shiny, for about
> ten minutes, but mostly
>
> it's just
> gray skies up there—
>
> clouds moving
> their dark edges
>
> endlessly across
> the sky; a drying wind,
>
> and no rain.
> Dammit.

I've raised five children through adolescence to adulthood, a fulfilling, but never an easy task. I've had the joys and pressures of working as an editor and publisher with many skilled and successful authors. I've learned a lot about indifference to my work as a poet, even in the church; I should say *especially* in the church. In addition, I've experienced a turbulent inner life—wounds of the spirit, bereavement. Depression. At such times I've been comforted to know that even Jesus suffered doubt, rejection, frustration, fatigue, despair, even abandonment by God his Father.

You may attribute my uneven progress (I sense there *has* been progress) to the instability of the artistic temperament. And you may be right. I am a poet. Perhaps I wouldn't *be* a poet without the highs and the lows. Perhaps the poet's hypersensitivity to both despair and delight, pain and pleasure, ugliness and beauty, meaning and absurdity, color my relationship with God. Perhaps I'm a bit like David the psalmist, another poet, another individual with "a heart after God," a yearning spirit, who also had a bumpy journey. In poetry and life David soared and plunged, both.

On a holiday in the British Virgin Islands recently I wrote:

The Pink Hibiscus

In the space of a single psalm David's
emotional pendulum would often swing all the way
from lament to celebration. Was it an act of faith?
A surge of optimism? For myself, the oscillation
moves too often from doubt to faith and
back again; it's the stretch, the wide arc from soar
to swoop that disconcerts. Sometimes it seems
as if equilibrium comes only from
letting myself go numb. Then the distress
of melancholia fades into a fugitive dream,
along with old happinesses, spurts of elation—
they all dim into an echoing, indeterminate past.
Waiting for the nerves to tingle into life again.

And more of the same, even here on a
tropical vacation. But right now a flushed hibiscus,
inviting a bee to its pink lip, its swollen stamen
angling up at me, wakens my eye to ardent color,
and the possibility of, once again, passion.

Where one part of me has always been eager to pin faith down where I can see it, examine it, and control it like a bug on board, another part of me is restless, shaking at the reins, wanting to explore all the other possibilities, knowing that even if I achieved it, watertight certainty is like legalism. It jettisons mystery, renders faith unnecessary, tries to grab the control from God's hands and set up a grid of human rules instead. Such predetermined codes of conduct and thought may give us a false sense of safety, but they build up fortress battlements against the free and unpredictable movements of the Spirit of God. Faith is more like charting a course through the turbulent waters of Puget Sound, among all the islands and hidden reefs. We can see the islands and steer our craft clear of obvious obstacles, but the underwater rocks and sandbars, appearing and then vanishing with the tides, are mysteries we cannot fathom, places where we must trust the charts and the skipper's experience rather than clear sightings.

These conflicting seismic rumblings have shaken my Christian certainties over the years. But my internal spiritual incongruities finally erupted, with the force of a volcano, when out of the blue, Harold, my husband of thirty-three years, father of my five children, a man of God who had never smoked, was diagnosed with lung cancer. During the sixteen traumatic months between the diagnosis and his death, I began for the first time to keep a daily, reflective journal. Those journal entries appeared in *God in the Dark,* a painful book to write, in which I grappled with the problem of suffering, with the reality of God's presence, his love, and his power, and with the devastation of seeing my heart-companion diminishing in body, drawing further into himself, being cut off from me. And as he was wasting away, I was caught again between believing in divine power for his healing, and facing my own profound fears and doubts that God was real and that he would be there for us.

How did Henri Nouwen enter the picture for me? A close friend gave me a copy of *The Genesee Diary,* the journal Nouwen kept during his seven months of seclusion in a Trappist monastery. There he attempted to come to grips with his own deepest questions, to strip away the glittering image that had been projected by his role as a gifted and popular writer and speaker (". . . how much of my own life was motivated by self-glory"), to draw closer to God. I felt immense reassurance as I learned that some of my questions had been his questions too (it's always a gift to me to discover a kindred spirit). His very personal published journal, like my own never written for publication and perhaps more candid and forthright as a result, allowed me the privilege of glimpsing his unguarded soul and learning with him as he learned from God and his brothers, the monks, that "the central things in life, although spiritually perceptible, remain invisible in large measure and can very easily be overlooked by the inattentive, busy, distracted person that each of us can so readily become."[1]

As an active writer, teacher, and speaker, I immediately identified with Nouwen when he brooded, in his introduction to *The Genesee Diary:* "Maybe I spoke more about God than with him. Maybe my writing about prayer kept me from a prayerful life. Maybe I was more concerned about the praise of men and women than the love of God. Maybe I was slowly becoming a prisoner of people's expectations instead of [one who was] liberated by divine promises." With him I knew from experience that only by "stepping back and allowing the hard question to touch me even if they hurt," would I begin to *know,* to come slap-up against my own bedrock realities.

As one who had known doubt and uncertainty about my faith, I felt Nouwen's comments about Thomas, the rationalist, the disciple of doubt, forcefully: "Didymus, the name of Thomas, means 'twin', as the Gospel says, and . . . all of us are 'two people', a doubting one and a believing one."[2] Although Thomas found it difficult to accept the reality of Jesus' resurrection, "he kept faithful to the community of the apostles. In that community the Lord appeared to him and strengthened his faith."[3] During Harold's illness and my bereavement, I found this to be a fruitful pattern for my own dilemma. In spite of my hard questions, my Episcopal parish family became for me, week by week, the context in which my

experience confirmed Nouwen's observation, "In times of doubt or unbe-
lief, the community can 'carry you along,' so to speak; it can even offer
on your behalf what you yourself overlook, and can be the context in
which you recognize the Lord again."[4]

It's still true. As Nouwen says, "The way to 'God alone' is seldom traveled alone." The body of the church reinforces its individual parts when
they are weak, including me, just as when I have a toothache on the right
side of my mouth I am prompted to let the left side take over the chew-
ing for a while. Often I have felt this strength of being "carried along,"
like a small boat in a flowing current, by the community of faith. Every
week at the Eucharistic feast I participate in the old exchange: At Communion I bring to the altar all my flaws and failings, handing over to God
my fears and skepticism and inadequacy, and Christ offers me himself
instead, feeding me body and blood, his food for my soul, which strengthens me for the journey of the coming week, as I "feed on him in my heart,
by faith." Kneeling at the Communion rail I feel like a little bird being
fed crumb by crumb from God's infinite loaf, taking in enough nourishment to keep me going until the next sacramental meal. If I am unable
to take Communion, I sense the spiritual impoverishment that precedes
assaults of doubt—doubt in God, and self-doubt.

I sense that Nouwen had in himself these aspects of "the twin."
Throughout his life he felt torn in opposite directions—attracted to the
life of the eminent scholar and theologian, with high-level teaching
responsibilities, multiple speaking engagements (which provided multiple opportunities to feed his need for approval and respect), sought
after for his spiritual wisdom by numerous correspondents and acquaintances, yet on the other hand yearning for the deeper relationship with
God which was precluded by his own busyness. Speaking and writing
to a wide audience about intimacy with God required such expenditure
of emotional energy that his own intimacy with God would suffer and
seemed diminished—at which point he would write compellingly about
such spiritual atrophy and its remedies and incur a further flood of invi-
tations to speak!

This cycle may have been partly responsible for the restlessness and
dissatisfaction which recurred at intervals throughout his life until his
death in 1996. His ardent desire was to come home to himself and to
God, as his book-length meditation inspired by Rembrandt's painting,
The Return of the Prodigal, affirms. One biography of Nouwen is subti-
tled "A Restless Seeking for God." In a conversation with a friend, he
admitted that two voices competed within him—the call to succeed and
achieve, and the call to rest and enjoy being God's beloved. Dissatisfaction with himself and his spiritual progress pushed him from project to
project, from faculty appointments at Notre Dame, Yale, and Harvard,

to his monastic seclusion in the Genesee, to mission work in Latin America, and finally to ministry in the L'Arche community in Ontario, Canada, where for the first time Henri seemed to find a measure of contentment. While our confidence is that Henri has finally come home to God, we may feel uncomfortable with the kind of impasse which much of his life reflected. And we feel even more uncomfortable as we recognize and face it in our own experience.

A different perspective, perhaps a truer way of viewing the conflicts in his life and ours, is suggested in Nouwen's book *The Wounded Healer*. Once again, the paradox presents itself: We are full of flaws and failings. We have been badly hurt and we need healing. We want unconditional love, but we strive to fulfill our own conditions to achieve it. Yet without the vulnerability and humility that accompanies our woundedness, how can we bring comfort and healing to others all around us who have been battered and bear bruises similar to our own? One solution: our ability to help lies in our very vulnerability. As we admit our inadequacies and our own need for help, not only can each of us identify with others in the same condition, they can identify with us and know that we understand and sympathize. Perhaps this was one reason why Jesus entered our humanity, to bare himself in the very arena in which we had been assaulted and damaged, and suffer the same assaults himself, "tempted in everything as we are," which gives us greater confidence in his love and understanding. "The leadership about which Jesus speaks is of a radically different kind from the leadership offered by the world. It is a servant leadership . . . in which the leader is a vulnerable servant who needs the people as much as they need him or her."[5]

I have to ask, as I face tugs of the heart in different and competing directions, much as Henri Nouwen did, how many of us suffer from similar disjunctions—self-defeating or deep emotional needs which we attempt to satisfy with affirming human relationships and achievements instead of affirmation from the heart of God? Do we all allow the conflicts of other people's loud urgencies to drown out the small voice within us that calls us to listen for God in quietness? I must admit that even though I am able, from time to time, to retreat and be still, and to be rewarded by a sense of interior spiritual and artistic richness and serenity, that very stillness and retreat seems the most difficult of all life objectives to achieve.

Over the years, whenever I have reread *The Genesee Diary,* I have found a personal and profound wisdom and a way of penetrating to the heart of my own needs. Like many of the students who have been participants in journal-writing workshops I have offered, I find Nouwen's *Diary* a wonderful model for entering the process of personal reflection, discovering insight, and growing in maturity, self-understanding, and

God-awareness through a journal. Like Nouwen, I feel that keeping a consistent, personal journal is a form of prayer; as I write, honest and transparent to myself and God, I may become conscious of the divine presence directing my thoughts and conclusions. I sense that God is with me in the intimacy gained on these private pages. I can deal with emotional difficulties as I write from the inside out. I can also grow artistically and spiritually, as my secret thoughts find their most compelling avenues of expression.

And to students hesitant to start a journal because they are intimidated by the blank pages, or who think they have nothing profound or valid or interesting to say, I quote these words, excerpted from Nouwen's *Reflections on Theological Education:*

> Most students ... think that writing means writing down ideas, insights, visions. They feel that they must first have something to say before they can put it down on paper. For them writing is little more than recording a pre-existent thought.
>
> But with this approach true writing is impossible. *Writing is a process in which we discover what lives in us. The writing itself reveals what is alive*... [italics mine]. The deepest satisfaction of writing is precisely that it opens up new spaces within us of which we were not aware before we started to write. To write is to embark on a journey whose final destination we do not know. Thus, creative writing requires a real act of trust. We have to say to ourselves, "I do not yet know what I carry in my heart, but I trust that it will emerge as I write." Writing is like giving away the few loaves and fishes one has, trusting that they will multiply in the giving. Once we dare to "give away" on paper the few thoughts that come to us, we start discovering how much is hidden underneath ... and gradually come in touch with our own riches.[6]

Such words free us, nudging us into the kind of confidence in the process which eases our way into writing as a way of discovering and articulating who we are before God. They urge us to trust God and our own hearts, and such trusting results in fresh and surprising insights which bring great personal enrichment for ourselves, and through us to those whom our lives touch. Often after reading one of his books, Nouwen's silver words seem to hang in the air over my days, reassuring, refreshing as a shower in drought time. Blessing me, or challenging me.

Let me describe some of the life circumstances in which Henri Nouwen and I intersected as my thoughts and prayers followed his. Like Henri, I struggled for most of my life with my own yearnings for approval, affirmation, recognition. Paradoxically, those yearnings grew like an addiction to a drug the more approval, affirmation, recognition I received.

Like him, I realized that the only resolution to such deep needs was to let Jesus himself fill that lonely, hungry place inside me, to feel his approval, to rest in that alone, and to discover the soul-satisfaction of communion with God. I was convinced that I needed to lift my heart away from myself, to set my love free to rise singly and purely to God. Like Henri I wanted intimacy with God, but my very active life, full of diverse and compelling interests, has all too often robbed me of the quiet, meditative time that is the prerequisite for such intimacy.

This is a dilemma which has not yet found its ultimate resolution in my life, and may not while I am mortal. But I have come to believe that as long as the desire is there, as long as I don't become apathetic and complacent, I am being drawn toward the Being in whom my ultimate longings *will be* satisfied. Hunger may draw me to a restaurant. Thirsty on a hike, I am attracted to a mountain stream. Wanting more of God and never quite getting enough of him is like a magnet with a relentless pull. With him I'm learning more of what Eugene Peterson calls "passionate patience"—investing enough trust in God that I am more content to leave what I cannot understand or know for sure in the realm of mystery.

Now that Henri is in heaven, I am deeply happy that he has found what he was searching for, and that I may some day join him. Thanks to him I'm willing to wait for my existential questions to be answered in *kairos,* that time beyond time when my knowing approaches my being known by God.

Human as we are, inextricably hemmed into our physical selves, able to perceive the outside world only through our senses, unable to get outside of ourselves to evaluate our performance or to see ourselves objectively, there may always be a conflict between how we view ourselves (as despicable, self-serving, mixed in motivation and action) and how others see us (wise, experienced, godly, loving). This problem is exacerbated by our almost unconscious desire to put our best foot forward, to present ourselves in the best light, at the same time disguising our true motives or attitudes. Nouwen addresses this disjunction of the self in *The Inner Voice of Love.*

This problem with the insatiable *self,* the terrible interior gnawing need to be noticed, to be known, to be recognized as having unique gifts, has been an affliction for most of my adult life. I have always felt its negative shadow on even minor achievements. Responsibility for this might be laid at the feet of a family for whom my performance, academically and spiritually, was of paramount importance.

Excellence was expected, and more than excellence; our excellence was to be exceptional. This is a heavy burden. Somehow, my brother and I, siblings born late in the lives of our missionary parents, managed to achieve, at least outwardly, what was required of us. Moving between cultures and climates supplied me with a broad backdrop for creative expression, but such shifts, such leavings and cleavings were not without emotional stress, and as we migrated from continent to continent in our youth, large gaps were also left in our learning; our comings and goings seldom coincided with the beginnings and ends of school terms. Our parents, as well as requiring our academic success, were, however, superbly confident. "You kids are bright. You'll catch up," became a watchword in our family. Somehow, we did. But our parents' confidence in us seldom rewarded us with praise, which was thought to contribute to vanity and bigheadedness. If I only achieved the honor roll, but not the *high* honor roll, my mother was likely to stop speaking to me for weeks. No matter what I did, some flaw was found. The blanket I knitted for her was an inch narrower on one end than the other. The strawberry jam didn't jell quite firmly enough. The needlepoint footstool I worked for a year to complete wasn't quite the right green to go in her living room.

Perfection and its consequent prize of approval, though an unattainable goal, became almost an obsession with me, one that still plagues me today. The drive to achieve, to do something unique and unrepeatable, to do something so well, better than anyone else, so that others would respect and value me, would even *like* me more, had for years been the objective of my life. And failure to reach that pinnacle covered me with the rags of shame and guilt. In this context Nouwen describes the second temptation to which Jesus was subjected in the wilderness, a temptation "to do something spectacular," Nouwen says, "something that could win him great applause." Nouwen depicts Satan, who says to Jesus, "Throw yourself from the parapet of the temple and let the angels catch you and carry you in their arms." Then Nouwen enters the story: "But Jesus refused to be a stunt man. . . . 'Don't put the Lord your God to the test,' he said."

The attractions the tempter offered Jesus continue to offer themselves today.

> When you look at today's Church, it is easy to see the prevalence of individualism among ministers and priests. Not too many of us have a vast repertoire of skills to be proud of, but most of us still feel that, if we have anything at all to show, it is something we have to do solo. Stardom and individual heroism, which are such obvious aspects of our competitive society, are not at all alien to the Church. There too the dominant image is that of the self-made man or woman who can do it all alone.[7]

Piercing words! And Nouwen himself felt the shock of entering the secluded monastic life in the Abbey of the Genesee, where "solitude becomes really hard when you realize that nobody is thinking about you anymore."[8] In imagination, I put myself so easily in his place and felt the sting of becoming unspectacular, insignificant. Of vanishing from the world. Of being erased by absence from the consciousness of others.

Another thing. I used to "catastrophize" difficulties out of all proportion, to allow relatively minor rebuffs or perceived rejections to send me spiraling down into depression and despair. I have often felt like a loaded, cocked pistol, ready for some emotion, some small finger of negative feeling to pull the trigger. Nouwen, quoting his Genesee abbot John Eudes, in a similar predicament, commented that it is

> not that your feelings are totally illegitimate. In fact, you might have a good reason to feel rejected. But the problem is that your response has no proportion to the nature of the event . . . Little rejections like these open up a huge chasm, and you plunge right into it, all the way to the bottom."[9]

Instead, Eudes counseled, we should learn to *nuance* our responses, to learn to see ourselves and our situation more truly, through God's eyes, and find a more authentic perspective. I remind myself of this often, and it has helped me immeasurably; the plunge into darkness and emotional chaos has been halted. And I often pray that the Holy Spirit will help me to see myself as my heavenly Father sees me—absolutely clearly, acknowledging my flaws, but encouraging me with great love, and a desire to see my potential fulfilled.

An impatient, often restless person, I've had to learn a great deal about slowing down and waiting, often frustrating processes that seem like a waste of time. Yet as I read the Psalms, they are full of waiting: "Our soul waits for the LORD—our help and our shield." "I shall always wait in patience and shall praise you more and more." "Be strong, take heart and wait for the LORD." "I lay my requests before you and wait in expectation." "My soul waits for the LORD more than watchmen wait for the morning, more than watchmen wait for the morning." (In that repeated phrase we feel the watchers' eager anticipation for daybreak after what seems like an endless night.) Waiting seems to be an inevitable part of the human condition, especially frustrating in this age in which we have been conditioned to demand, and expect, instant gratification in almost every arena of life.

I only began to come to terms with waiting, and to learn its enormous value, after listening to a Nouwen tape on "The Spirituality of Waiting." And I like to couple Nouwen's words in the tape, "Waiting is a period of learning. The longer we wait, the more we hear about him for whom we are waiting," with Eugene Peterson's paraphrase of Romans 8:22–25: "Waiting doesn't diminish us any more than waiting diminishes a pregnant mother; we are *enlarged in the waiting*" (italics added).

I have begun to understand that during the times of waiting God is as vibrantly at work within us as new life and growth is at work within an expectant mother. If, through the Spirit of God, we have been united with the Father in dynamic relationship, if God has sown his gospel seed in us, then Jesus *is being formed within us,* you and me, little by little, day by day, just as a human embryo grows to become a fetus and develops incrementally, though invisibly at first, into a human baby. But we all need to *wait* if the Word is to become flesh in us and our potential is to mature into the reality for which we were created.

It was in this context of procreation and birth that Nouwen gave me a vital metaphor for understanding and dealing with my own finite knowledge of God, a human limitation which had in part led to my existential questions about divine reality. During an address at an arts conference he gave an illustration which printed itself vividly in my imagination. He told of twins, waiting, seedlike, in their mother's belly, warm, protected, blind in the amniotic dark, unknowing about anything that lies ahead for them. As I listened to these introductory words, my heart gave a quiver; I had a feeling about where his narrative was leading, and that it might present me with a new understanding of my present human darkness and my ultimate place in God. The twins tell each other how much they feel at home in their fetal state, contented in their secure comfort in the womb, floating in warm fluid, yet safely tethered by their umbilical cords. But as their faculties and bodies develop they begin to wonder, to ask questions about their future. Finally, one of them says to the other, "Have you heard? Someday soon we're going to be pushed out into the light, and there'll be this . . . this thing called a *mother.* We'll see her face!"

Nouwen's story gave me the needed analogy. Now, in this life, we are all like seeds in the place of unknowing in the womb of God, growing towards our ultimate release into the light of God's presence, where we'll "know as we are known," where we'll see the Parent's face.

Recently I bought a copy of Nouwen's *In the Name of Jesus.* Much of the substance of that little book (Nouwen does so much in the narrow space of his short paperbacks!) deals with Henri's own lessons in giving away what power God gave him, sharing it with those who are powerless, in this book the severely disturbed, mentally handicapped, or physically disabled people of L'Arche Community in Ontario, Canada.

This directive, to give our power away, goes directly against our twentieth-century cultural grain. There is much sociopolitical discussion about how the disenfranchised are to achieve "empowerment." This process often seems to boil down to the seizing of power for themselves by people, or cultures, or nations, frequently by violent and destructive means. As Nouwen says: "One of the greatest ironies of the history of

Christianity is that its leaders constantly gave in to the temptation of power—political power, military power, economic power, or moral and spiritual power—even though they continued to speak in the name of Jesus."[10] All this despite the fact that the Nietzschean view of the lust for power as the underlying principle of life and evolution directly opposes the Christian view.

Power has always been obsessive, whether in international political feuds or in personal relationships, but the idea of "empowerment" has become a cultural catchword in this generation in particular. This may be because in the past there have been such outrageous abuses of power, of dictators over their populaces, of church leaders over members of their congregations, of parents over their children, of husbands over their wives. Perhaps some redress was deemed necessary. When we feel powerless, the thing we desire most fiercely is to gain (or regain) a sense of control and autonomy over our own lives.

We can talk endlessly about power for good versus power for evil, but it has long been understood that no matter what its motivation, personal power may corrupt, and the struggle for power for its own sake nearly always creates conflict which results in the destruction or annihilation of another.

Is this the result that God had in mind when he spoke our radiant world into being? The magnificent, continuing act of Creation shows an astonishing kind of power for beauty and for good. And when, in the supreme Creative Act, God sent the Son into our world, en-fleshed, and provided for the ongoing presence of Jesus in the Holy Spirit, there was never a hint manifested of destructive or selfish power. The gift of God's power was bestowed on us to help us change in ways that all our own effort and energy could never achieve, to lift us out of the kingdom of darkness and release us into the realm of light. As the apostle Peter put it in Acts 10, "God anointed Jesus . . . with the Holy Spirit and power ... he went around doing good and healing all who were under the power of the devil" (v. 38), which describes the classic confrontation of destructive, evil power with the power of good to heal and make whole.

What makes the temptation of power so seemingly irresistible?

We hear a lot these days about "upward mobility"—that desire for elevated status, greater wealth, enlarged influence, increased control. And the social scientists today have cajoled us into a new idolatry—the worship of self, of our *selves*. Now, I know that it's important for us to grow a healthy self-image. I absolutely acknowledge that we should be able to regard ourselves with respect for our integrity, our personal growth. We need to live out the image of God in us by loving ourselves as God has loved us, unconditionally. But I believe that our self-absorption and self-ism, like so many other corrective measures, have been taken to an extreme. With self-ism as the new idolatry, with becoming empowered as the new objective in life, with material values having risen to the top rung of the ladder of success, with anything that we cannot see, touch, prove, and *use* being discounted as irrelevant, spiritual and moral values have been dismissed or marginalized in this age of upward mobility.

How refreshing it is, in this context, to think of the *downward mobil - ity* of Jesus, who left behind the magnificence and richness of heaven, who stripped himself of his sovereign splendor, who was willing to undergo poverty and abuse and rejection, to be out of step with his age. I listen to the prophetic words of Isaiah: "He will not cry or lift up his voice, or make it heard in the street; a bruised reed he will not break, and a dimly burning wick he will not quench" (42:2–3). No arrogant power demonstrated there! Jesus most often works quietly, healing gently, restoring us even when we feel most weak and useless.

In Philippians 2 we read the astonishing description of how Jesus relinquished power. The passage begins with these radical words of the apostle Paul, as Eugene Peterson renders them in *The Message:*

> Do me a favor: Agree with each other, love each other, be deep-spirited friends. Don't push your way to the front; don't sweet-talk your way to the top. Put yourself aside and help others get ahead. Don't be obsessed with getting your own advantage. Forget yourselves. . . . Think of yourselves the way Christ Jesus thought of himself. He had equal status with God but didn't think so much of himself that he had to cling to that status no matter what. Not at all. When the time came he set aside the privileges of deity and took on the status of a slave, became human.[11]

The NRSV concludes the passage like this: "He emptied himself . . . and became obedient to the point of death—even death on a cross."

Jesus allowed himself to be categorized as a criminal, relinquishing any reputation for respectability. In the Greek the word translated to "empty oneself" has the sense in this passage of a waterfall *contin - ually pouring itself* over a cliff edge, an inexhaustible flow of living water. This is the kind of Jesus love which Henri Nouwen exemplified so truly, so consistently. He knew the ultimate power of continually sharing his power with the powerless, as he did for his friend in Latin America and in the L'Arche Community near Toronto, Canada, at the end of his life—a period he graphically describes in his small volume, *In the Name of Jesus.*

Richard Wilbur metaphorically expressed the same principle—the power released by brokenness—in his brief poem "Milkweed," one of "Two Voices in a Meadow":

Anonymous as cherubs
Over the crib of God,
White seeds are floating
Out of my burst pod.

What power had I
Before I learned to yield?
Shatter me, great wind:
I shall possess the field.[12]

My one face-to-face encounter with Henri Nouwen vividly illustrates this last conviction—that if God gives us power, it is so we may give it away to others. Several years ago I was designated as the "point person" to coordinate a conference on religion and the arts in Berkeley, California, with many prominent writers, artists, and lecturers scheduled to participate. But six weeks before the scheduled conference date all our attempts to find a leader for the culminating worship service had failed. In a phone discussion, the name of Henri Nouwen came up. "But he's in such demand, I'm sure he's already booked solid," I demurred. Greg Wolfe, the editor of the journal *Image,* which was sponsoring the event, responded, "It's a long shot, but let's invite him anyway. The worst he can say is no." Copies of the magazine and an outline of conference events were forwarded to Nouwen in Canada and almost immediately on receiving them he called us, declaring enthusiastically: "It's just the kind of thing I love to do. Of course I'll come!"

My next move was to write and ask him about his choice of music and Scripture readings to accompany his message. His answering letter dumbfounded me. His suggestion: "Let's do it the other way around. You tell me what your theme is and what songs and Scripture readings you'd like, and God will help me fit my message into your plan." Talk about a servant spirit. Talk about giving up the power of control! I thought, *Here, in the flesh, is the kind of humility and humanity and flexibility that I have been glimpsing in his writing.*

How well this man had been learning his own lessons! Nouwen had lamented, in *The Genesee Diary,*

> When I think of the many lecture invitations I declined with the argument that I had no time to prepare, I see now how I looked at every speaking engagement . . . as a new performance that calls for new preparation. . . . This attitude leads to fatigue and eventually to exhaustion. . . . Now I see that I was all mixed up, that I had fragmented my life into many sections that did not really form a unity. The question is not, "Do I have time to prepare?" but, "Do I live in a state of preparedness?"[13]

And when we met the day before the conference was to begin, he was as human and eager to please as a wise child. He showed me some notes he'd jotted down; "Do you think this metaphor will work? It's right out of my own life, but does it go well with the plans you've made?" He kept coming back for approval, and even asked me to pray with him about an idea he wanted to present, living out what he was to write later in *In the Name of Jesus:* "I have found over and over again how hard it is to be truly faithful to Jesus when I am alone. I need my brothers and sisters to pray with me, to speak with me about the spiritual task at hand." Farther on in the same volume he tells us, "The leadership about which Jesus speaks is of a radically different kind from the leadership offered by the world. It is a servant leadership . . . in which the leader is a vulnerable servant who needs the people as much as they need him or her."[14]

There in the empty chapel before the meetings started we sat in a pew, and God was present in an almost tangible way as this appealing but unassuming servant of God asked humbly for help, for clarity of thought, for integrity, for the power of the Spirit. And when the time came for him to speak, he was ignited with that power. Love and wisdom streamed from him, and we were powerfully affected for good and for God.

Every time I go back and view the videotape of that service, I am moved and challenged again. And I keep having to apply to my own life Henri's words, written in the context of Christ's temptations in the wilderness:

> The temptation to consider power an apt instrument for the proclamation of the Gospel is the greatest of all. We keep hearing from others, as well as saying to ourselves, that having power . . . is a good thing. With this rationalization crusades took place; inquisitions were organized; Indians were enslaved . . . splendid cathedrals and opulent seminaries were built; and much moral manipulation of conscience was engaged in.[15]

And again, speaking of Jesus' words to Peter in John 21:18, "Someone will take you where you would rather not go," Nouwen comments, "These words are the words that made it possible for me to move from Harvard to L'Arche. They touch the core of Christian leadership and are spoken to offer us . . . new ways to let go of power and follow the humble way of Jesus."[16]

And once again I give thanks not only that our minds had intersected as I'd read his words on the printed page but that when our paths had crossed and we had joined hands in ministry, he had shown me, unselfconsciously, a living model of wisdom, grace, and obedient servanthood that reminded me of Christ himself.

And I sense that God, through Henri Nouwen, isn't through with me yet.

GETTING STARTED WITH NOUWEN

Easy entry into the mind and heart of Henri Nouwen is achieved in his journal, *The Genesee Diary: Report from a Trappist Monastery,* in which he is winningly transparent to his own perceived flaws. His best-selling books, testimony to his connection with human needs, include *Life of the Beloved: Spiritual Living in a Secular World,* *Return of the Prodigal Son,* and *The Wounded Healer. Life-Signs: Intimacy, Fecundity and Ecstasy in Christian Perspective* opens up major emphases in his writings on spirituality. Nouwen was a prolific writer, and many of his other books, such as *In the Name of Jesus,* *The Road to Daybreak,* and *With Open Hands* are equally rewarding. Compilations of his meditative sayings include *Bread for the Journey* and *Show Me the Way: Readings for Each Day of Lent. Nouwen Then* is a recent anthology of personal reflections by friends of Nouwen, and *Henri Nouwen: A Restless Seeking for God* by Jurgen Beumer is a more complete biographical overview of his writing and ministry.

5

PAUL TOURNIER
The Power of the Personal

J. Keith Miller

A "C-minus!" I couldn't believe it! I'd been a good student all my life and had spent hours developing, writing, and editing this, my first sermon for a homiletics class in seminary. I was angry, but, more than that, I was confused. This sermon represented the way I had always thought preachers should preach, sharing their own personal experience, strength, and hope along with the biblical message. But my professor of preaching had dismissed my sermon as being unacceptable.

After pointing out some structural mistakes that I could agree with, he leaned back in his chair, drummed his fingertips together, and said, "The reason your grade was a C-minus was because you were 'personal.' You used the first person singular to describe the problems with which you were dealing." He paused and then went on. "In the first place, using

---

J. Keith Miller is a widely known lecturer and author. His more than fifteen books include the best-sellers, *The Taste of New Wine, The Becomers, Please Love Me,* the recently published *The Secret Life of the Soul,* and several books cowritten with his wife, Andrea Wells Miller, and Bruce Larson.

the first person singular in a sermon is *not effective*. And besides, it is not in good taste." He pushed my sermon across the smooth surface of the large desk.

Still, in the years to come I could not shake the notion that one's own feelings and experiences of pain, fear, anger, guilt, shame, sadness, and joy could be drawbridges over which a communicator could carry the message and love of God into the deepest levels of people's lives. I felt that the world and the church had become depersonalized and that people were growing more and more isolated. Somehow the stance of the "expert" communicator expounding abstract concepts or telling laymen how they should live seemed to further the depersonalizing process. Worse, the message of God's healing love didn't appear to be catching the attention of the modern world—even many of those already in the churches.

I knew that what I needed personally was a model: someone who was seriously trying to be God's person and to have intellectual integrity but who also faced the kinds of fears, problems, and failures that I faced. Evidently, this was not a combination to be found in a single Christian communicator. People seriously committed to God either did not have the kind of struggles I had or considered them too insignificant to be mentioned. I had met some other strugglers who, like me, were trying to slug it out with this paradox, but we were all nobodies. I had never run across a communicator with any authority who admitted to this strange predicament of feeling unable to be whole, in spite of the power and joy to be found in the gospel.

Then, in 1965, Dr. Paul Tournier came to Laity Lodge in the remote hill country of southwest Texas for a conference. I was director of the conference center. And although I had heard of Paul Tournier, I had never read anything he had written.

The first evening he spoke, the "great hall" at the lodge was filled with psychiatrists, psychologists, M.D.s of all varieties, Christian ministers, and lay leaders from various professions. The air was almost electric with expectation, and I realized how much the conference guests were looking forward to hearing this man whose books they had read. Many of the guests had traveled hundreds of miles for this weekend. We had turned down a number of requests to attend, and still the group had overflowed into the motel in the nearest town. As we all gathered for the first session, I wondered how well Tournier would be able to cross the language barrier from his French through an interpreter to us. I had no idea what content to expect.

Then he began to speak. Within five minutes the room had faded, and we were transported into another world. A little boy was describing his struggle with loneliness and self doubt almost sixty years before in a country several thousand miles away. You could have heard a pin drop on the stone floor. I sat behind the speaker near the huge fireplace and looked past Paul Tournier into the eyes of almost a hundred sophisticated American professionals. Inside those eyes, wide open, I could see a roomful of other lonely little boys and girls reliving their own struggles for identity and worth.

After fifteen or twenty minutes had passed, a strange thing began to happen, something I have never seen happen before or since. As Paul spoke in French, we found ourselves nodding in agreement and understanding—before his words were translated. We trusted him so much, and felt he understood us so well, that we knew at a subconscious level we would resonate with what he was saying. He described problems, doubts, joys, meanings, fears—many of which still existed for him—and spoke of them naturally, as if they were the materials God normally worked with in his healing ministry among all people, Christians included.

Before us was a man who did not even speak our language, a man in his sixties who wore a wrinkled tweed suit, and was exhausted from a whirlwind trip across America. And yet as he spoke fatigue, age, clothes, and language difference all faded into the background. He turned periodically to make eye contact with those of us behind him. I was mainly conscious of his sparkling eyes, his personal transparency, and a glow of genuine caring about his face. As he spoke, I felt and heard love, and the truth of God about my own life.

I found myself having to fight back tears—tears of relief and gratitude, and release from my solitary burden. Because of my own struggles, I had sensed that, to be healed, we need more than good medical advice or even excellent psychological counseling. We need presence. Vulnerable, personal *presence*. I knew the Bible claimed that was what God gave us in Jesus Christ and the Holy Spirit: his own presence to heal and strengthen us. And I had felt that somehow we Christians were to be channels to convey that healing presence personally to other people's lives through our own openness and vulnerability. But in Paul Tournier I met at last a living model of the kind of communication I was trying in a stumbling, uncertain way to find.

I made two decisions during that conference. First, I would go back to school to get some psychological training. Second, as soon as I finished a manuscript I was working on, I would read some of Tournier's books. I was already in the process of writing a book for new Christians about living in a personal relationship with God. Other books of this sort seemed to me overly pious, and they did not deal with the "stumbling blocks" that had bothered me as a new Christian. After Tournier's visit, I completed the manuscript of that, my first book, with great enthusiasm.

And when I sent my manuscript to the publisher, the next thing I did was to read *The Meaning of Persons.* Again, tears. For years I had been looking for books whose authors were real and transparent so that I could identify with their problems and move toward healing in Christ. The closest thing I had found was Augustine's *Confessions,* which is what had finally persuaded me to write a book about my own struggles as a contemporary Christian. But if I had read Tournier first, I doubt I would have felt the need to write that manuscript, *The Taste of New Wine.*

Knowing that a man existed who loved God and yet who also faced his own humanity and used the discoveries and methods of scientific investigation did something for me. And knowing that, at least partially because of Christ, this man could afford to be honest about his own struggles helped push me far beyond my small horizons of security and faith.

From that day forward Paul Tournier became a mentor and friend, until his death in 1986. We traveled and spoke in conferences with other Americans and Europeans in Spain, Portugal, Italy, and Greece. His work has influenced me deeply. But more, his life and his way of personal dialogue gave me a direction for living as a Christian which has brought more hope and courage than I could have imagined.

※

Paul Tournier was born in Geneva. His father served as the minister for many years at St. Peter's Cathedral, where John Calvin had preached and taught three hundred years earlier. But young Tournier's father died when Paul was very young. As the lonely orphan boy studied Calvinistic theology, he was plagued by feelings of unworthiness. He committed his life to Christ at the age of eleven, after an evangelistic sermon. He read Calvin's *Institutes* and got involved in church work, becoming a student leader and speaker far beyond his own home congregation. But by his own admission his religion remained cold, impersonal, and unsatisfying.

Then, after graduation from medical school, Tournier met some members of the Oxford group and began to learn to talk to others about his insecurities as well as his theological formulations. He also began to spend an hour a day in silent meditation before God. Gradually, a change took place in this brilliant young professional. He began to listen to his patients in a different way. And as he did he noticed that their deeper issues were not the physical symptoms they presented to him but rather the inner spiritual conflicts of their lives and relationships.

Tournier, who saw himself as a scientist practitioner, didn't feel it was proper for him to deal with spiritual issues in his office. So one day he invited a patient to come to his home in the evening so they could have a personal dialogue in front of the fireplace. Before long, Tournier the physician discovered that the truly significant healing was taking place as a result of these conversations in his home. In 1937 he wrote all his patients, telling them that his work had led him beyond the diagnosis and treatment of physical complaints to the deeper problems of the human personality. He said that he believed the understanding of persons could never come about by objective study but only through personal dialogue. In that dialogue a spark of life and healing might be kindled.

As time went on, collected experiences and observations formed the basis for Tournier's first book, *The Healing of Persons*. Friends urged him not to have the book published. It was too personal and would embarrass him and hurt him professionally, they said. He was tempted to abandon it. But he could not deny the healing that his patients and he were experiencing in the dialogue of the person. So he sent the book off and it started a worldwide movement called *"Groupe Medecine de la personne."* In the United States this movement is called the Medicine of the Person Group and maintains an active network among physicians who strive to combine scientific excellence with faith through the dialogue of the person.

Tournier saw the pathway of life as proceeding through sets of powerful, contradictory forces. At each step, one hears opposites calling, like the Sirens of Greek legend. And each of us adopts a pattern which causes us to respond characteristically to life with either a *strong* or *weak* reaction (e.g., being talkative or secretive, being resistant or surrendering). All of life, said Tournier, can be seen as dialogue and dialectic.[1] His books reflect the various ways the polar opposites in our lives pull on us, creating an ongoing dialogue and dialectic which we may experience as a kind of spiritual/mental warfare.

Tournier uses the word *person* to describe the experiencing center of an individual that travels through the field of opposing forces. These forces, or inner voices, battle to capture and control the individual's allegiance.

The *person,* as vulnerable as a child, develops a repertoire of behaviors that form a sort of mask or protection. By fulfilling the expectations of important others, the *person* seeks to protect itself from attack and rejection. Tournier calls this overlay of protective adapted behaviors the *personage.* But unlike the American use of the term "mask," the *personage* both reveals and hides the *person.* We give people glimpses of our real selves even as we hide ourselves from them.

Every encounter calls for a choice (often unconscious) of whether to be a *person* or *personage.* But as the *person* behind the *personage* travels through life, it encounters a series of dilemmas, like magnets lined up on either side of a long hallway. For example, there is the choice between keeping control or letting loose: Shall we cling to the security and control of the past or shall we turn loose and move forward in faith as we seek a personal identity and a place in God's will? In *A Place for You,* Paul uses the image of a trapeze artist who must turn loose of one bar, one security, to fly forward to the next.[2] He suggests that we pay money to watch trapeze artists because they live out our inner question: If I turn loose and surrender, will I fall? Will I be able to grasp the new bar of security that God swings toward me, in the form of a new challenge or opportunity, and thus move forward spiritually? Or shall I tighten my grip on the people, places, and things in my past and keep attempting to control them? The inner struggle between the *person* and the *personage* we have constructed to please others sets us up for making some major choices before we can move on to wholeness.

Tournier saw a unity and purpose in the struggle of dealing with apparent contradictions. As an individual learns to live through the alternations of life, first resisting change, perhaps, but then learning to surrender control of the past and move ahead—in this very process something (someone) very wonderful and beautiful is born. That, in fact, is how the authentic *person* begins to form.

The development of the *person,* of course, takes place not in isolation but in relation with other people. And when others encounter the presence of a *person* who is not veiled by his or her *personage,* that helps to create the conditions for intimacy and deep dialogue about the problems and joys, the awesome secrets of life. Paul's counseling was based on this sharing of persons.

Still, the development of the *person* is not complete until it goes through the same process of encounter and alternations (i.e., resisting and then surrendering) as it enters a relationship with God. And this relationship allows the *person* in a human being to catch glimpses of the *Person* of God. Moreover, it unlocks in human beings the ability to receive and give love, and to transmit something of the spiritual, healing strength of God. This dialogue often introduces a consciousness of grace and a creative impetus into that individual's life. Tournier believed that Jesus, through the Holy Spirit, represented the experienced *Person* of God. In addition, through the sharing of their authentic human *persons,* people of faith put others in touch with the hidden, intimate Person of God.

When I first approached Paul Tournier's work, I was immediately taken with his clarity of insight into the human situation. As a student of psychology, I respected his theories of a personal journey conducted through the inner dialogue of opposites. But suddenly, as he was describing a counseling situation in his books or lectures, Paul would begin to speak of God, and of the patient's (and doctor's) relationship with God. At first all my psychological warning bells went off, and I said to myself, "Oh no, Paul. You would have convinced some psychologists if you hadn't brought God in." (I thought this even though as a Christian I was delighted that he did bring God in.)

But after a while I realized that he was being consistent, as a psychologist and a thinker. He had accepted the hypothesis that God is. Having accepted that hypothesis, he could not in fact represent reality in his thinking if he did not discuss the patient's (and doctor's) relationship with God as a real part of a person's need and God's response. He did so with humility and with a clear understanding of the differences between faith and the generally accepted tenets of science. It was exciting for me to hear a brilliant scientist thus bring in evidence of God's healing presence on the same basis as any other evidence related to personal healing.

✖

All of Tournier's insights into the *person*—the inner dialogue, the relationship with others, the encounter with God—came together in his conception of therapy. A healing dialogue of persons takes place when one individual, say, a physician or minister, listens to another. Then the physician begins to reveal a brief glimpse of his or her *person* by sharing the painful, frightening, lonely feelings and experiences of his own life that are normally hidden behind the *personage*. This mutual sharing in an appropriate atmosphere of trust can lead to a wholly different order of dialogue, one in which the secret inner pain and fears of the patient are exposed to the vulnerable, nonjudgmental love of another person. The presence and acceptance of this other person channel a transcendent and healing force into the *person* of the patient—and of the counselor. By exposing his or her own inner conflict, the physician takes away the patient's fear of the patient's own inner warfare. This deep identification of two *persons* on the journey through life provides the matrix for psychological and emotional healing and growth.

There is no way to codify or describe precisely what Tournier did in his therapy sessions because it varied according to the nature and development of his patient's *person*. As one who took counsel with him, I can say that Tournier seemed simply to join me in my situation. He did not "strip" or reveal secret things that were not relevant to my issues, but he became a companion on the journey through life with me. He told of his own loneliness and of the fear in his life and relationships. And although we spoke of possible directions to move, he was never "directive" in the sense of giving advice. I always had the feeling I was finding my own way, with him as a helpful older companion on the journey— and yet his presence and insights made all the difference. It was a paradox. And that is one of the mysteries of the medicine of the person.

Although Tournier the physician used all of his technical skill and insight, his willingness to walk on the journey with the patient introduced a new dimension of discovery and companionship which I have found largely missing in my encounters with physicians and therapists.

Tournier's writings stress the role that "secrets" play in the development of the *person*. Understanding this role helps explain how the healing process operates, whether between a client and therapist or simply between two friends. Secrets affect the development of the *person* from infancy onwards. Before a child is born it is only a part of its mother. But even after the umbilical cord is cut, the child remains for a long time absolutely tied to its mother. In fact his or her *person* is in many ways only a reflection of the mother.

When the child learns to talk, he or she tells the mother everything, even secrets that he or she will tell no one else. Years pass. The child grows and goes to school, a major step toward independence. The child's developing *person* begins to recognize that he or she is having thoughts and experiences that Mother is not. Sooner or later there comes a confusing need to free a little from the mother. Suddenly the child may not want her to get to know everything. Little by little the child will have to separate from the parent in order to become an individual before it is possible to become a *person*. And the child's secrets will be the indispensable instruments of this emancipation.

By keeping secrets from the parents, the child gains an awareness of being distinct, of having an individuality, of being a *person*. Secrets provide the child a way of escaping from the all-powerful grip of parents. The child now knows something that no one else knows—not even father and mother. At last the child possesses something that is the child's very own.

Therefore, learning to manage secrets—learning to keep them to oneself, and to give them up only willingly—constitutes the first movement in the formation of the individual *person*. There is a private place for hopes and dreams that doesn't have to conform to other people's expectations.

As the individual stores away secrets, however, he or she also develops the masks and facades of the *personage* to hide the secrets of his or her *person*. Revealing the inner truth might prove embarrassing, or cause the child to be laughed at or rejected. The *person* and *personage* begin to split.

Take the subject of sex as an example. The young person trying to find out about its secrets is often flooded with physical feelings he or she doesn't understand and that cause embarrassment. Sometimes the child may even believe that he or she has a shameful illness—yet the child is obsessed with sex and wants desperately to penetrate its secrets. But because of the fear of discovery (everyone else seems evasive or much less interested), the child learns to hide or even repress sexual interests and desires behind a *personage*. This protective *personage* may appear "asexual" or, paradoxically, it may appear hypersexual in order to cover fears of sexual inadequacy.

Many individuals go all through life without truly confronting their sexual nature and its deep longings. Lonely, frustrated, and gnawed by guilt, such a person may avoid true intimacy and openness with people because of his or her prison of secrecy (or, in some cases, because of guilt about real or imaginary sexual sins involving masturbation, sexual fantasies, and even early sexual experiments). At all costs, the unacceptable secrets must stay hidden.

The split between *person* and *personage* caused by secrets follows the individual throughout life. When marriage comes, for instance, the newlyweds need their privacy and their secrecy. They begin to develop a marital *personage* which they present to the world but also a joint *person* which represents their secret life together. And any attempts by a parent to correct or pry into that secrecy, or to give advice that seems to impinge on the developing marital *person,* can bring devastating (and surprisingly strong) reactions to the prying parent or in-law. The couple may even cut such parents out of their real lives.

Secrecy has such enormous power because, when violated, it threatens individuality. Totalitarian regimes understand this well: out of contempt for the individual, they systematically violate secrets. And, at a more basic level, everyone knows the dishonor of trying to seize another person's secrets through force or trickery. Perhaps the hesitation and fear that many people feel about going to a psychiatrist or even a minister for counseling comes from our sense that such a person may be able to pierce our secrets.

※

Yet we cannot, and must not, keep our secrets forever. Just as keeping secrets is the first stage in becoming a separate individual, and thus a mature *person,* the second is to choose another or others and make them close friends by *telling* one's secrets. It is the autonomous "freedom" to tell that constitutes the *person,* not just the act of "telling."

A person develops, therefore, as the result of a delicate balance between holding one's tongue and speaking. One who reveals secrets easily is not necessarily mature, for those who open their hearts too freely rarely tell secrets of a liberating nature. On the other hand, one who never divulges, but limits talk to impersonal ideas, forfeits growth. The opposing actions of withdrawing and giving of self alternate throughout a person's life.

How much should a person tell? Paul Tournier felt that this revealing of the secrets of the person is an art, and like all arts must be learned by each individual through practice. Unlike the animals with their reflex actions, human beings can learn to hide or delay their true reactions. We meet and talk together, with much opportunity for telling secrets. But since we also fear being known, we play a kind of charade game. We partially hide behind our *personage,* giving only vague clues as to the hopes, dreams, and pains of our person. We may test the waters by revealing something authentic about ourselves, but if people laugh or appear shocked, we'll pretend we were only joking.

Occasionally, however, something happens to break through this game of hide-and-seek. For example, a person may one day speak to you in an intimate tone that you've never heard before, telling you what he or she never dared tell anyone. You are touched. Ordinarily, this person is so reserved. You sense a mark of extraordinary confidence. Of all people, this individual has chosen you for a confidant. At that moment a deep bond connects the two of you. You have a friend.

But more has happened than a new connection between two separate individuals. Something very basic has taken place within each of you, for it is by means of such genuine and intimate encounters that one becomes a *person.* No one discovers himself or herself in solitude. It is only by giving of self that one can find oneself. And to tell a secret is to give one's self. It is the most precious gift, the one that touches the deepest chords of humanity. By overcoming the natural resistance to open one's heart, overcoming timidity and constraint, the individual human being becomes a *person.*

At the same time, you the listener have become more of a *person,* because someone has chosen to entrust you with a secret. And this trust arouses in you a desire to reciprocate, freeing you too of your restraint. In this atmosphere of unusual confidence you can tell some hidden secret. And in this exchange of secrets, each partner grows stronger, more mature.

Of course, one must choose a confidant or confessor very carefully. If a person confides a precious secret to someone who can't keep it, the disclosure is a betrayal, and may block personal growth as much as the telling might have encouraged it. The violated person may withdraw for years, or forever, from such personal encounter.

There are no clear-cut "little" secrets or "big" ones—their importance depends solely on how they affect us. And as we go through life the secrets about which we feel shame, guilt, resentment, or fear may eat away inside us. A person may drink alcohol secretly, though professing not to. Another, a respectable married person and parent, may masturbate, visit a prostitute, or have an affair. Another may cheat on tax statements or have a childish hobby. A strong person may have a weakness which only his or her mate may know about and exploit. There are a thousand cowardly, despicable thoughts and acts that we surprise our-

selves by engaging in. And as the weight of these intimate se
increases, especially as they contradict the public image of our *person -
age,* our *person* is trapped and inhibited from growth. If the secrets prove
too painful, we repress them, hiding them even from ourselves.

✖

What can one do who longs to be known—and yet is blocked by the
fear that his or her secrets might destroy the very relationship or dream
for which the inner person longs? It is this point that Paul Tournier
addresses with his insights into the person-dialogue with God. This "I-
thou" dialogue with God may come years after one has been an active
member of a church.[3] Sensitive people often become aware in midlife
that, however well they may have succeeded in making themselves
known to another person, deep within lies much more to know and to
reveal about their *person.*

Tournier believed that the Christian God, unlike those of the philosophers, chose to reveal his deepest self to each of us—through his *person,*
Jesus Christ, and through his Word, the Scriptures. This revelation
makes possible in return our revelation of ourselves to God.

But since God wants us to be whole *persons,* we also must learn the
process of keeping our secrets, of withdrawing from him, else our confession of secrets will not have the value of a free act. So in healthy Christian lives we find in our relationship with God this alternation of refusal
and surrender so necessary to the formation of a *person.* That is evidently why God respects our revolts, our reticence, our disobedience, for
these alone confer a genuineness on our witness, our confessions, and
our adoration. Paul once told me, "He who has never doubted has never
found true faith either. He who has never said no to God cannot genuinely say yes to him."

In dialogue God speaks to each of us, revealing both the falseness of
our *personage* and the reality and plan or potential of our natural *per -
son.* The dialogue may be difficult, and threatening, for within it we discover potentials we must strive to realize, and honesty and vulnerability we must risk.

But in this dialogue with God we find ourselves freed for a deeper dialogue with others who are also trying to become the people God intended
them to be. We find authentic "fellowship." And deeper interpersonal
help and love become possible because of the double movement of the
person coming out of secrecy in response to God and to people.

Withdrawal and surrender—the alternating pattern applies to the
developing of *person* in relations with people and also with God. Realizing this has been a great relief to me, because previously I always felt
guilty when I needed to withdraw from people and even from talking

with God. I have learned that God, too, follows the patterns of revealing himself and then silence. He has not "gone," as many seem to think, but rather is giving us the chance to act in faith: the freedom to follow with fidelity what we have been given, or to turn and run as prodigals, or to return and surrender to a new phase of the growth of the *person.*

✖

At one time I immersed myself in the thought and life of Paul Tournier with the idea of writing a book about him. As I shared some crucial experiences of my own with this gentle giant, and heard about his life, my thinking about what it means to live and share as a mature human being gradually changed. I saw that my early attempts to be "personal" in communicating the gospel had pointed in the right direction, but I did not know then about the great areas of denial in my life. These kept me from seeing how dishonest I was with myself, because I was not in touch with my own sin and manipulative self-centeredness. I learned that it is in the vulnerable person-dialogue, with people and with God, that I may come to discover what is behind the wall of my denial and begin truly to know myself, my *person,* so that I can share authentically with God and people.

Perhaps it is at the mysterious level of the *person* that we are most clearly made in God's image, with the potential for strength and yet for gentleness and "weakness." The apostle Paul, for example, learned that God's power "is made perfect in weakness" (2 Cor. 12:9). In the Bible, and especially in the life, death, and resurrection of Jesus, God gives us the model for sharing of *persons* and of resistance and surrender. Jesus' life illustrates the first stage of detachment from his parents as he established his identity, and then the stages of personal connection with his disciples. He shows us the way of intimacy and integrity in order that we may share ourselves and God's love. The mystery of faith is that in this intimate sharing we discover the power of God on the human scene, the Power of the Personal.

GETTING STARTED WITH TOURNIER

More than twenty of Paul Tournier's books are available in English. I would recommend starting with *The Meaning of Persons*. Or, if you are interested in the relation between the physical and the mental/spiritual aspects of healing, *The Healing of Persons* would be a good place to begin. For Christian physicians a follow-up book would be *A Doctor's Casebook in the Light of the Bible*. Two books which have been especially meaningful to me personally are *Guilt and Grace* and *A Place for You,* the book Tournier was writing and speaking about at Laity Lodge when I met him. If you want to go further, you will find books on many aspects of life—from the impact of naming a child in *The Naming of Persons* to facing the aging process in *Learn to Grow Old.*

6

MUSINGS
On a Life with Poetry
Robert Siegel

hen I was young and uneasy under the campus elms, rest-less with the vague hankerings of youth, I took an English course—two rather, having escaped freshman biology by an exam. I had always enjoyed reading: from the Oz books to Ishmael's voy-age out of Nantucket and Hamlet's mouthing of his question. But I could not have guessed what awaited me as I lugged the two tomes of *Major British Authors* from the bookstore to my room in Smith Hall. Concealed between the sober blue covers lay lines of poetry that would change the course of my life that year, and continue to affect it now.

One of the first of these hidden mines went off while I was reading Chaucer. After I had penetrated the slight barrier of his Middle English, with its curious spelling and pronunciation, I found *The Canterbury*

Robert Siegel is a poet whose books include *In a Pig's Eye* and *The Beasts & The Elders* and the fictional works *Alpha Centauri, Whalesong, White Whale,* and *The Ice at the End of the World.* Formerly a professor of English at the University of Wisconsin-Milwaukee, he also has taught at Dartmouth, Wheaton, Princeton, and Goethe University in Frankfurt.

Tales disturbingly modern, the characters, except for their odd dress and turn of speech, suspiciously like people I knew—warts and all. (To this day the wart on the nose of the miller, black, with three red hairs, is the wart that comes first to mind when I see the word.) But nothing there prepared me for the effect of two lines in "The Knight's Tale." In this story a young knight laments the death of his friend, crying out,

> What is thys world? What asketh man to have?
> Now in his love's armes, now in his colde grave?[1]

For an eighteen-year-old hundreds of miles from home and several states from the girl he hoped to marry, that was the question—far more so than Hamlet's. Two years earlier, a friend of mine had died of polio shortly after leaving for college. Now I myself was barely two weeks gone from home and an eternity (it seemed) from the one face I desired to behold. In those two balanced lines of Chaucer the extremes of human experience flashed before me, almost as if the poet had sifted through all of life and fastened upon its two essential parts: on the one hand, the indescribable presence of love, on the other, the unimaginable absence of death. The glory of the sunlit day and the blackness of night that swallows it.

Love and death, one and then the other—it was all there in the twin images of warm arms and a cold grave. As I stared at the words, Peter's face flashed before me, a face radiant with humor as I had last seen it on a debate trip months before his death from the three-day virus. Rather than evoking horror, though, these lines gave me a peculiar pleasure. Read repeatedly, they produced a dizzy feeling of detachment, the cold pleasure of being snatched, like Chaucer's Troilus, above the starry spheres to see all things in their smallness. I felt like Julian of Norwich when God showed her "a little thing, the size of a hazelnut, in the palm of my hand, and it was as round as a ball. I looked at it with my mind's eye and I thought, 'What can this be?' And the answer came, 'It is all that is made.'"[2]

I walked from my room to Dr. Brown's class in a trance after reading these lines. Over the weeks, the feeling slowly faded, only to wax again later that fall when (miraculously, it seemed) the girl from home visited my southern Ohio campus. Walking through the Granville Burying Ground with her, examining the tombstones of those who perished in the milk fever of 1834, I felt it again. So intense were the contrasts of that scene, I can without effort recall the scritch of dried-up leaves blowing across fallen slate, the smell of apples in decay, the gray lid of clouds, her cool fingers in mine, and the blue loden coat she wore over a lighter blue sweater. I still feel the lumpy turf under our shoes and see the faint white puffs of our breath as we tried to read aloud the blurred epitaphs, stumbling among the gravestones thrust up like crooked teeth. Her light hair and gray blue eyes held in them the brightness and clarity of the sky and absent sun and for that reason seemed fragile to me, and all the more dear.

Among the broken slates, it struck me how brief and fleeting indeed was the life of man. The lines from Andrew Marvell carved themselves across my brain:

> But at my back I always hear
> Time's wingéd chariot hurrying near;
> And yonder all before us lie
> Deserts of vast eternity.[3]

With a warm breath rapidly cooling in that rising damp, I proposed. The murmured words rose and vanished in the overarching gray. Specifically, I proposed that we elope to Michigan, where two could get a marriage license under the age of twenty-one.

"Yes," she said. "Yes," also in a whisper, and we were silent, clasping hands over the dead.

Fortunately, later that day Ann had the good sense to reconsider.

I remember the cool touch of her cheek as we kissed good-bye at the train the next day, the rough feel of her loden wool against my neck, and, later, the unfamiliar taste of salt creasing down my face as I drove the fifty miles back to campus: "Now in my love's armes, now in my colde grave."[4]

It was a time when poetry opened up life, and life, poetry. With each author and literary period I felt myself immersed in a new way of looking at everything: whether through the luminous images of Spenser's *The Faerie Queene,* the passionate wit of Donne, the sweetly reasoned couplets of Pope, or the transcendent vision of Wordsworth, who saw splendor in the grass, glory in the flower.

Poetry permeated my life. Whenever the analytical materialism of some professors broke the world into hard lifeless pebbles, poetry melted it down and gave it back mint-fresh. Poetry was the golden currency from the mines of academe. Strangely, most of the academic world (it struck me then as well as now) spend their lives measuring the slag heap from those mines.

Meanwhile, for me, the mysteries of love, death, and what Shakespeare's Cleopatra calls "immortal longings" pulsed through all the lines worth remembering. The best teachers, like Dr. Merle Brown (or the much different Mr. Keating in *Dead Poets Society*) do not forget the mysteries of poetry, or that they are felt upon the pulses. Dr. Brown taught me something else too, which I can only identify as intellectual passion—that moment when thought becomes feeling and feeling thought. Yet, sadly, the field of English has never lacked for those who forget these truths, teachers well caricatured by the poet Yeats:

> Old learned, respectable bald heads
> Edit and annotate the lines
> That young men, tossing on their beds
> Rhymed out in love's despair.[5]

My own version of the Great Chain of Being, stretching up from the void to God, showed poetry occupying a place just above man's and a little lower than—perhaps even with—the angels'. For me poetry was a necessary part of that ladder which Plato and those later in cahoots with him (such as Augustine, Spenser, Milton, Wordsworth, and Shelley) saw reaching up from the vegetable kingdom to divine Love. A year or so later, I became aware that these "immortal longings" that I met in poetry were intimately involved with the new religious direction in my life.

One considerable source of spiritual insight was Spenser's *The Faerie Queene*—especially Book I where the Red Crosse Knight in his search for Una, or Truth, is constantly tricked by false appearances. His confusion and roundabout way through the land of faerie struck me as true to the misleading appearances of the world I encountered and to my own bumbling pilgrimage among conflicting worldviews. Most of these, like the behaviorism of my psychology course, were reductionistic: they held up a part of the truth as the whole. They left out, or too easily explained away, the essential struggle of the will and the actual weather of personal experience. (I recall W. H. Auden's remark that as a boy he didn't believe in witches, giants, and ogres, and only as an adult did he discover they really exist.)[6] Red Crosse is gradually led out of his confusion and when the old man Contemplation shows him a vision of Jerusalem, his eyes are "dazed . . . Through passing brightness."[7] For me, Spenser's poetry itself provided that surpassing brightness.

An equally important point about the Red Crosse Knight's adventures has stuck with me: whenever Red Crosse thinks he has all things neatly put together and in their final order, someone or something comes along and knocks him off his horse. Whoever is in control, it is not Red Crosse. He learns humility: the mystery is greater than his apprehension of it.

The light I felt shining through Spenser's poetry and that of others obviously had a source beyond the poet's world, or even the world of faerie, where it shone more intensely. These were not the highest rungs on the platonic ladder of being.

In his "Elegiac Stanzas" Wordsworth speaks of "The light that never was, on sea or land, / The consecration, and the Poet's dream."[8] In a literal sense, that light never was on land or sea, as sunlight can be, but shone through them from a deeper source. That was the light I felt coming through poetry, a light showing from inside them and ultimately from beyond them. In the experience of most of us, the light can be elusive, as Wordsworth laments in his "Intimations of Immortality" ode,

> Whither is fled the visionary gleam?
> Where is it now, the glory and the dream?[9]

Yet it is the same light responsible for "splendor in the grass" and "glory in the flower." It is a light beyond our control and in its furthest reaches dissolves into mystery.

At a critical time in my own development I read the seventeenth-century Henry Vaughan and found that the light I felt shining through most poetry might also be found in God, where it was paradoxically described as "a deep but dazzling darkness":

> There is in God (some say)
> A deep, but dazzling darkness; As men here
> Say it is late and dusky, because they
>   See not all clear;
> O for that night! where I in him
> Might live invisible and dim.[10]

The last two lines had an intoxicating effect, an effect more usually available to me through the light I sensed in nature. Later, while attending college in Illinois, I would spend whole afternoons in the Morton Arboretum feeding on lines from Marvell's "The Garden," where in contemplation the mind

> creates, transcending these,
> Far other worlds and other seas,
> Annihilating all that's made
> To a green thought in a green shade.[11]

The effect of the last two lines was indescribable, almost an alteration of being—a quietus, a raptus.

Sometimes the light was transmuted, taking the form of a voice, like that of the ineffable nightingale in Keats's ode which, through song, creates homesickness for a land from which we are all exiles:

> Perhaps the self-same song that found a path
> Through the sad heart of Ruth, when, sick for home,
> She stood in tears amid the alien corn.[12]

(Of course, as the poem's later lines suggest, this light, this voice, if not tracked to its source, could be misleading, charming "magic casements, opening on the foam / Of perilous seas, in faery lands forlorn."[13] In this regard I think of the false lights that mislead the Red Crosse Knight in his meanderings through faerie, and the "fair appearing good"[14] that deceives Eve in the Garden and all of us at one time or another.)

The source of the light was most frequently named in the poems of Gerard Manley Hopkins, the Jesuit poet who celebrated the unique beauty (what he called "inscape") of each particular thing and found each a vehicle for divine glory:

> The world is charged with the grandeur of God.
> It will flame out, like shining from shook foil.[15]

Hopkins celebrated the light which shone from each individual thing—a wave of the sea, an eyelash—and urged his readers likewise to "Give beauty . . . back to God, beauty's self and beauty's giver,"[16] however near at hand or unusual the thing showing it:

> Glory be to God for dappled things . . .
>
> For rose-moles all in stipple upon trout that swim
> Fresh-firecoal chestnut-falls, finches' wings . . .
> Whatever is fickle, freckled, (who knows how?)
>   With swift, slow: sweet, sour; adazzle, dim;
> He fathers-forth whose beauty is past change.
>   Praise him.[17]

But it was in the poems of T. S. Eliot, like myself a child of the twentieth century, that I found a pattern similar to my own. I discovered that the paradisal glimmerings in poetry had drawn him on a quest for the same source I had found in Spenser. His poem "The Waste Land," concerned a quest for the modern equivalent of the Holy Grail in a landscape darker, but no more deceptive, than that the Red Crosse Knight wandered. In "Ash Wednesday" and the *Four Quartets,* Eliot's quest ends with the discovery of one like the mythical Fisher-king, whose wounds heal the sick land and give water to the dehydrated soul:

> The wounded surgeon plies the steel
> That questions the distempered part;

Beneath the bleeding hands we feel
The sharp compassion of the healer's art.[18]

Four Quartets concludes, like Dante's *Divine Comedy,* with a vision of paradise regained:

The end of all our exploring
Will be to arrive where we started
And know the place for the first time.
Through the unknown, remembered gate
When the last of earth left to discover
Is that which was the beginning;
At the source of the longest river
The voice of the hidden waterfall
And the children in the apple-tree
Not known, because not looked for
But heard, half-heard, in the stillness
Between two waves of the sea.
Quick now, here, now, always—
A condition of complete simplicity
(Costing not less than everything)
And all shall be well and
All manner of thing shall be well
When the tongues of flame are in-folded
Into the crowned knot of fire
And the fire and the rose are one.[19]

As Eliot wrote, "In my beginning is my end." Eventually poetry led me to try to capture in poems of my own (however fleetingly) the light I glimpsed in others—especially that light as it comes through familiar things. I learned the ordinary, the homely, even the grotesque, can reveal it, along with the sublime. In "Rinsed with Gold, Endless, Walking the Fields," I celebrate, among other things, the quality of sunlight on a fine September afternoon:

Let this day's air praise the Lord—
Rinsed with gold, endless, walking the fields,
Blue and bearing the clouds like censers,
Holding the sun like a single note
Running through all things, a *basso profundo*
Rousing the birds to an endless chorus.

Let the river throw itself down before him,
The rapids laugh and flash with his praise,
Let the lake tremble about its edges
And gather itself in one clear thought

88

To mirror the heaven and the reckless gulls
That swoop and rise on its glittering shores.

Let the lawn burn continually before him
A green flame, and the tree's shadow
Sweep over it like the baton of a conductor.
Let winds hug the housecorners and woodsmoke
Sweeten the world with her invisible dress,
Let the cricket wind his heartspring
And draw the night by like a child's toy.

Let the tree stand and thoughtfully consider
His presence as its leaves dip and row
The long sea of winds, as sun and moon
Unfurl and decline like contending flags.
Let blackbirds quick as knives praise the Lord,
Let the sparrow line the moon for her nest
And pick the early sun for her cherry,
Let her slide on the outgoing breath of evening,
Telling of raven and dove,
The quick flutters, homings to the green houses.
Let the worm climb a winding stair,

Let the mole offer no sad explanation
As he paddles aside the dark from his nose,
Let the dog tug on the leash of his bark,
The startled cat electrically hiss,
And the snake sign her name in the dust

In joy. For it is he who underlies
The rock from its liquid foundation,
The sharp contraries of the giddy atom,
The unimaginable curve of space,
Time pulling like a patient string,
And gravity, fiercest of natural loves.

At his laughter, splendor riddles the night,
Galaxies swarm from a secret hive,
Mountains lift their heads from the sea,
Continents split and crawl for aeons
To huddle again, and planets melt
In the last tantrum of a dying star.

At his least signal spring shifts
Its green patina over half the earth,
Deserts whisper themselves over cities
Polar caps widen and wither like flowers.

In his stillness rock shifts, root probes,
The spider tenses her geometrical ego,
The larva dreams in the heart of the peachwood,
The child's pencil makes a shaky line,
The dog sighs and settles deeper,
And a smile takes hold like the feet of a bird.

Sit straight, let the air ride down your backbone,
Let your lungs unfold like a field of roses,
Your eyes hang the sun and moon between them,
Your hands weigh the sky in even balance,
Your tongue, swiftest of members, release a word
Spoken at conception to the sanctum of genes,
And each breath rise sinuous with praise.

Let your feet move to the rhythm of your pulse
(Your joints like pearls and rubies he has hidden),
And your hands float high on the tide of your feelings.
Now, shout from the stomach, hoarse with music,
Give gladness and joy back to the Lord,
Who, sly as a milkweed, takes root in your heart.

—ROBERT SIEGEL

As for the girl I left at home when I went to college? In my end is my beginning. Not long ago I ran across a poem of hers which reflects some of what I've been trying to say—how poetry puts things together that seem separate and unconnected and how a light then shines through them.

Her poem is about Glen Columbkille, the ruins of St. Columba's fifth-century monastery on the west coast of Ireland where the saint erected a stone cross and church on a mound sacred to the Druid religion and several others before it. From this mound and the beehive stone huts around it, his monks fanned out as missionaries to all Europe during the Dark Ages. Of Glen Columbkille the poet asks,

What is there about this place that lies at
The tip of earth and summons the sea to nest
Its limits, a masher bird feathering her brood?
St. Columba . . . wedged the Celtic
Cross on the pile of stones some ancient
Druid tribe used to bury their dead.
The beehive huts stand like giant cabbages
Waiting for the harvest that came and left . . .

For time waits here, stone upon stone upon stone.

When I read that, I remembered those earlier stones she and I had gazed at walking through the cemetery one November afternoon, where time also waits, stone upon stone. I felt a twinge of nostalgia, but not all that much, for as I confessed at the outset, poetry has shaped my life. That same girl I left at the train station in Marion, Ohio, four years later became my wife. Together Ann and I have three daughters, all beyond the age she and I were when we encountered Chaucer's knight and Keats's nightingale—and so perhaps are the words of poems made flesh.

GETTING STARTED WITH POETRY

Bookstores, like libraries, usually have a special poetry section. Your librarian will be glad to help you find the classics and your bookstore clerk will help you find newer works in *Books in Print*. The collected works of Spenser, Wordsworth, Hopkins, Eliot, and others are easily available. There are so many good anthologies of poetry it is difficult to mention just one or two. But the W. W. Norton company is noted for its large and helpful ones, such as *The Norton Anthology of Poetry* or *The Norton Anthology of Modern Poetry*. There are also pocket-size paperbacks under titles such as *Great Poems of the English Language*. I should also mention *The Oxford Book of Christian Verse*. To understand more of how poetry works, a reader might try X. J. Kennedy's *Understanding Poetry*.

7

JOHN MILTON
Sing Heavenly Muse

Emilie Griffin

Lately I have started reading John Milton again with something like the ferocity I had as an undergraduate in the late fifties. My motives are different now, but the passion, the fervor, the longing is much the same.

In those days, I think, I wanted to decipher experience, and I seized upon any writer—novelist, dramatist, essayist, or poet—who could give me a clue; I devoured writers for their insights, then cast them aside, while I attempted to digest the meaning. In this needy spirit I consumed Milton for perhaps a year or two, making him my chief poet and interpreter of reality. I understood him little, though I thought I saw right through to the heights with him. Later on, I would know what I had missed, how much had slipped through my consciousness, ungrasped.

Emilie Griffin is the author of, among others, *Clinging: The Experience of Prayer, The Reflective Executive: A Spirituality of Business and Enterprise, Spiritual Classics* (with Richard Foster), and *Doors into Prayer: An Invitation.* She lives in Louisiana with her husband, William Griffin.

Now, possibly, the way I experience Milton has something to do with darkness in the spiritual life. Recently I have been praying through his sonnet that begins, "When I consider how my light is spent / 'ere half my days in this dark world and wide."[1] This poem, known as the sonnet "On His Blindness," is rather like the cry of the psalmist; it takes God to task for the things in our own experience that baffle us, the limits on our lives we had not expected, the boundaries we never foresaw when we were young.

At other times I imagine that my love of John Milton has less to do with darkness than with light. A flood of light and beauty cascades through his work. He is one of the few writers who has captured a celestial vision. His angels are stunningly real. They make sudden appearances. They speed through the universe. The universe itself is bright with meaning in Milton's imagination. I love Milton, I then suppose, because of the scope of his vision, the size of his imagination. I love him not only for his insights but for insight itself: for seeing that "the mind is its own place, and in itself / can make a heaven of hell, a hell of heaven."[2]

At yet other moments, my feeling for Milton has nothing to do with any of these things. Instead I am drawn by his weaknesses, his glaring flaws of character. Milton is ambitious. Arrogant. He dares to be the best poet and thinker of his generation. He insists he will take hold of the epic poem and transform it. He shows off his brilliance at Cambridge, writing poems about his destiny. He is outraged with himself for not having achieved greatness by his twenty-third year. He is everything false and presumptuous that I was as an undergraduate, and later. (Milton never outgrew his pomposity, either. Later in life he made an extended trip through Europe, explaining to the Italians and others what a great poet he was, though he had hardly written enough verse to justify even being considered a minor one!)

Milton simply will not entertain the possibility of failure. Triumph dominates his vocabulary. He strikes attitudes, he poses, he condescends. And I sometimes fear I am exactly like him! Afraid of my peers, wanting to be liked by them, afraid to be nicknamed and teased by them, I am for all the world like Milton, who earned the nickname, "The Lady of Christ's College." I get impatient with my teachers when I know more than they do; I blaze with virtue and accomplishment; I am determined to win, forever snatching at victory and despising defeats, even little ones. I am grandiose. I have no sense of proportion. I want to possess the world, to embrace it, to conquer it. I am, in a word, proud.

Yet I am not simply *that* Milton but also still another one. The one who has no sense of the future, no consolations to cling to, no assurance of success. The one who is constantly baffled by the course his life is taking.

Who feels a tension in his life between the high call to poetry and the plain requirement to earn a living, to pursue some necessary occupation, to do the will of God and not his own. Then I identify most with the Milton of no-vision, not the Milton of high imagination and grandeur. I feel with Milton most in fidelity and failure; least in the business of being the greatest epic poet of the English language. Always, he holds out to me the virtues I long for, and is cramped by vices that I recognize as my own.

※

Striking isn't it, that a twentieth-century woman could be so moved by the figure of a writer born in 1608 in Cheapside, London, who spent most of his life reading, writing, and engaged in political life? What could possibly link us, even in imagination? What intensity of heart was it, what depth of soul that first captured me when I curled up under the trees of Newcomb College in New Orleans with a copy of Milton's poetry and all my life spread before me? How did the persona of the passionate young man with the long hair and the beautiful face seize upon my affections? How was it that I managed to walk with him through Cambridge, enter into the mind of his moving elegy, "Lycidas," the comic spirit of "L'Allegro," and darker spirit of "Il Penseroso"? How was it that I first attempted sonnets under Milton's tutelage? How was it that on some level John Milton, some three hundred years my elder, first opened up for me an understanding of the life of faith?

Most of all, I must suggest it all came about through reading Milton, rather than just thinking about reading him and being afraid to try. Milton is much maligned. People tell you he is too difficult, too intellectual, too heady, too obscure. In fact he is a spellbinder—but only to those who are willing to actually take up the book and read!

Reading Milton, I find, is something like praying. Before you begin there is a kind of tension. Something you can't put your finger on gets in the way. A reluctance builds before you actually open the book, a little murmur reminds you of all the things you could be doing instead. Reading Milton, the murmur suggests, is a tiresome duty, one that takes much effort and yields little pleasure. Milton is only for scholars, for people in universities who have papers to write on individuals dreadfully out of date. You may remember that line from George Bernard Shaw's play, *Man and Superman,* characterizing *Paradise Lost* as a long poem that no one has ever read all the way through. But if you're lucky, you also remember that onstage it was the devil who said it.

If you take hold of the moment and shove temptation aside, however, something enticing lies in store. Milton offers a journey into the imagination that is full of high drama and entertainment, rich with conflict and dread. With Milton, you plunge into a vast and visual cosmic realm. Much to your surprise, you find spiritual insight there.

I enjoyed watching this discovery take place a short while ago with a friend of mine who wanted to learn something about poetry. This man is a professor of systematic theology and philosophy, well educated in many fields. Yet poetry had somehow eluded him. One evening, at my suggestion, we tried reading Book I of *Paradise Lost* out loud. Milton reads wonderfully out loud. The verses have a resonance and power that spill out when the words are spoken. At the same time you can hear the structure of the verse as it moves from line to line. Soon, however, you forget the verse and are caught up in seeing the action unfold. Hell is spread out before you in a strange panoply. Devils swarm there, planning a rebellion against God Almighty. A rich mythology, both classical and biblical, comes bristling to life.

All this invited my friend to enter a new and exciting realm. He was fascinated by the sheer ambition of the project, something on the same scale as great philosophy or music. How could a work of such proportions have existed for centuries without his knowing something about it? Who was this John Milton, anyway, and why wasn't his work better known? It was as if Plato or Aristotle had fallen off the list of great philosophers and was residing in some obscure corner of the library, unappreciated, almost forgotten.

As part of my own rediscovery of Milton, I took a paperback edition of *Paradise Lost* and *Paradise Regained* on a plane flight recently. There is nothing more satisfying than Milton at thirty-seven thousand feet, where creation is flung out in all its grandeur. With astonishment you remember that Milton "saw" it all long before airplane travel and when he was totally blind. His vivid description of *terra firma*—especially Eden, that privileged spot—from the archangels' point of view is breathtaking.

Milton takes scenes and characters from Scripture and enhances them, adding new luster without disturbing our sense of the Bible as it is. Take his description of the Archangel Raphael on his way to earth to counsel Adam and Eve:

> Down thither prone in flight
> He speeds, and through the vast ethereal sky
> Sails between worlds and worlds, with steady wings
> Now on the polar winds, then with quick fan
> Winnows the buxom air; till within soar
> Of towering eagles, to all the fowls he seems
> A phoenix, gazed by all . . .

> At once on the eastern gulf of Paradise
> He lights, and to his proper shape returns
> A seraph winged; six wings he wore, to shade
> His lineaments divine; the pair that clad
> Each shoulder broad, came mantling o'er his breast
> With regal ornament; the middle pair
> Girt like a starry zone his waist, and round
> Skirted his loins and thighs with downy gold
> And colors dipped in heaven: the third his feet
> Shadowed from either heel with feathered mail
> Sky-tinctured grain.[3]

In Scripture, archangels simply appear. In Milton, they actually travel.

But my relationship to Milton goes deeper than poetic figures. The heroism of his angels, the blazing erotic beauty of Adam and Eve in their primordial innocence, the poet's grasp of Scripture and pagan mythology—I admire all these, but for me the power of Milton goes beyond them. What makes me care about Milton is his depth of spirit, his understanding of human frailty, of suffering, of temptation, of the mystery of God.

Especially when I was young, my ambitions were global. I wanted to conquer the world, to hold it in the palm of my hand. My plan was to use the force of my talent to stun the world and bring it to heel, not eventually, but right away. In some dim part of myself I must have known these grandiose dreams were spiritual temptations. In Milton himself, as in his work, I saw this for the first time.

True to the pattern of aspiring writers in every generation, he wanted early recognition and what we would call stardom: fame. At the same time, he had the spiritual understanding I lacked. Fame, he knew, was the trickiest spiritual challenge. In "Lycidas," his elegy on the early death of his schoolmate Edward King, Milton wrote:

> Fame is the spur that the clear spirit doth raise
> (Thee last infirmity of noble mind)
> to scorn delights, and live laborious days.[4]

I have not been able to think about fame since, without remembering it as the last infirmity. In another poem, a sonnet written about the time of his twenty-third birthday, Milton laments that he has achieved so little:

> How soon hath time the subtle thief of youth
> Stolen on wing my three and twentieth year
> My hasting days fly on with full career
> But my late spring no bud or blossom sheweth.[5]

But the poem which begins as a cry for recognition ends with measured spiritual reflection:

> Yet be it less or more, or soon or slow
> It shall be still in strictest measure even
> To that same lot; however mean or high,
> Toward which time leads me, and the will of heaven;
> All is, if I have grace to use it so,
> As ever in my great taskmaster's eye.[6]

Still another way I identified with Milton was in the conviction he had from earliest childhood that he was marked for greatness. I can remember as a child identifying with Samuel in the temple, when he heard the Lord's voice speaking directly to him. There is no way to know how Milton came to believe in his own destiny. Clearly both Milton and his family believed he had been singled out for some studious and literary work, called by God to some special prophetic task. No doubt such a "call to greatness" is part of ego development in all young children. But Milton (and I) took it very seriously.

As a child, Milton burned the midnight oil to read every book he could; he attended school and was also tutored at home. I had been taught to read at the age of three by a great-aunt, an elementary school teacher who believed in early reading. By my family I had been led to believe I was a gifted child. There was pleasure in this, and challenge, but also a quality of differentness that brought its own pain. Here again I was like Milton. At Cambridge he was called "The Lady of Christ's College" for his sensitive, feminine appearance. I also knew what it was like to be treated as an outsider—in my case, for intellectual pretensions, for using rarefied vocabulary, and talking less about events than about ideas.

Later in life, as blindness descended, Milton wrote:

> When I consider how my light is spent
> Ere half my days in this dark world and wide
> And that one talent which is death to hide
> Lodged with me useless, though my soul more bent
> To serve therewith my Maker and present
> My true account, lest he returning chide
> Doth God exact day-labour, light denied,
> I fondly ask; But patience to prevent
> That murmur, soon replies, "God doth not need
> Either man's work or his own gifts, who best
> Bear his mild yoke, they serve him best, his state
> Is kingly. Thousands at his bidding speed
> And post o'er land and ocean without rest;
> They also serve who only stand and wait."[7]

Reading that poem for the first time, I thought Milton presumptuous to suppose his talent was "death to hide." Yet privately I thought the same of my own talent. Also, once I was consciously a Christian, I felt a constant tension between wanting to do something great for the Lord and honestly admitting I wanted to be great for my own sake. Lucifer's defiant words, "I will not serve," expressed Milton's own rebellious spirit and mine.

Yet, as Milton's life shows, grandiosity may hide beneath it a genuine gift, the chance of a humility that shapes it to God's service. Milton did that, reaching far beyond the ordinary tasks of life to devote his talent to the service of God. To be shaped by Milton's life is to learn humility and trust. This poet with youthful arrogance, overweening ambition, global knowledge, and remarkable discipline still accomplished little in poetry, his chosen path, until late in life. Then, in spite of disease, blindness, and old age, he kept on working. He rose at four to pray and meditate. Others read to him and he dictated his verse epics to his daughters. Milton pushed on, yet never fully knew the effect of his life's work. He poured himself out to be a great epic poet but never knew he had attained his goal. Trusting to God, he endured to the end. As for *Paradise Lost,* its publication fetched him the tidy sum of five pounds.

✳

Spirituality was only one part of my exchange with Milton. His ideas affected me just as strongly. A propagandist and a man of politics, Milton was one of the great thinkers and writers on freedom. His most famous speech, to Parliament, the *Areopagitica,* dealt with freedom of expression. Though a Puritan who served under Oliver Cromwell, Milton strongly opposed banning books. "He who destroys a good book kills reason itself, kills the image of God as it were, in the eye." As Milton saw it, a good book is "the lifeblood of a master spirit, embalmed and treasured up on purpose to a life beyond life."[8]

This strong belief in freedom arose out of Milton's views on freedom of the will. A loving God had designed freedom and given it to men and women in spite of his foreknowledge that they could and would abuse it. We, therefore, should follow God's example. Also, Milton had no confidence in morality gained under compulsion; for him, it was no morality at all. Arguing that goodness should be tested in the marketplace, he said, "I cannot praise a fugitive and cloistered virtue."[9] Milton insisted on the value of goodness freely chosen: "Were I the chooser," he said, "a dram of well doing should be preferred before many times the forcible hindrance of evil-doing. For God more esteems the growth and completing of one virtuous person than the restraint of ten vicious ones."[10]

Virtue was one of Milton's great themes, dealt with touchingly in *Comus,* an early work written to be performed as a masque at Ludlow Castle in 1634. *Comus* is a dramatic poem with music to be performed outdoors. The work was commissioned by the Egerton family, whose near relatives, Lord and Lady Castlehaven, had been involved in a sex scandal. Castlehaven, a homosexual, had been arrested for buggery, for collaborating in the rape of his wife by one of the servants (who was also his own homosexual partner); and for collusion in the rape of his daughter. (Clearly, our own era has no monopoly on sexual aberration.) It is possible that the Egerton family chose the theme of virtue for Milton's masque because they wanted to cleanse the family name. Certainly they wanted to proclaim the good reputation of the Lady Alice Egerton. I prefer to suppose that Milton suggested the theme. Certainly it was one of his ongoing themes: virtue as dazzling, beautiful, compelling, and a powerful protection against the assaults of wickedness.

To complete this account of John Milton, and of the me I see in his reflection, I must mention one more character: Dr. Mildred Christian, my professor at Newcomb College, who brought Milton fully to life for me. No one in Miss Christian's classes could fail to notice her love of John Milton; nor could anyone fail to notice her personal resemblance to an angel. White-haired, pink-cheeked, with flashing blue eyes, this diminutive woman was filled with authority. And her voice, speaking or singing, was glorious. To excite us about Milton as artist and songwriter, she sang the songs of his *Comus* from the lecture platform. For us as students she personified something Miltonic: a blazing core of goodness, a flash of understanding and humor, a breadth of knowledge and memory for detail.

Even now I can hardly read a passage of Milton's work without recalling some insight or observation of hers. She knew the man: his self-involvement, his foibles, his ambition, his grandiosity. She painted him, warts and all: being rusticated (sent to the country) from Cambridge for a time, perhaps because he thought he knew more than his tutor; going through stormy times in his several marriages; writing tracts in behalf of divorce to justify his own position in domestic quarrels. Miss Christian never tried to disguise Milton's male chauvinism. She let us know he was not the best of politicians and no genuine diplomat, that he was flawed as an orator despite his gift of rhetoric. Even so, she showed us a man worth admiring, a poet whose lyric vision soared, whose mastery of epic was unmatched, whose love of God was passionate and deep. This was a man who conceived a life's work courageously and set about it fearlessly—a man to follow and imitate.

"Milton, thou shouldst be living at this hour,"[11] Wordsworth wrote in England of 1802. No doubt Wordsworth meant that the England of his time needed Milton's political and poetic vision ("We are selfish men; / Oh! Raise us up, return to us again").[12] For me, in another place and time, Wordsworth's words hold true. Writers today specialize in showing the smallness of man. God, too, has been considerably scaled down. Set against all these, Milton with his grand vision reminds me that with God all things are possible. Wordsworth, who modeled his writing on Milton in many ways, expresses his own love of Milton well:

> Thy soul was like a Star, and dwelt apart;
> Thou hadst a voice whose sound was like the sea:
> Pure as the naked heavens, majestic, free,
> So didst thou travel on life's common way,
> In cheerful godliness; and yet thy heart
> The lowliest duties on herself did lay.[13]

Wordsworth's choice of Milton as mentor confirms my own. Better still, Wordsworth's reflection on Milton's life reminds me of the ordinariness of the writer's path, traveling with visions of grandeur along a common way. Perhaps most of all, both Milton and Wordsworth show me that poetry, and the diligence it takes, can become a task for faith, a form of life commitment often lacking in glamour or consolation. Fidelity in darkness, fidelity in light, the mind living in its own place which is God's place—these are the lessons I draw from my own love of Milton and the love that other writers have shown for him along the intervening centuries.

Milton helps me to see the writer's life and her craft in dialogue with her Maker.

GETTING STARTED WITH MILTON

To read Milton for enjoyment, I would suggest starting with his English sonnets, which are few in number and show a bit of Milton's lightness and humor; next, "L'Allegro" and "Il Penseroso." "Lycidas" is a relatively short work with much to recommend it. Then, plunge right in to *Paradise Lost*. Any good paperback collection should include all these works, as well as *Paradise Regained* and *Samson Agonistes*. *The Life of John Milton* by A. N. Wilson is available in hard cover from Oxford University Press. Also, C. S. Lewis's *A Preface to Paradise Lost* and the commentaries by James Holly Hanford provide genuine insight.

8

WILLIAM SHAKESPEARE
The Sweetest Prince of Them All
William Griffin

I first got into Shakespeare—or perhaps I should say, Shakespeare first got into me—by virtue of performance. I can remember seeing a professional production of *The Merchant of Venice* at the Brattle Street Theatre in Cambridge, Massachusetts, in the spring of 1949. A freshman in high school at the time, I hadn't read it before I saw it, and hence was not prepared for, among other things, how easily the actors would recite the lines and how natural they would make the poetry sound:

William Griffin has done major biographical work on C. S. Lewis and Billy Graham, and modern translations of Thomas à Kempis's *Imitation of Christ* and Augustine of Hippo's *Sermons for Advent, Christmas, New Year's, Epiphany*. He lives in Alexandria, Louisiana.

> How sweet the moonlight sleeps upon this bank!
> Here will we sit and let the sounds of music
> Creep in our ears. Soft stillness and the night
> Become the touches of sweet harmony.
> Sit, Jessica. Look how the floor of heaven
> Is thick inlaid with patines of bright gold.[1]

I was fourteen years old, loved baseball, wasn't allowed out nights, and had no girl friends in my near acquaintance . . . but when I heard words like these spoken from the tiny stage of the Brattle Theatre, I was transported to another world: not to the sixteenth century Venice of history, but to a Venice, I learned later, that existed only in Shakespeare's mind. This one production of the play and my subsequent reading of it put that second Venice into my own mind forever.

I was also held in suspense by the twists of the play's plot, simple as they were. I was not able to guess which of the three caskets would hold the portrait of Portia. But it seemed only fair, as the play and production developed, that the Prince of Morocco picked the golden casket, only to find in it "a carrion Death." It seemed only right that the Prince of Aragon would select the silver casket, only to find in it "the portrait of a blinking idiot." It seemed only just that Bassanio, a maritime merchant who looked like a matinee idol, should humbly ask for the leaden casket, and that he should find therein "fair Portia's counterfeit."

In 1951 I had the unexpected good fortune to visit New York over a holiday weekend with my best friend of the time, Joey Dever. Our parents, who probably wanted to visit a night club, insisted that we do something cultural. They stashed us in the last row—the only seats available—of the Winter Garden Theatre. There Joey and I saw Laurence Olivier and Vivien Leigh in *Antony and Cleopatra*. I say *saw* because the theater was enormous, and I probably heard little. But what I did hear was intoxicating. Cleopatra was a "morsel for a monarch"; Mark Antony was "the noble ruin of her magic"; both were running up and down the Nile in royal barges with poops of beaten gold. Shakespearean speech was beginning to seem a passport, if not to a better, then at least to a better-spoken, world.

After high school, prayerfully answering what I felt was a vocational call, I entered the Society of Jesus, hoping to serve God as a Jesuit and a priest. For eight years I received an extravagant classical education, being exhorted beyond my competence in the Oxford-Cambridge tradition. The lingua franca of this experience, except for recreational times, was Latin.

First stop on the pilgrimage, in the summer of 1952, was Shadowbrook, the name given to the Andrew Carnegie estate in Lenox, Massachusetts. Located halfway up a hill, it looked down upon a classy lake in the near distance and in the far distance off to some hills named Indian Head. Serendipitously, the property was within a trombone slide of Tanglewood, the site each summer of a music festival, the Boston Symphony presiding.

In this happy place I spent four years. I can still remember a bunch of us, a raggle-taggle bunch of male youth with immortal longings, standing on an upper porch in frayed soutanes and shredded cinctures (they gave the newest arrivals the oldest clothing), looking down the lawn through the trees, some of them sculptured, to the roadway around the lake, along which raced all sorts of rich young people in red convertibles, golden tresses traipsing after them in the careless wind.

As we watched this scene, played out like a recitative on August afternoons, someone on the porch would ask of the youth speeding by, many of them our peers in age, the inevitable question: "But are they happy?" A second of thoughtful silence would pass, and then we would laugh ourselves silly. Perhaps it was something of this incongruity that made it possible for the young celibates even to contemplate the staging of a romantic comedy.

At the end of the novitiate, which had to be in the summer of 1954, after having pronounced first vows as a Jesuit on July 31, we put on, I believe for the edification of the fourth-year men, "The Lamentable Comedy and Most Cruel Death of Pyramus and Thisby," the play within a play that appears in the fifth act of *A Midsummer Night's Dream*.

A bunch of "rude mechanicals," as Shakespeare called them, assembled in a clearing to rehearse the script. Peter Quince appointed himself the director and handed out the parts. He appointed Bully Bottom the weaver to play Pyramus, Francis Flute the bellows mender to play Thisby, Robin Starveling the tailor to play Thisby's mother, Tom Snout the tinker to play Pyramus's father, and Snug the joiner to play the lion. In addition to his duties as director, Quince would play Thisby's father.

The humor of the one-act play was, of course, preposterous. Shakespeare was burlesquing the classical myth of a flaming love that could not possibly fail but inevitably did so. It was the stuff tragedies had been made of since Sophocles, but in the hands of Shakespeare and these country bumpkins it would turn into—what else?—comedy. As a result, the playlet and the play that surrounded it, when first performed at, as some think, an aristocratic wedding in 1594 or 1595, sweetly satirized the lunacy of love. What we young celibates were doing with such foolishness escapes me to this day—I was the chief perpetrator—and the frame of mind we were in on that summer day of 1954 was not one of the firstfruits of the *Spiritual Exercises* of Ignatius Loyola.

After the production, and indeed after the poorly provisioned but richly enjoyed party that followed, just before the night prayers, I gave the group of third- and fourth-year Jesuits, of whom I was now one, "points" for meditation. That is to say, I proposed some thoughts for the hour's meditation the following morning, flowing more or less directly from the evening's histrionics.

I remember taking for my text "Put on the Lord Jesus Christ" (Rom. 13:14 RSV). Browsing through Liddell & Scott's *Greek-English Lexicon* (by this time I had five years of Greek and read Homer and Sophocles and some of the Greek Fathers), I noticed that the Greek verb used by Paul in this context had at least two possible meanings. The more obvious was that the Christian should put on the Lord Jesus Christ the way a Roman legionary would put on the leathern armor—helmet, breastplate, greaves, shield—of his profession. The less obvious was that the Christian should put on the Lord the way an actor on the Greek and Roman stages put on a character. Not one New Testament exegete in ten thousand has ever noted the latter meaning. Indeed, it's more in the realm of connotation than denotation, but it's real.

Parenthetically, at the time Paul was writing, the soldier had been a low-comedy character on the Greek and Roman stages for perhaps 250 years. The Roman playwright Plautus created the character of the Braggart Soldier, a man-slayer and would-be lady-killer, who roamed about the world seeking whom he might seduce; since he was lucky in neither war nor love, his only weapons seemed to have been bombast and braggadocio.

Now, some thirty-five years later, I have stumbled across my typewritten text from that midsummer night in 1954:

"Put on the Lord Jesus Christ" (Romans 13:14). As you know, St. Paul took this figure from the life of an actor. It is a strange metaphor, but like the theater world, it is fascinating because "there's no business like show business!" When you consider the actor's patient and laborious reading of a part, his hours of reflection and brooding meditation; when you consider his attempts to see in his imagination his character's deportment and body-acting, to hear with his imagination how he will employ the full spectroscope of his voice, and how he will avoid confining his tones to a monotonous grey; when you consider his private practice before mirrors, his constant use of a recorder: all that he may for the brief "two hours' traffic on our stage" (Prologue, *Romeo and Juliet*) sink his own personality and "put on" before an audience Hamlet or Oedipus; then will you understand what St. Paul means by "putting on the Lord Jesus Christ."

Rereading this paragraph some decades later, I find the style somewhat florid, and indeed feel my face becoming flushed, realizing that I may have borrowed parts of that paragraph from a British book (the

punctuation and the spelling of the word "grey" are definite give-aways).
The point I was trying to make, though, seems to have validity still.

Not long after I quoted Paul, I quoted Shakespeare, or at least one of
his characters, Jaques, the dyspeptic philosopher with the Tidy-Bowl
name in *As You Like It.*

> And all the men and women merely players;
> They have their exits and entrances;
> And one man in his time plays many parts,
> His acts being seven ages.[2]

Reading the manuscript of my points for meditation, I am surprised
to discover that I had managed to work in quotations from such other
Shakespearean plays as *Hamlet, All's Well That End's Well, Much Ado
about Nothing, Coriolanus, Macbeth, Troilus and Cressida, King Lear,
Romeo and Juliet,* and *Antony and Cleopatra.*

Sometime during this period I began to read the rest of Shakespeare's
plays. It was probably during a recuperation. Shadowbrook, known
locally as the "Ruby of the Berkshires," burned down one cold March
night, its red terracotta roof at the climactic point of the inferno descending en masse from the fourth floor to the basement. I was one of the few
casualties, burns covering 35 percent of my body. It gave me, I would
say to commiserating visitors, bundled as I was in bandaging, a whole
new perspective on Lamb's "Dissertation on Roast Pig."

After the skin grafts and the cosmetic surgery, after the gauze and
the Vaseline, I set myself a reading schedule of a play a day, and in the
day-to-day reading I discovered not only a better-spoken world but a bet-
ter-worded world, in which the diamonds were metaphors. Now, at that
time, my everyday world was disciplined both physically and spiritually; intellectually, it was lean, linear, even the study of literature, logicked right down to the last enthymeme. And so to walk into a world
where metaphor was king was escapism at its most Houdini. Like Puck,
I could "put a girdle about the earth in forty minutes."[3]

Early on in the reading, I felt the hot blasts of Shakespearean rhetoric, soliloquies shot as if from culverins that splattered all over my face.
I heard Shylock's plea for Hebraic dignity in *Merchant of Venice;* Marcus
Antonius's eulogy over the corpse of Caesar, not burying his body but
praising his life; the Chorus's wishing for "a Muse of Fire that would
ascend / The brightest heaven of invention" at the beginning of *Henry V.*[4]

Across Shakespeare's tragic stage I learned to walk gingerly, without slipping. Those vile jellies, Gloucester's gouged-out eyes from *King
Lear,* were rolling about underfoot. And that was no banana peel on the
floor—that was Lavinia's tongue untimely ripped from her pretty mouth

in *Titus Andronicus.* A pound of Antonio's tenderest flesh would certainly have hit the floor like a flank steak if Shylock had had his way in
Merchant of Venice.

Tripping was always a possibility—there were bodies everywhere, Mac-
donwald unseamed from the nave to the chops in *Macbeth,* Desdemona
strangled silkily on her couch in *Othello,* Polonius bloodied behind the
arras in *Hamlet,* Caesar daggered by a multitude of senatorial hands in
the tragedy that bears his name. For reasons that only my psychiatrist
could know for sure, if indeed I could afford one, I reveled in the violence.

Across Shakespeare's comic stage I could walk, but not without falling
down in laughter. I felt at home with such characters as the brace of self-
inflated constables, Dogberry in *Much Ado about Nothing* and Anthony
Dull in *Love's Labour's Lost;* the porter who tippled in *Macbeth;* the braggart soldier, Sir John Falstaff, in the *Henry IV* plays, who pranked about
and eventually drank himself to death with such whiskered and whiskied
companions as Bardolph, Peto, and Pistol; the grave-digging clowns in
Hamlet; Malvolio, the yellow-stockinged steward in *Twelfth Night* who
set a new standard in personal vanity; Charles, the well-spoken but
unbribable wrestler in *As You Like It;* the nonsensical Gobbos, elder and
younger, in *The Merchant of Venice;* Autolycus the ballad-monger and
"snapper-up of unconsidered trifles" in *The Winter's Tale;* Sweet Ann
Page, a daughter "with seven hundred pounds of possibilities" in *The
Merry Wives of Windsor;* Nell in *Henry IV, Part I* and Doll in *Henry IV,
Part II,* the sort of quick-witted and quick-sheeted prostitutes one was
led to believe were found in any companionable tavern.

After the fire and after the recuperation, I moved from western to
eastern Massachusetts, to Weston College, where young Jesuits studied philosophy for three years, with side orders of science and literature,
and four years of theology. I was well on my way toward a master's degree
in philosophy, with a thesis on the notion of freedom in Nikos Kazantza-
kis's *The Odyssey: A Modern Sequel*—existentialism *a la grecque.*

I can remember spending afternoon recreations—instead of knocking
the living daylights out of a baseball, which I loved, or rambling around
Thoreau's Walden or Emerson's Concord, which I loathed—going down
to the underground auditorium, whose dimensions matched exactly the
chapel above, and entering one or another of the rooms flanking the foren-
sic stage. This was where the tape recorders and record players were
kept, bulky boxes from the staticky dawn of audio electronics, and where
the seminarians were supposed to perfect their speech.

One day in the latter half of 1956, I can remember playing the newly
released album of *Richard III,* the soundtrack from Olivier's film. (I can't
remember how I got a copy of it—I must have smuggled it in.) Listening
in the semidarkness, I had what I can only call a mystical experience of

a minor sort. Olivier's diction made the ossicles of my inner ear dance. At one moment, when he said the word "sprang'st," I thought I heard him say "s-p-r-a-n-g-s-t," his darting tongue and quavering lips leaping from letter to letter—one vowel sandwiched somewhere among seven consonants—until he had produced an auditory whole. I heard, or thought I heard, everything, including the apostrophe. I changed the way I listened—and indeed the way I spoke—forever.

In those golden years at Weston, we seminarians were subjected to "Speech," a course traditionally entrusted to the man who spoke, not the purest, but the poorest. Besides classroom sessions in that nonsubject, none of which I can remember now, there was reading in the refectory. Hundreds of men would pass into the hall, millions of dollars of education on the hoof. They were a tough audience and indeed a hungry one. On nonfeast days they would have to endure a passage from the Latin Vulgate during the soup course, followed by some chapters from a current nonfiction book until the rector perceived that the last dessert dish had been licked clean. At that point, the *Martyrology* was read, commemorating the birthdays in the Lord of the saints of the day.

The reader of the day climbed up some steps into a carved wooden pulpit and tried to handle the several books on and about the lectern with some decorum. Alas, he was doomed to fail. At least once a week he made a fool of himself by bumping the live microphone with the folio-sized Vulgate, thus sending a sort of sonic boom around the lofty hall, or by nudging the nonfiction book onto the floor below with a loud crash, or by just losing his grip on the *Martyrology,* thus letting it slip under the chair in the pulpit where it could be retrieved only with contortion.

This reading in the dining hall was a loathsome job to many, but I felt drawn to it, volunteering for it as often as I could. Whenever I mispronounced a word, which was often at first, the Elmer Fudd of Jesuit phonics, sitting at the faculty table at the far end of the hall, cut the electrical current of the public address system, and through the intercom I would hear his voice whisper something like, "We-peat, mister: the word is péjorative, not pejórative." Then he restored the juice, and I repeated the corrected pronunciation and carried on.

But I survived and prospered—perhaps I should say, Prosperoed—mastering more alternate pronunciations than Merriam-Webster ever dreamed of—"hárass" instead of "haráss"; "pérfect" instead of "perféct" in the verb form; and the initial "e" in "pejorative" could be pronounced as either a long or a short vowel—all of which invariably turned out to be British rather than American ones. And all this while I was listening to Olivier's voice, recording my own voice in imitation, and beginning to sound like someone who no longer hailed from Massachusetts.

It was about this time, 1958–1959, that the album memorializing John Gielgud's one-man show entitled "Shakespeare's 'Ages of Man'" appeared. I must have smuggled this album into the seminary, too, for I remember spending hours listening to him soliloquize as Romeo, Prospero, Clarence, Richard II, Hamlet, Lear. If Olivier could be said to mouth Shakespeare's lines athletically, then Gielgud could be said to sing the lines gracefully. Goddard Lieberson, the Columbia Masterworks producer, even went so far as to put a paragraph entitled "John Gielgud As Musician" on the album cover. This was soon followed by another Gielgud album, "One Man in His Time."

The Shakespeare passages in both albums I assiduously typed out on an Olympia portable, a German typewriter that demanded one's pinkies press down with fascistic force to elevate the cast iron platen high enough to make the uppercase letters. Eventually I bound the pages between two stiff cardboard covers salvaged from the umpteenth volume in the *New York Times Crossword Puzzle* series. In time, and not too much time at that, I was able to master both Olivier's and Gielgud's delivery and could give a fair imitation of both, even reciting passages that I had never heard either of them do.

What was happening, of course, was more Shavian than Shakespearean, more Pygmalion than Pericles. By changing my speech I was, in a very short time, changing my social class. By getting the Irish immigrant and New England Yankee out of my accent, *by pahking my cah in a place other than the Hahvahd yahd,* I was moving upward rapidly. By mastering Shakespearean sound, the most difficult, or at least the most sophisticated, in the oral language, I was turning myself into a gentleman—or so I thought at the time. I don't know what type of social gathering I imagined I might someday be in, but if anyone challenged my right to be there, I would have only to open my mouth, and they would fall back, realizing that I was one of them or even that I was better than they.

All this was very serious at the time, but as I look back, I find my expectations were grandiose. The Jesuits were, for the most part, a classless society, in which almost no one cared how he sounded. What one said was surely important, but to speak well was to court affectation, which would, if left untended, lead one down the sort of "primrose way to the everlasting bonfire" described by the porter in *Macbeth*.[5]

Of all the books I read about Shakespeare during this time, I can remember only two that were helpful. First was *Principles of Shakespearean [sic] Production* by G. Wilson Knight, the book I had probably burglarized when preparing those points for mediation after "Pyramus and Thisby." Pictured on the back cover, if I remember correctly, was Knight himself sitting on a motorcycle. The pages of the Penguin paperback edition were turning to sepia, its binding was becoming unglued, and its smell was that of must, but the argument it contained was anything but musty. Knight insisted, as I recall, that whenever they entered the lists with each other, Performance should unhorse Poetry. That is to say, the exigencies of production had priority over the regulations of poetry when it came to determining meaning.

C. S. Lewis argued much the same in "Hamlet: The Prince or the Poem?" the Annual Shakespeare Lecture of the British Academy in 1942. He suggested that most Shakespearean criticism had been hopelessly academic, virtually ignoring the dramatic elements that made a play effective. What remained with him decades after reading *Hamlet* for the first time, were the simple things:

> Night, ghosts, a castle, a lobby where a man can walk four hours together, a willow-fringed brook and a sad lady drowned, a graveyard and a terri-ble cliff above the sea, and amidst all these a pale man in black clothes (would that our producers would ever let him appear!) with his stockings coming down, a dishevelled man whose words make us at once think of loneliness and doubt and dread, of waste and dust and emptiness, and from whose hands, or from our own, we feel the richness of heaven and earth and the comfort of human affection slipping away.[6]

The second helpful book was *Shakespeare's Imagery and What It Tells Us* by Caroline F.E. Spurgeon, originally published in 1935. On the cover of the Beacon Press paperback, the edition I had, was an illustration of what appeared to be a mandrake, an herb credited with human attributes and subjected to numerous superstitions, not the least of which was aiding women to conceive. Perhaps it aided Miss Spurgeon to count and categorize Shakespeare's myriad of images, but I'm not sure it helped her interpret them. Appended to the work, appearing after the Index, were charts showing the range and subjects "in five of Shakespeare's plays" (Chart I), "of Marlowe's images in their exact proportion" (Chart II), "of Bacon's images" (Chart III), and so on.

The eleventh chapter, "Shakespeare the Man," I found especially interesting. Since there seemed to be fewer biographical details about Shakespeare than there were for, say, Jesus himself, I looked forward to whatever she might have been able to glean from his works. As a hint of what was to come, she used, as an epigraph to the chapter, some words from *Love's Labour's Lost:* "He is a marvelous good neighbor, faith, and a very good bowler."[7]

If I may reduce her argument to its simplest form, she considered William Shakespeare a sort of Humpty-Dumpty, and having shoved him off the wall, she was trying to put all his images back together again. It was an exercise in what Lewis was already calling, in the 1930s, the "personal heresy," the doctrine that one could traverse backward through time and indeed through works eventually to arrive at the personality of the author. I was grateful that Spurgeon had taken such a good whack at it . . .

> The figure of Shakespeare which emerges is of a compactly well-built man, probably on the slight side, extraordinarily well coordinated, lithe and nimble of body, quick and accurate of eye, delighting in swift muscular movement. I suggest he was fair-skinned and of a fresh color, which in youth came and went easily, revealing his feelings and emotions. All his senses were abnormally acute, especially—probably—those of hearing and taste.
> He was healthy in body as in mind, clean and fastidious in his habits, very sensitive to dirt and evil smells. Apart from many indirect proofs of these facts in the plays, no man could have written his images on sickness, surfeit, gluttony, dirt and disease, who had not naturally a strong feeling for healthy living, a like for fresh air and "honest water" (*Timon of Athens,* 1.2.58), and who was not himself clean, temperate and healthy.[8]

I drank in this description when I first read it. It made the "sweet swan of Avon" sound like Ignatius Loyola's idea of the perfect Jesuit, right down to the minutiae enunciated in the Society of Jesus' "Rules of Modesty," wherein, among other things, wrinkles on the forehead, and indeed much more on the nose, were to be frowned upon. Miss Spurgeon continued:

> He had, in short, an excellent eye for a shot, with bowl or arrow, and loved exercising it. He was, indeed, good at all kinds of athletic sport and exercise, walking, running, dancing, jumping, leaping and swimming.[9]

She seemed to be saying that Shakespeare was what he wrote; indeed that he was some sort of superman, an Elizabethan Ian Fleming creating a sort of Jacobean James Bond. That is to say, he didn't make up a great deal of what he wrote. His ability to image-ize and metaphor-ize was not really well developed. All he had to do was draw on personal experience. I don't think I believed that at the time I first read Spurgeon, and I certainly don't believe it now. He could just as well have been olive-skinned, corpulent, and crapulous. He could have had a bad eye for a bowl as well as for an arrow and would rather have died than bathe. In other words, he could have been more like his comic characters than his historic or tragic characters.

According to Spurgeon, Shakespeare's inner man, as seen in his images, could be summed up in five words: sensitiveness, balance, courage, humor, and wholesomeness.

Those words sounded like a passage from the martyrology that was read every day in the refectory. If I had to find Shakespeare in his works, I don't think I could do it; it would be like trying to pinpoint Yahweh in the Hebrew Scriptures. He's everywhere and nowhere at one and the same time. It would be better, it has always seemed to me, just to acknowledge his shadowy presence and press on.

If, however, I were to pick some words of my own to describe the essence of Shakespeare's quality or character as seen in his plays, I would pick prudence, temperance, fortitude, and justice—the moral virtues, chiefest of them anyway, that have generally been acknowledged, from Plato's time onward, to operate in the order of nature. A random example of this would be Portia, admonishing Shylock in the fourth act of *The Merchant of Venice:*

> The quality of mercy is not strained,
> It droppeth as the gentle rain from heaven
> Upon the place beneath . . .[10]

In addition to the moral virtues, I would also pick imprudence, intemperance, unfortitude, and injustice; that is to say, the moral vices operating in the order of fallen nature. As a forceful example of this I would cite Lear's railing against what he perceived as his youngest daughter's ingratitude: "How sharper than a serpent's tooth it is / To have a thankless child."[11]

So much for Knight and Spurgeon, but there was a third book. . . .

The longer I studied Shakespeare, and the deeper I delved into ascetical theology, the more I wondered why, since he was writing in a Christian age, more of his characters weren't Christians and more of his plots didn't take Christian turns. It was a foolish question, I suppose, but it was not unlike the conundrums with which Christian academics usually bedeviled their students. Are there Christians in the Old Testament? Can Job be considered a Christian hero? Can Oedipus be considered in any sort of sense a Christian tragic hero? And what about *King Lear,* a Christian play in which there are only British pagans?

I began to formulate my answer to questions like these when I read, as part of spiritual reading, Jean Daniélou's *Les saints "païens" de l'Ancien Testament.* In it the French theologian developed the theory of "seminal Christianity." Job and the other holy people of the Old Testament were Christians, contended Daniélou, if not in full chronological bloom, then at least in a seminal way, having drawn all the spiritual nourishment they could from the rather flinty soil in which they had been planted.[12]

If there was any validity to this theory of seminal Christianity, and there appeared to be some, then it was only a hop, skip, and jump to "seminally Christian humanism," a concept that would allow the Christian critic to perceive Christianity, however dimly, not only in *Oedipus Tyrannus* some centuries before the Christian era but also in *King Lear,* which may represent drama in its fullest bloom in the Christian era.

From there it wouldn't take a biathlonic effort to perceive the religious content—employing similar theories from Justin Martyr's *logos sper - matikos* to Karl Rahner's *anonymous Christian*—of many of the literary and dramatic artifacts produced from the beginning of the Christian era down to the present day that are not presentationally Christian.

By way of example, I think of a recent episode from the television series "The Equalizer," in which a character named Robert McCall, retired from a secret service, now tries to Robin Hood his way back into society. Having tracked down one of the perpetrators of a heinous crime, and indeed having shot him almost to death, he pleads with the dying man. "Just consider, for one moment, just consider that there is a God, and tell me where the hostage is!" Shakespeare, I loathe it.

It has been many years since I was a Jesuit, and in that time I have done many non- and even un-Shakespearean things. His presence, however, has been forever with me in a number of memorable ways.

First, almost everything I know about English adjectives I learned from him, especially how to make them out of nouns; in this brief essay I would hearken the reader back to such nouns-cum-adjectives as *whiskered* and *whiskied.* I learned also how to make verbs out of nouns, and I would call your attention to such noun-cum-verbs in the last few pages as *daggered* and *logicked.* The same is true with adverbs.

Second, the result, inevitable perhaps, given so much reading and memorizing of Shakespeare's iambic pentameter, is that I have been inoculated—Shakespeare might have said "pricked"—with the ictus of the iamb. Phrases of mine, clauses, sentences, even paragraphs—including the ones in this essay—sometimes can be scanned to reveal chains of iambs. They can even be parceled into pentameters by anyone crazy enough to want to do so. I've no idea what this means today, whether it may be considered either as *arrière-garde* or *avant-garde.*

Third, years after I had decided that the Jesuits would pursue their goals more surely without my humble efforts than with them, I came to a realization. It was in a quiet moment—I don't think it was a moment of prayer. I realized just why characters like Sir John Falstaff and Justice Shallow, Launcelot Gobbo and Bully Bottom so appealed to me. It was that I too was a buffoon and that I would have to live with my buffoonery, aching like Oedipus, limping like Achilles, wearing original sin like an ass's head over my own for most of the rest of my public life.

Fourth, every year on the anniversary of Shakespeare's birth (he was baptized on April 26, 1564, and hence his birth, unrecorded, has been placed at April 23), I pay homage to the Droeshout engraving, which appeared originally on the title page of the First Folio, printed in 1623. Somewhere, decades ago, in a modestly priced packet of materials about Shakespeare, I discovered a poster-sized enlargement of that portrait, measuring twenty-two by twenty-six inches and had it framed in black metal. Since then, it has occupied the primary position on the wall nearest my writing desk in whatever city. Every April 23 I attach to the glass in the frame, on the spot over Shakespeare's breast, an instant stick-on bow the color of Christmas-red.

Fifth, Shakespeare's presumed birthday was also his death day. He died on April 23, 1616, at the age of fifty-three. The register in the Stratford church, dated April 25, 1616, noted the interment of *"Will. Shakespere, gent."* As a long-time admirer and sometime imitator of the sweetest prince of them all, I could hope for nothing more appropriate on this side of the grave than to have my own burial recorded with the words *"Will. Griffin, gent."*

GETTING STARTED WITH SHAKESPEARE

Go to a bookstore and pick up a paperback edition of a play, any play—a Penguin or Pelican, a Signet Classic or a Bantam Rooster. There's Barron's *Shakespeare Made Easy,* and there's *The Contemporary Shakespeare Series* with modernized text for moderns with low language capabilities. The *Viking Portable Shakespeare* would fit into a pocketbook or attache case, but I don't think either could contain the not-so-portable, almost elephant-octavo *Oxford Shakespeare.* Helpful are either *Tales from Shakespeare* or *Outlines of Shakespeare's Plays.* Shakespeare's recordings are instructive, like John Gielgud's "Ages of Man" or "The Rape of Lucrece and Other Poems" read by Richard Burton, Edith Evans, and Donald Wolfit, or "*Macbeth* with Anthony Quayle" or "*Measure for Measure* with Ralph Richardson" or "*Romeo and Juliet* with Albert Finney and Claire Bloom." Shakespeare's films are entertaining, like *Othello* with Orson Welles as the murderous Moor, *King Lear* with Paul Scofield as the leathery King, *Julius Caesar* with Marlon Brando as a mumbling Mark Antony, *A Midsummer Night's Dream* with Jimmy Cagney as Bottom and Mickey Rooney as Puck, *Much Ado about Nothing* with Kenneth Branagh as Benedick and Emma Thompson as Beatrice. In the end, it's better to go looking for the man and his works by yourself than to accept the recommendation of a stranger. Wherever you begin the conversation with Shakespeare, that's the place for you.

9

JOHN DONNE
As He Lay Dying

Philip Yancey

No matter where I start, I usually end up writing about pain. My friends have suggested various reasons for this phenomenon: a deep psychological scar from childhood that has not yet come to light, or perhaps an additional melancholy chromosome. I do not know. All I know is that I set out to write about something lovely, like the diaphanous wing of a mayfly, and before long I find myself back in the familiar shadow of pain, writing about the mayfly's brief, tragic life.

"How can I write about anything else?" is the best explanation I can come up with for my fixation. Is there a more fundamental fact of human existence? I was born in pain, squeezed out through torn and bloody tissues, and I offered up, as my first announcement of life, a wail. I will likely die in pain as well. Between those brackets of pain I live out my days, limping from the one toward the other.

Philip Yancey, former editor of *Campus Life,* now writes regularly for *Christianity Today* as editor-at-large. His numerous books include *Where Is God When It Hurts, Fearfully and Wonderfully Made, Disappointment with God, I Was Just Wondering, The Jesus I Never Knew, What's So Amazing about Grace?,* and most recently *Soul Survivor.*

Before writing the book *Where Is God When It Hurts,* I spent a month in a seminary library exploring what other people had written. In that library, books about "the problem of pain" filled five long shelves. While browsing in this library of pain I noticed a curious trend: the nineteenth century seemed to mark a watershed in approach to the subject. Earlier works—including some of the greatest writings on pain, by Calvin, Luther, Augustine, Aquinas—had in common an attitude of resigned acceptance, even reverence. These sought to "justify the ways of God to man." The authors wrote with utter confidence, as if the sheer force of their reasoning could calm emotional responses to suffering. Having "solved" the riddle of pain, why wallow in existential angst?

But beginning with the nineteenth-century writings, God was bumped from a "friend of the court" position to the box reserved for the defendant. Modern books, setting forth a mountainous accumulation of evidence against God, took on the tone of a brief for the prosecution. "How can you possibly justify yourself, God?" these angry moderns seemed to say. Evidently, the ancients had not solved the problem at all.

As I read these books in sequence, the change in tone seemed remarkable. The earlier, reverent books had been written in an age when the average person lived thirty-five years, when surgeries were performed without benefit of anesthesia or antiseptic, when bubonic plague ravaged whole continents. And yet the modern authors—who lived in princely comfort, toiled in climate-controlled offices, and hoarded elixirs in their medicine cabinets—were the ones smoldering with rage.

After reading through several shelves full of such works, I came across a startling exception to the ancient modern division: John Donne's *Devotions upon Emergent Occasions.* Although written in 1623, the book seemed as "modern" in outlook as any I had yet encountered. The great Elizabethan poet and preacher composed it in bed, without benefit of notes, convinced he was dying of bubonic plague.

I have studied Donne's *Devotions* many times since, and I have learned to use it as a guide in thinking about pain. It is trenchant without being blasphemous, profound without being abstract or impersonal. It combines the raw humanity of modern treatises with the reverent sagacity of the ancients. John Donne has changed forever the way I think about pain.

※

How shall they come to thee whom thou hast nailed to their bed?
John Donne was a man acquainted with grief. During his term as Dean of St. Paul's Cathedral, London's largest church, three waves of the Great Plague swept through the city. (Donne's own illness turned out to be a spotted fever like typhus, not bubonic plague.) The last epidemic

alone killed forty thousand people. Thousands more fled to the country-side, transforming whole neighborhoods into ghost towns. Mangy, half-crazed prophets stalked the deserted streets, crying out judgment, and in truth nearly every one believed God had sent the plague as a scourge. Londoners flocked to Dean Donne for an explanation, or at least a word of comfort.

Donne had, in fact, grown up in the school of suffering. His father had died in John's fourth year. The Catholic faith of his family was a crippling disability in those days of Protestant persecution. Catholics could not hold office, were fined for attending mass, and were often tortured for their beliefs. (The word *oppressed* derives from a popular torture technique: unrepentant Catholics were placed under a board onto which heavy boulders were heaped until they literally pressed the life out of the martyrs.) After distinguishing himself at Oxford and Cambridge, John Donne was denied a degree because of his religious affiliation. His brother died in prison, serving time for having sheltered a priest.

At first Donne responded to these difficulties by rebelling against all faith. A notorious Don Juan, he celebrated his sexual exploits in some of the most frankly erotic poems in all of English literature. But finally, riven by guilt, he renounced his promiscuous ways in favor of marriage. He had fallen under the spell of a seventeen-year-old beauty so quick and bright that she reminded him of sunlight.

In a bitter irony, it was just when Donne decided to settle down that his life took a calamitous turn. When Anne More's father found out about the arrangement, he determined to break his new son-in-law forever. He got Donne fired from his job as secretary to a nobleman and had him, along with the minister who performed the wedding ceremony, thrown into prison. In black despair, Donne wrote his most cryptic poem "John Donne, Anne Donne, Un-done."

Once out of jail, Donne, now blackballed, could not find further employment. He had lost his chance to serve in the court of King James. For nearly a decade he and his wife lived in poverty, in a cramped house that filled with their offspring at the rate of one per year. Anne was subject to periodic depression, and more than once nearly died in childbirth. John, probably malnourished, suffered from acute headaches, intestinal cramps, and gout. His longest work during this period was an extended essay on the advantages of suicide.

Some time during that gloomy decade, John Donne converted to the Church of England. Later, his career blocked at every turn, he decided to follow the king's advice by seeking ordination as an Anglican priest. He was forty-two. Contemporaries gossiped about his "conversion of convenience" and scoffed that he had "wanted to be Ambassador to Venice, not Ambassador to God." But Donne gradually grew reconciled to his calling. He earned a Doctor of Divinity degree from Cambridge, promised to write no more poetry, and devoted himself instead to parish work.

The year after Donne took his first parish job, Anne died. She had borne twelve children in all, five of whom died in infancy. Donne made a solemn vow not to remarry, lest a stepmother bring them further grief. He preached Anne's funeral sermon, choosing as his text these words, poignantly autobiographical, from the Book of Lamentations: "Lo, I am the man that have seen affliction."

This, then, was the priest appointed by King James to St. Paul's Cathedral in 1621: a lifelong melancholic, haunted by guilt over the sins of his youth, failed in all his ambitions (except poetry, which he had forsworn), sullied by accusations of insincerity. He hardly seemed a likely candidate to inspire the nation in plague times. Nonetheless, Donne applied himself to his new task with vigor, arising every morning at four and studying until ten at night. In the era of the first King James Bible and William Shakespeare, educated Londoners honored eloquence and elocution, and in these Dean John Donne had no equal. He delivered sermons of such power that soon the vast cathedral was crowded with worshipers.

Two years later, the first spots of illness appeared on Donne's body, and doctors diagnosed the plague. For six weeks he lay at the threshold of death. The prescribed treatments were as vile as the illness: bleedings, strange poultices, the application of vipers and pigeons to remove evil "vapours." During this dark time Donne, forbidden to read or study but permitted to write, composed the book *Devotions*.

Some writers report that the knowledge of imminent death produces a state of heightened concentration, somewhat like an epileptic fit; perhaps John Donne felt this as he worked on his journal of illness. The writing lacks his usual rigorous construction. The sentences—dense, strung together in free association, overladen with concepts—mirror the feverish state of Donne's mind. He wrote as though he had to pour into the words every significant thought and emotion that had ever occurred to him.

Donne gave some order to his wildly roaming thoughts by dividing each of the *Devotions*' twenty-three chapters into three parts: a Meditation describing his circumstance, an Expostulation hinting at a biblical perspective, and a Prayer recording his spiritual struggle with God. That tripartite form allowed him to render his emotional state with absolute honesty, to explore the theological questions of pain, and then to attempt some sort of resolution with God.

"Variable, and therefore miserable condition of man! This minute I was well, and am ill, this minute," the book begins. Anyone confined to bed for more than a few days can identify with the series of circumstances, petty yet overpowering, that Donne describes: a sleepless night, doctors in whispered consultation, church bells tolling out a death announcement (Am I next?), the false hope of remission followed by the dread reality of relapse.

The mood of the writing changes quickly and violently. Fear, guilt, and the sadness of a broken heart take turns chasing out all inner peace. Donne frets over his past: Has God "nailed him to bed" as a mocking punishment for past sexual sins? In his prayers he tries to muster up praise, or at least gratitude, but often fails. For example, one Meditation begins valiantly as Donne seizes upon the hopeful thought that, in sleep, God has given us a way to "get used to" the notion of death. We lose consciousness and yet rise again the next day refreshed and mended. Is that not a picture of what will happen to us after death? But he suddenly realizes that the illness has robbed him of even this emblem: "I sleep not day nor night. . . . Why is none of the heaviness of my heart dispensed into mine eye-lids?" Insomnia has left him an unbroken span in which to worry over death, but no rest to renew him for that worrying.

I have read some of Donne's sermons as well as his *Devotions,* and the difference between the two reminds me of the difference between two books by a more contemporary writer, C. S. Lewis. *The Problem of Pain* shows Lewis at the height of his intellectual powers, tackling the most daunting philosophical questions with scrupulous logic. But years later, after his own wife died of cancer, Lewis wrote another book, *A Grief Observed,* which he published under a pseudonym. It covers the same topic, but in a very different style, as if another hemisphere of the brain had taken over the writing process. The latter work is a rambling personal journal of human emotions extended to the breaking point— stretched beyond the breaking point.

In style and tone, Donne's *Devotions* resembles Lewis's personal journal rather than his philosophical treatise. He pictures himself as a sailor tossed capriciously about by the towering swells of an ocean in storm. Occasionally he gets a glimpse of faraway land, only to lose it with the next giant wave.

Other writers have described the vicissitudes of illness with similar power; what sets Donne's work apart is his intended audience: God himself. In the tradition of Job, Jeremiah, and the psalmists, Donne uses the arena of his personal trials as a staging ground for a no-holds-barred wrestling match with the Almighty. Somehow, whether directly or indirectly, God is involved in human suffering. For Donne, as he looks back on life, the facts do not add up. After spending a lifetime in confused wandering, he has finally reached a place where he can be of some service to God, and now, at that precise moment, he is struck down by a deadly illness. Nothing appears on the horizon but fever, pain, and death. What to make of it?

In *Devotions,* John Donne calls God to task. "I have not the righteousness of Job, but I have the desire of Job: I would speak to the Almighty, and I would reason with God."[1] Sometimes he taunts God, sometimes he grovels and pleads for forgiveness, sometimes he argues fiercely. But not once does Donne leave God out of the process. The presence of God looms like a shadow behind every thought, every sentence.

※

Give me, O Lord, a fear, of which I may not be afraid.

I have interviewed many people whose lives are defined by suffering, and in every case they have described to me a crisis of fear, a crisis of meaning, and a crisis of death. The central reason I keep returning to Donne's *Devotions* is that the book continues to yield new insights into these primal confrontations with the mystery of suffering.

Dr. Paul Brand, with whom I coauthored two books on the human body, cites fear as the single greatest "enemy of recovery." He has explained to me the anatomical details of how the effects of an emotion based in the mind can filter down into the lower recesses of the body and produce cellular changes that will alter the perception of pain. A person with an exaggerated fear of hypodermic needles, for example—Dr. Brand admits he is one—feels more pain from the injection than does a diabetic who has learned to take injections every day. The physiology is the same in both persons; fear makes the difference.

One would think that advances in medicine since John Donne's day would vastly reduce our fears. Now we can give an exact diagnosis for most ailments, and we can supply tranquilizers and anesthetics to soothe the fears. But, in Dr. Brand's words, "In many ways our advanced state of medicine has served to increase the problems of fear and helplessness. Patients are put in private rooms and made to lie in bed all day with little to think about other than their sickness. They are surrounded by an imposing array of sophisticated instruments with tentacles that reach inside their own bodies. Outside, in the hallway, they may hear physicians and nurses discussing a prognosis in lowered voices. The physician comes into the room and studies graphs and figures that have no meaning whatever to the patient. The patient is poked and studied and bled and charted, 'all for your own good,' of course. Little wonder his fear does not subside."[2]

John Donne experienced the same "disconnected" sensation that sets in when doctors hover over a patient. He felt like an object, like a map spread out across a table, pored over by cosmographers. He imagined himself separated from his own body and floating above it, from which vantage point he could observe the disintegrating figure on the bed. Indeed, as the illness progressed, he felt himself to be a statue of clay, its limbs and flesh melting off and crumbling into a handful of sand. Soon nothing would remain but a pile of bones.

Most of the time Donne had to battle such fears alone. In those days victims of contagious diseases were subject to quarantine, and as Donne lay on his bed he wondered if God, too, was participating in the quarantine. He cried out, but received no answer. Where was God's promised presence? His comfort? Always, in each of the twenty-three meditations, Donne circles back to the primary issue underlying his suffering. His real fear was not of the tinny clamor of pain cells all over his body; he feared God.

The very posture of illness reduces us to a kind of subhuman state of bedridden creatureliness. No longer the proud creatures who walk erect and fashion tools, we lie flat, spread out helpless before our Maker. Thus humbled, we cannot avoid thinking about God. "Why me?" we ask. "What does God have against me? And what's he trying to tell me anyhow?"

Donne asked the "Why me?" question over and over again. Calvinism was still new then (amazing thought!), and Donne pondered the notion of plagues and wars as "God's angels." But he recoiled from that idea: "Surely it is not thou, it is not thy hand. The devouring sword, the consuming fire, the winds from the wilderness, the diseases of the body, all that afflicted Job, were from the hands of Satan; it is not thou."[3]

Yet he never felt certain. The *not knowing* caused much inner torment. Guilt from his spotted past lurked like a demon nearby. Perhaps he was indeed suffering as a result of some sin. And if so, was it better to be scarred by God or not visited at all? How could he worship, let alone love, such a God?

Donne never really resolves the "Why me?" questions in his book, and my years of inquiries into the problem of pain have convinced me that none of us can resolve those questions. The Bible surely gives no clear answer: even in God's summation speech to Job, at a moment that begged for such an answer, God refrained. Answers to "Why?" questions seem beyond the reach of humanity—in fact, that was God's main message to Job.

Although *Devotions* does not answer the intellectual questions about suffering, it does record Donne's emotional resolution, showing us a step-by-step process of transformation. At first—confined to bed, churning out prayers without answers, contemplating death, regurgitating guilt—he can find no relief from omnipresent fear. Obsessed, he reviews every biblical occurrence of the word *fear*. As he does so, it dawns on him that life will always include circumstances which incite fear: if not illness, financial hardship, if not poverty, rejection, if not loneliness, failure. In such a world, Donne has a choice: to fear God, or to fear everything else.

In a passage reminiscent of Paul's litany in Romans 8 ("For I am convinced that neither death nor life, neither angels nor demons . . . will be able to separate us from the love of God ..."), Donne checks off his potential fears. Great enemies? They pose no threat, for God can vanquish any enemy. Famine? No, for God can supply. Death? Even that, the worst human fear, is no permanent barrier to those who fear God.[4] Donne concludes that his best course is to cultivate a proper fear of the Lord, for that fear can supplant all others. And that is why he prays, "as thou hast given me a repentance, not to be repented of, so give me, O Lord, a fear, of which I may not be afraid."[5]

In his wrestling with God, Donne has changed questions. He began with the question of *origin*. Who caused this illness? And why?—for which he found no answer. His meditations move ever so gradually toward the question of *response*. The crucial issue, the one that faces every person who suffers, is that same question of response: Will I trust God with my pain, even my fear? Or will I turn away from him in bitterness and anger? Donne decided that in the most important sense it did not matter whether his sickness was a chastening or merely a natural accident. In either case he would trust God, for in the end *trust* represents the proper fear of the Lord.

Donne compared the process to his change in attitude toward physicians. Initially, as they probed his body for new symptoms and discussed their findings in hushed tones outside his room, he could not help feeling afraid. But in time, seeing their compassionate concern, he became convinced that they deserved his trust. The same pattern applies to God. We often do not understand his methods or the reasons behind them. But the underlying issue is whether he is a trustworthy "physician." Donne concluded yes.

As Donne explains, the decisive reason for trusting God traces back to his Son, Jesus. Illness opens up a great gulf between ourselves and a God who knows nothing like weakness or helplessness. A sense of *distance* from God may creep in that only underscores our frailty and magnifies our fears. But in Jesus we have a Great Physician "who knows our natural infirmities, for he had them, and knows the weight of our sins, for he paid a dear price for them."

How can we rightly approach a God we fear? In answer, Donne holds up a phrase from Matthew's story of the women who discovered the empty tomb after Jesus' resurrection. They hurried away from the scene "with fear and yet great joy," and Donne saw in their "two legs of fear and joy" a pattern for himself. Fear was surely in the air at the time of the resurrection. One glance at the angel ("his appearance was like lightning") forever shattered the safe, terrestrial lives of Jesus' friends. Those women saw with their own eyes the vast distance between immortal God and mortal man—but, lo, it was a distance to inspire joy. That all-powerful God had conquered death: Jesus stood at the edge of the garden, alive again. For that reason the women felt both fear and great joy. And for that reason John Donne found at last a fear of which he need not be afraid.[6]

I once talked with a Catholic priest who had just performed the funeral of an eight-year-old girl. His parish had prayed and wept and shared pain with the family for more than a year as the girl fought a futile battle against cancer. The funeral had strained the emotions, the energy, and even the faith of the priest. "What can I possibly say to her family?" he said to me at the time. "I have no solution to offer them. What can I say?" He paused for a moment, and added this. "I have no solution to their pain; I have only an answer. And Jesus Christ is that answer."

Make this . . . very dejection and faintness of heart, a powerful cordial.

Viktor Frankl, survivor of a Nazi concentration camp, expressed well the second great crisis faced by people who suffer: the crisis of meaning. "Despair," he said, "is suffering without meaning." And in a society like ours, saturated with comfort, what possible meaning can we give to the great intruder, pain?

What is the meaning of AIDS? A loud public debate rages over that one, but what about the meaning of progeria, the bizarre abnormality which speeds up the aging process and causes a six-year-old child to look and feel eighty? Or what is the meaning of cerebral palsy, or strep throat? What is the meaning of an earthquake, or a freak January tornado?

Most of us can see only a negative "meaning" to suffering: it is an interruption of health, an unwelcome brake on our pursuit of life, liberty, and happiness. Visit any card shop and you will get the message unmistakably. All we can wish for suffering people is that they "Get well!" But as one woman with terminal cancer told me, "None of those cards apply to the people in my ward. None of us will get well. We're all going to die here. To the rest of the world, that makes us invalids. Think about that word. Not valid."

What is the meaning of terminal cancer?

John Donne, thinking himself terminally ill, asked such questions, and his book suggests the possibility of an answer. The first stirrings came to him through the open window of his bedroom, in the form of church bells tolling out a doleful declaration of death. For one paranoid instant Donne wondered if his friends, knowing his condition to be more grave than they had disclosed, had ordered the bell to be rung for his own death. But he quickly realized that the bells were marking a neighbor's death from plague.

A short time later, sounds from the funeral service itself drifted in amongst the street noises. Donne croaked out a feeble accompaniment to the congregational singing of psalms, and then he wrote Meditation XVII on the meaning of the church bells—the most famous portion of *Devotions*, and indeed one of the most celebrated passages in English literature ("No man is an island. . . . Never send to know for whom the bell tolls; it tolls for thee").

Donne realized that although the bells had been sounded in honor of another's death, they served as a stark reminder of what every human being spends a lifetime trying to forget: We will all die. "When one man dies, one chapter is not torn out of the book, but translated into a better language; and every chapter must be so translated; God employs several translators; some pieces are translated by age, some by sickness, some by war, some by justice; but God's hand is in every translation, and his hand shall bind up all our scattered leaves again for that library where every book shall lie open to one another. . . . So this bell calls us all; but how much more me, who am brought so near the door by this sickness."

C. S. Lewis used the phrase "pain, the megaphone of God" to express the singular ability of pain to break through normal defenses and everyday routines.[7] Donne expressed something similar: "I need thy thunder, O my God; thy music will not serve thee."[8] The tolling of the bell was, for him, an advance echo of his own death. For the dead man, it was a period, the end of a life; for Donne, clinging to life, it was a penetrating question mark. Was he ready to meet God?

The tolling of that bell worked a curious twist in Donne's progression of thought. Up to that point he had been wondering about the meaning of illness and what lessons he should learn from it. Now he began contemplating the meaning of health. The bell called into question how he had spent his entire life. Had he hallowed the gift of health by serving others and God? Had he viewed life as a preparation, a training ground, for a far longer and more important life to come—or as an end in itself?

The megaphone of pain, or thunder of God, caused Donne to reexamine his life, and what he saw had the force of revelation. "I am the man that have seen affliction,"[9] Donne had told the congregation at his wife's funeral. But it now seemed clear that those times of affliction, the periods of sharpest suffering, had been the very occasions of spiritual growth. Trials had purged sin and developed character; poverty had taught him dependence on God and cleansed him of greed; failure and public disgrace had helped cure worldly ambition. A clear pattern emerged: pain could be transformed, even redeemed. Above all, his lifelong struggle with vanity and ambition appeared in a new light. Perhaps

God's own hand had blocked his career—a devastating disappointment at the time—in order to prepare him for the ministry.

Donne's mental review next led him to reflect on present circumstances. Could even this pain be redeemed? His illness prevented him from many good works, of course, but the physical incapacity surely did not inhibit all spiritual growth. He had much time for prayer: the bell reminded him of his less fortunate neighbor, and the many others suffering in London. He could learn humility, and trust, and gratitude, and faith. Donne made a kind of game of it: he envisioned his "soul" growing strong, rising from the bed, and walking about the room even as his body lay flat.

In short, Donne realized he was not "in-valid." He directed his energy toward spiritual disciplines: prayer, confession of sins, keeping a journal (which became *Devotions*). He got his mind off himself and onto others.

What Donne experienced parallels exactly the process prescribed in the major New Testament passages about suffering. In Romans 5, James 1, and the Book of 1 Peter, the writers direct the readers' attention away from misery and self-pity, focusing instead on what suffering can produce. It can produce patience, for example (a virtue attainable only in conditions that ordinarily provoke impatience). Character, perseverance, hope, discipline, faithfulness—all these qualities grow only in mixed soil.

The *Devotions* record a seismic shift in Donne's attitude toward pain. He began with prayers that the pain be removed; he ends with prayers that the pain be redeemed, that he be "catechized by affliction." Such redemption might take the form of miraculous cure—he still hoped so—but even if it did not, God could take a molten ingot and through the refiner's fire of suffering make of it pure gold.

God had demonstrated that power beyond all argument, Donne notes, in the death of his Son. The shed blood of Christ had become a *salus mundo,* a kind of toast of health to all the world. In the end, even the unimaginable suffering of the cross was fully redeemed: it is by his *stripes* that we are healed.

✵

Though so disobedient a servant as I may be afraid to die, yet to so merciful a master as thou I cannot be afraid to come.

Two great crises spawned by Donne's illness, the crisis of fear and the crisis of meaning, converged in a third and final crisis, the crisis of death. The poet truly believed that he would die from his illness, and the cloud of impending death hangs over every page of *Devotions.*

We moderns have perfected techniques for coping with the crisis of death, techniques that doubtless would have caused John Donne much puzzlement. Most of us construct elaborate means of avoiding the crisis altogether. As shown by our exercise regimens and nutrition fetishes, we treat physical health like a religion, while simultaneously walling off death's blunt reminders—mortuaries, intensive care rooms, cemeteries. Living in Elizabethan London, John Donne did not have the luxury of denial. Each night huge carts clattered through the streets to collect the bodies of that day's plague victims; their names appeared in long columns in the next day's newspaper. No one could live as though death did not exist.

On the other hand, some modern health workers have taken the opposite tack, proposing that *acceptance,* not denial, is the ideal attitude toward death. After Elisabeth Kübler-Ross established acceptance as the final stage in the grief process, scores of self-help groups sprang up to help terminally ill patients attain that stage. One need not read long in John Donne's work to realize how foreign such an idea might have seemed to him. Some have accused Donne of an obsession with death (thirty-two of his fifty-four songs and sonnets center on the theme), but for Donne, death was always the Great Enemy to be resisted, not a friend to be welcomed as a natural part of the cycle of life.

The *Devotions* record Donne's active struggle against accepting death. Despite his best efforts, he could not really imagine an afterlife. The pleasures that he knew so well all depended on a physical body and its ability to smell and see and hear and touch and taste.

Donne took some comfort in the example of Jesus, "my master in the science of death,"[10] for the Garden of Gethsemane hardly presented a scene of calm acceptance either. There, Jesus sweat drops of blood and begged the Father for some other way. He too felt the loneliness and fear that now haunted Donne's deathbed. And why had he chosen that death? The purpose of Christ's death brought Donne some solace at last: he had died to effect a cure.

The turning point for Donne came as he began to view death not as the disease that permanently spoils life, but rather as the only cure to the disease of life. For sin had permanently stained all life, and only through death—Christ's death and our own—can we realize a cured, sinless state. Donne explored that thought in "A Hymn to God the Father," the only other writing known to survive from his time of illness:

> Wilt thou forgive that sin where I begun,
> Which was my sin, though it were done before?
> Wilt thou forgive that sin, through which I run,
> And do run still: though still I do deplore?
> When thou hast done, thou hast not done,
> For, I have more.

Wilt thou forgive that sin which I have won
Others to sin? and, made my sin their door?
Wilt thou forgive that sin which I did shun
A year, or two: but wallowed in, a score?
When thou hast done, thou hast not done,
For I have more.

I have a sin of fear, that when I have spun
My last thread, I shall perish on the shore;
But swear by thy self, that at my death thy son
Shall shine as he shines now, and heretofore;
And, having done that, thou hast done,
I fear no more.

The word-play on the poet's name ("thou hast *done*") reveals a kind of acceptance at last: not an acceptance of death as a natural end but a willingness to trust God with the future no matter what. "That voice, that I must die now, is not the voice of a judge that speaks by way of condemnation, but of a physician that presents health."

John Donne did not die from the illness of 1623. He recovered and, though in a weakened state, put in eight more vigorous years as Dean of St. Paul's. His sermons and other writings often returned to the themes touched upon in *Devotions,* especially the theme of death, but never again did they express the same sort of inner turmoil. In his crisis, Donne managed to achieve a "holy indifference" about death: not by discounting death's horror—his sermons contain vivid depictions of those horrors—but rather by a renewed confidence in resurrection.

If Jesus' death had made possible a permanent cure for sin, his resurrection made possible a permanent cure for death. Donne liked to use the analogy of a map. Spread out flat, a two-dimensional map radically separates East from West. The two directions appear irreconcilably distant. But curve that same map around a globe, a far more accurate representation, and the farthest eastern point actually touches the farthest western point. The two are contiguous.

The same principle applies to human life. Death, which appears to sever life, is actually a door opening the way to new life. Death and resurrection touch; the end is a beginning.

Death be not proud, though some have called thee
Mighty and dreadful, for, thou art not so . . .

One short sleep past, we wake eternally,
And death shall be no more, Death thou shalt die.

Seven years after the illness which inspired *Devotions,* Donne suffered another illness which would severely test all that he had learned
about pain. He spent most of the winter of 1630 out of the pulpit, confined to a house in Essex. But when the time of the Passion approached
on the church calendar, Donne insisted on traveling to London to deliver
a sermon on the first Friday of Lent. The friends who greeted him there
saw an emaciated man, looking far older than his fifty-eight years. A
lifetime of suffering had taken its toll. The friends urged Donne to can-
cel the scheduled sermon, but he refused.

Donne's first biographer, his contemporary Izaak Walton, sets the
scene at Whitehall Palace on the day of Donne's last sermon:

> Doubtless many did secretly ask that question in Ezekiel, "Do these bones
> live?" Or can that soul organise that tongue? . . . Doubtless it cannot. And
> yet, after some faint pauses in his zealous prayer, his strong desires
> enabled his weak body to discharge his memory of this preconceived med-
> itations, which were of dying; the text being, "To God the Lord belong the
> issues from death." Many that then saw his tears, and heard his faint and
> hollow voice, professed they thought the text prophetically chosen, and
> that Dr. Donne had preached his own Funeral Sermon.[11]

Donne had often expressed the desire to die in the pulpit, and he
nearly did so. The impact of that sermon, "Death's Duel," one of Donne's
finest, did not soon fade from those who heard it. To John Donne, Death
was an enemy that he would fight as long as strength remained in his
bones. But he fought with the confident knowledge that the enemy would
ultimately be defeated.

Carried to his house, Donne spent the next five weeks preparing for
death. He dictated letters to friends, wrote a few poems, and composed
his own epitaph. Acquaintances dropped by, and he reminisced. "I cannot plead innocency of life, especially of my youth," he told one friend,
"but I am to be judged by a merciful God, who is not willing to see what
I have done amiss. And though of myself I have nothing to present to
Him but sins and misery, yet I know He looks upon me not as I am of
myself, but as I am in my Savior . . . I am therefore full of inexpressible
joy, and shall die in peace."[12]

Izaak Walton contrasted the image of John Donne in those final
days—his body gaunt and wasted but his spirit at rest—with a portrait
he had seen of Donne at age eighteen. The portrait showed a dashing
young cavalier, bedecked in finery, brandishing a sword. Its inscription,
notes Walton, had proved ironically prophetic of Donne's difficult life:
"How much shall I be changed before I am changed!"

A carver came by during those last few weeks, under orders from the church to design a monument for the Dean. Donne posed for him in the posture of death, a winding sheet tied around him, his hands folded over his stomach, his eyes closed. The effigy was carved out of a single piece of white marble. After Donne's death, workmen mounted it over his funeral urn in St. Paul's Cathedral.

I have seen John Donne's monument. It was the only object in the entire cathedral to survive the Great Fire of 1666, and it can still be viewed in the ambulatory of St. Paul's behind the choir stalls, a white marble monument set in a niche in the gray stone. Tour guides point out a brown scorch mark on the urn dating from the fire. Donne's face wears an expression of serenity, as though he attained at last in death the peace that eluded him for so much of life.

> Our last day is our first day; our Saturday is our Sunday; our eve is our holy day; our sunsetting is our morning; the day of our death is the first day of our eternal life. The next day after that . . . comes that day that shall show me to myself. Here I never saw myself but in disguises; there, then, I shall see myself, but I shall see God too. . . . Here I have one faculty enlightened, and another left in darkness; mine understanding sometimes cleared, my will at the same time perverted. There I shall be all light, no shadow upon me; my soul invested in the light of joy, and my body in the light of glory.[13]

GETTING STARTED WITH DONNE

Almost four centuries later, John Donne's *Devotions upon Emergent Occasions* remains in print in several editions and is available in paperback at most college bookstores. Unfortunately, there is no good annotated version available, and it will take some effort to understand the archaic language and difficult allusions. Donne's *Complete Poems* are also readily available—these are well annotated—and include some outstanding religious poems. His surviving sermons have been collected in an expensive ten-volume edition, and a one-volume paperback sampler, *Sermons on the Psalms and the Gospels.*

10

HANS CHRISTIAN ANDERSEN
Shaping the Child's Universe

Walter Wangerin Jr.

W hen I was a child, I spake as a child, I understood as a child. When I became a man I put away childish things, but the man I became was shaped in childhood, and that shape remains forever.

Fairy tales shaped me. I have since "put them away." That is, the adult is a mostly rational creature, aware that fairy tales are not "real" but are a fantasy, an entertaining escape from the problems of the real world. As a man, I make such tales an object of my attention and maintain an analytical control over them: I read them. I interpret them; they don't

Walter Wangerin Jr. occupies the Jochum Chair at Valparaiso University as writer-in-residence and is the speaker for Lutheran Vespers, an international radio show. His first book of fiction, *The Book of the Dun Cow,* won the American Book Award. A sequel followed, *The Book of Sorrows,* as well as the fictional *Miz Lil and the Chronicles of Grace,* and *The Orphean Passages.* Other works include *As for Me and My House, Ragman and Other Cries of Faith, The Manger Is Empty, Crying for a Vision, Mourning into Dancing, Reliving the Passion,* and numerous children's books. Most recently, he has published *The Book of God: The Bible as a Novel* and *Paul: A Novel.*

interpret me. I master the tales, placing them within my memory and my experience exactly where I wish them to be. Fairy tales dwell within the adult.

But as a child all full of wonder I approached the fairy tale as something real indeed. Children meet the problems of the world with their imaginations, and the fairy tale honors and feeds and abets the imagination. I accepted its invitation to enter in, and dwelt within the tale. As a child I never analyzed the tale I read; I felt it; I sank inside of it; I lived its experience through to the happy conclusion, thereby enacting the solutions of imagination.

The fairy tale was like a well-built house which I inhabited, safe and strong and significant. The problems outside didn't vanish when I entered that house, but its walls protected me from immediate danger. More wonderfully, when I viewed those "real world" problems through the windows of the fairy tale, they shrank to proportions equal to my child's size, and I discovered marvelous ways to triumph over them. By the art of the tale and by the power of my magic imagination, I became a citizen and a survivor in an otherwise confusing universe—and sometimes, even, a hero.

Once upon a time my mother was the problem. She, the largest figure of the real world, was beautiful beyond my deserving, and I loved her. I, the oldest child of all her brood, would truly have died for her, could it assure her happiness. But things were not so simple in those days, and I despaired of solving the problem of my mother, until a tale revised my comprehension of the world and whispered to me the secret of mothers in general.

In the dark of the evening my mother would come to tuck me into bed. When she sat on the side of the bed, her weight would sink the mattress and roll me close to her. I felt the warmth of her body. I felt the coolness of her hand upon my forehead. I smelled the holy cloud of perfume that surrounded her. I heard her low voice, thick with the thrill of loving me, and I would nearly weep with the sweetness of the occasion. How often she murmured good night to me in those days; yet always the word was new and exquisite, because this was my beloved.

We prayed together. She wore a deep red lipstick. When we finished praying, she would bend down to me and kiss my cheek, leaving the sign of her lips in red. And then she might go out for the evening, but I could get up and run to the mirror and gaze at her love for me and carry the knowledge back to bed and fall asleep contented. Her lipstick smelled of roses.

In the morning I woke and went downstairs and sought my beloved again. How many mornings I did so, forgetting the problem which every morning I encountered!

She was in the kitchen, standing at the counter stuffing lunch bags. Her bathrobe was snagged and ratty; her hair was wild; but again and again I neglected these signs and swam in the love of the night before.

"Mom," I would say, expecting the beauty to turn and smile on me. No answer.

"Mom? Mom?" I would repeat, prepared to say, I love you. But when I touched her to get her attention, it was a different woman altogether who rounded upon me.

"Wally!" she yelled. "Where have you been? You're late!" Lashless eyes, a forehead white with anger, a mouth made stiff, an odor of soiled sheets. "Move it!" this woman would cry. "Where's your shirt? If you're not ready when I leave, you're walking to school. Go!"

If I stood in stunned wonder, this woman would grow more furious, grab my shoulder, snap me around, and push me from her.

Often I moved to my room in confusion and dressed myself slowly, injured by the injustice of it all. I could not fathom the transformation. Who was my mother now? What had happened during the night? Most important what had I done to cause the change and to enrage her?

She meant her threat about walking. I sat with my socks in my hand, all lonely in the universe, until the car roared and beeped outside, and she and the other children drove away—and then my first feeling was panic, and the second was a bewildered guilt. I walked to school alone. I arrived there both solemn and silent, wounded by the real world, helpless to understand the problem that was my mother, let alone to solve it.

And as long as my mother was unsolvable, so was the whole world an impossibly complex and dangerous place. I didn't talk to my teacher. I withheld myself from the treacheries of friendship. I listened to everyone but spoke to no one.

One day the teacher read aloud a fairy tale whose fiction I entered, whose events I believed and experienced, whose view of the world resolved my own most troubled world—and (as a child, by the marvel of imagination) at last I understood my mother. I could love her again unhindered.

Snow White was the tale. It began with an image of simplicity and beauty, one perfectly congenial to my experience: a childless Queen sat and sewed at her castle window. It was snowing. The snow had drifted on the windowsill, and the window itself was open to the evening air.

The poor Queen pricked her finger with the needle. Three drops of blood fell onto the snow. The loveliness of those drops, crimson in the white snow, moved the Queen to tears and to a prayer. "Oh, let me have a child," she prayed, "with lips as red as blood and cheeks as white as snow." It was absolutely certain that this Queen was godly and good, that she would love forever the child of her yearning and of her blood.

131

I recognized that Queen and gave her my immediate devotion. I knew, in fact, that if she breathed on me, her breath would be scented with roses. And when next she bore a baby, I was not surprised. I recognized that baby too.

But then the poor Queen died, and the tale struck out in strange directions. The King remarried, and a second mother appeared, as beautiful as the first, perhaps, but wicked and so self-absorbed that she talked to her face in the mirror. It was sad that the first mother died, but somehow not astonishing. What did astonish and horrify me was that the face in the mirror spoke back to the stepmother. Here was a woman divided into two parts. One part asked and the other part answered, each one independent of the other. This seemed unnatural, and it frightened me.

For a while the two parts were in harmony. "Mirror, mirror, on the wall," said the stepmother, "who is the fairest of them all?"

"You are," said her image, and she was happy.

But in time the baby developed, grew lovely, grew so beautiful, in fact, that she surpassed the beauty of the stepmother; and then the two parts of this woman were divided, for the child had come between.

"Who is the fairest of them all?"

"Well," the face in the mirror replied, "Snow White is." Snow White: the child of that other mother, the Queen, the good and godly one!

Oh, how the stepmother howled at that knowledge, torn asunder by the innocent sweetness of a child. A forehead white with anger, a mouth made stiff—I recognized that woman too. I had met her often in the mornings, in the kitchen; and now I understood (as a child understands these things) her changes and her rages.

This is the explanation which imagination could accept: that I had not one but two mothers, an original and a stepmother, a Mother of the Evening who disappeared not once but ever and again, and a Mother of the Morning who possessed a different nature indeed. What a relief this insight was for me! No longer was my mother's transformation my fault. It was a simple, sad fact of existence—but a reversible fact, since the good and godly mother could spring new every evening, just as I could reread Snow White whenever I wished.

Moreover, even when the loving mother was absent, she still continued to exist—in me! My being was the issue of her prayer, her yearning, her bright red blood, and all her purity. I was the abiding beauty of that mother, which was precisely why the stepmother couldn't stand me. Should I think evil of myself? No. As the graceful offspring of my better mother, my very existence reminded my stepmother of worth and the virtue that she lacked. Not some shame in me, but rather my very innocence enraged the stepmother. I could endure her without guilt, for her anger now became understandable to me. I, the Snow White of the story, had destroyed her self-absorption.

Thus did I peer at the "real world" through the windows of a fairy tale, and thus did I find a certain fantastic sense in all of it, and the sense preserved me. Truly, this explanation of the double mothers is more subtle than I thought it through in childhood. I merely lived it. And I knew on some functional level that Snow White was "just" a fairy tale, that I was engaged in serious pretense. But the comfort it afforded me was actual: I loved better, walked freer, was a better, healthier child on account of it.

The child psychologist Bruno Bettelheim in *The Uses of Enchantment* has affirmed my private use of the fairy tale as something common to many children.[1] He writes that the structure of the tale (which is narrative and dramatic, not analytic and intellectual) orders and organizes the overwhelming chaos which children experience. Children are influenced by the tale, not because it rationally argues certain principles (scientific, moral, or spiritual), but rather because children identify with its characters and actually experience the events of the story, which mimic in imagination the difficult events of their own lives, but which also proceed to solutions that they on their own might never find.

If, therefore, I speak of the effect Hans Christian Andersen had upon my childhood, please understand that I am not slipping into a personal and irrelevant nostalgia. I'm describing deep influences upon my adulthood, the man and the writer and the Christian under heaven. For the story that shapes a child's universe also shapes the child—and by the child, the man thereafter. The memory of a burning fairy tale can govern behavior as truly as remembered fire will caution against fire forever.

This is how the tales of Hans Christian Andersen so mightily influenced me. They were my world for a while. They named and shaped the universe in which I dwelt, and something of that shape has remained forever: not the fantasy but the faith that created the fantasy continues even now to explain existence. By his fairy tales Hans Andersen welcomed me to his bosom, and I delivered myself for safekeeping unto him. Those things which were horrible and senseless in my external world were, in Andersen's world, horrible still; but his stories gave them a sense (often a spiritual sense) which I could grasp, by which the horror might be mastered, if not by me then by someone, by goodness, by God.

✳

When my father bought a thick, pictureless book containing all the tales of Hans Christian Andersen and began to read them to his children, he did me a kindness more profound than mere entertainment. He began to weave a world which genuinely acknowledged all the monsters in mine, as well as all the ridiculous situations and silly asides which I as a child found significant. Andersen was my whispering, laughing, wise companion when I most needed companionship.

Night after night my father would read a story in an articulate, baritone voice. Gently the voice invited me. Slowly I accepted the invitation and delivered myself to a wonderful world; I looked around, and lo, it was confident with solutions, and I was a citizen of some authority and reputation. I was no longer alone, no longer helpless. Even my foolishness seemed canny here. I could, with the soldier and his tinderbox, marry the princess, become a king—or, with the Little Match Girl, enter heaven.

Hans Andersen's stories, though simple on the surface, contain a precise and tender perception of personal development. They are honest about the hard encounter with the "real world"—honest about evil and the tendency to evil in each of us. Andersen did not coddle me, the "me" who was revealed within his fairy tales. He didn't sweeten the bitter facts which I already knew regarding myself. But he offered me hope, for in his tales, even when evil has been chosen, forgiveness may follow—therein lies extraordinary hope.

Never, never does Andersen compromise the truth of human experience for childish ears. He may tell it in outrageously fantastical terms. He may make trees to talk and darning needles to take trips, but they talk the truth and their trips are desperately familiar to children traveling toward adulthood. In his tales, love and loneliness are equally genuine. For me his stories offered sanctuary, a sacred place to dwell in for a while, almost a temple of the observant and merciful God.

Bruno Bettelheim observes that,

> The child is subject to desperate feelings of loneliness and isolation, and he often experiences mortal anxiety. More often than not, he is unable to express those feelings in words, or he can do so only by indirection: fear of the dark or of some animal, anxiety about his body. Parents tend to overlook ... those spoken fears.... The fairy tale, by contrast, takes these existential anxieties and dilemmas very seriously and addresses itself directly to them: the need to be loved and the fear that one is thought worthless; the love of life, and the fear of death. Further, the fairy tale offers solutions in ways that the child can grasp on his level of understanding.[2]

Even so did Andersen's tales express what otherwise was mute within me. If I found my feelings in his stories, then I was neither crazy nor alone. Someone shared my woe; someone invited me to chuckle at it. Andersen gave me a frame for things intangible, bewildering, elemental, and urgent. Without apology he structured his world with things of spiritual value: the eternal consequences of actions good or evil, the judging and the benevolent presence of God, the effective reality of repentance, the marvelous power of divine forgiveness. These things surrounded me when I dwelt with him.

✳

So, then, this is the way it is: Dad sits in a chair beside my bed, one lamp low at his shoulder, his pipe clamped between his teeth. Mostly, the room, an attic with slanted ceilings, is in darkness. The wind will whistle in the eaves before my father is finished reading tonight. We live in the north and the weather is winter. All that is to the good, because I will ride that black night wind.

"Ready?" Dad asks.

I nod. I curl tight beneath the covers.

"Once upon a time," Dad reads, "there lived in a village two men who had the same name; they were both called Claus. . . ."

Little Claus and Big Claus: this is the first of all the tales my father chooses to read to us. It's an astonishing beginning. There is violence here: horse killings, grandmother killings, old men sent to heaven, and a great rich fool apparently drowned. But the violence accords with nightmares of my own. And fantasies that I remember, otherwise secret and frightening, are here taken for granted. The spurts of childish rage which would blot out my enemies, but which I fear I can't control, appear here in the very order of things.

And the violence is funny! I listen and laugh till the tears run down my cheeks and my father laughs too. What is happening? Violence is being reduced to something manageable; and because I am the one laughing at it, scorning it, recognizing the blustering silliness of it, then I am larger than it, capable of triumphing over it. This story does not deny the monster in me or the cruelties of the general society. Rather, it empowers me.

As Dad reads my story, I identify with Little Claus. In contrast to the big and brutal Big Claus, I am poor and weak (though cleverer by half), hobbled by kindness while he is strong in amorality. In the beginning I have one horse and he has four. All week long he plows with all five, but on Sundays the team is mine. And because I am not sinless either, vanity makes me cry out "Giddy up, all my horses!"

This infuriates Big Claus. "Four of those horses are mine," he yells. "If you say that again, I'll knock your horse in the head, and then you will have none."

But I am not sinless. (This is a troubling and actual fact, both in my life and in this story—which makes, of course, the story true.) In spite of his threat, the passing of churchgoers stirs my vanity again, and I cry: "Giddy up, all my horses!"

So Big Claus comes and knocks my only horse dead.

Big Claus is an overtly violent man—as I, Wally, am too, in my secret soul. Although I may not like it, I find myself identifying with the brutal big man as much as with the clever little man. Dad is reading my own story in two ways, through two separate characters. But here is the magic of Andersen: his story divides the two tendencies within me, so that the one might be exorcised without destroying the whole of me.

Bettelheim again:

> In practically every fairy tale good and evil are given body in the form of some figures and their actions, as good and evil are omnipresent in life and the propensities for both are present in every man. It is this duality which poses the moral problem, and requires the struggle to solve it. . . .
>
> Presenting the polarities of character permits the child to comprehend easily the differences between the two, which he could not do as readily were the figures drawn more true to life.... Furthermore, a child's choices are based, not so much on right versus wrong, as on who arouses his sympathy and who his antipathy. The more simple and straightforward a good character, the easier it is for a child to identify with it and to reject the bad other.[3]

I like Little Claus. I want to be—I am—him. I dislike Big Claus. I sever myself from—and I am not—him, even though he represents a real iniquity in me. But within the story, by laughter and luck and cleverness (but call luck "grace"), I amputate this evil which I don't want to be.

And here is how I do it. I tan the hide of my murdered horse. I take it to market to sell it. On the way I have the "luck" to witness a farmer's wife involved in an impropriety with a deacon while her husband is absent: she's feeding the deacon a fine dinner in her kitchen.

Just before the farmer returns, she hides the dinner in the oven and the deacon in an empty chest. I see all this, and then the good farmer invites me inside for food.

"I'm sorry, dear, we have no food," says the farmer's wife.

But I, who am cleverer by half than deacons and wives and Big Claus too, step on the hide of my murdered horse. I make it squeak and interpret the squeaks as a prophecy that there is dinner ready-made in the oven. There is, and the farmer is amazed by my wonderful horsehide. Moreover, I step on it again, and it squeaks again, declaring that there's a devil-deacon in that chest. There is! So the farmer buys my horse's hide for a whole bushel of money and sends the deacon in a chest away with me. I'm so clever that I cannot quit this cleverness: when I come to a river, I pretend out loud that I'm going to toss the chest in. The deacon roars and pleads and bargains until I sell him his freedom for another bushel of money. I am rich.

And what do I do to the brutal Big Claus? Why, I use his stupidity and his greed against him. I borrow his measuring pail to measure all my money, then return it to him with a few coins stuck to the bottom.

"Where did you get all that money from?" cries Big Claus, his eyes popping out.

"Oh, that was for my horsehide. I sold it last night."

Immediately Big Claus hurries home and takes an ax and knocks all four of his horses in their heads. He skins them and runs to market to humiliate himself. Who would buy horsehides for bushels of money?

And so my story goes: I trick Big Claus into knocking his poor grandmother in the head. Ah, me, but the man is dumb! And his nature is violent altogether! Finally, I trick Big Claus into jumping into the river himself in search of a herd of cattle at the bottom, and so I am rid of dumbness, greed, and brutality all at once.

Dad closes the book. He turns out the light and leaves. But I am flying the night wind, living still in a good, good story—"good" in that evil is overcome and suffers its due, in that the Old Adam need not forever be my master. I may be forgiven—and free. But I discover the truth in experience, laughing till the tears run down my cheeks, not in remote and intellectual lessons which my poor brain can scarcely translate into "real life."

Hans Andersen has persuaded me of optimism, a tough and abiding optimism, not the Pollyanna sugar which merely sweetens the facts of evil and suffering, danger, and death. I would soon reject such optimism as fraudulent—even as a child I would. It would leave no print upon my personality. But Andersen's optimism both sees and redeems the evil. We travel through it, not around it, and I am impressed forever.

Many who read my writings today are inclined to call me "melancholy." They are wrong. Andersen's fantasies schooled me, rather, in realism. I know no resurrection except that first there's been a death. And as a writer, I cannot speak genuinely or deeply of resurrection except I speak the same of death and the sin that engendered death. That I can speak accurately of death without despairing is hardly melancholic. It is liberty—and victory ("O Death, where is thy sting?"). It is the evidence of the fundamental influence which Hans Christian Andersen had upon a child who did not analyze but lived such stories as Little Claus and Big Claus.

※

So night after night my father wreathes his head in pipe-smoke and reads to the whistle of the north wind, weaving for me experiences of genuine consolation. The number of these stories seems endless (in fact, there are 156), and that is important, for they seem to last a lifetime.

As long as I need them, they are here, ever the same and ever new—exactly as are the daily encounters of my life.

I cannot run. I am short, hampered by big buttocks, hunched with miserable coordination, generally inferior in the contests of children—as I say, unable to run. But in the track meets of fifth grade, they make me run the hundred-yard dash. It causes me a vomitous anxiety. I have nightmares of running underwater. My dreams are not untrue, for when the starting gun goes off, I stumble and am the last to leave the line; slowly, slowly I suffer my way to the end of the race, and when I arrive people have departed to run in other races. I am humiliated. Ellery Yurchuck cries out, "He walks like a girl!" I do. I burn with shame. Mary Enderby slaps my cheek. Only when school is out and I am staring in the mirror of my bathroom do I realize that she had drawn lipstick lips on the palm of her hand, and that a mocking kiss has clung to my cheek the whole day through. And I cannot do what other children do so thoughtlessly. I cannot run.

But Dad, in the nighttime, reads of a duckling more ugly than others, and I curl tight under the covers and listen with unspeakable sympathy for that duck.

"I know, I know," I murmur.

Soon, I am one of the ducklings.

The ugliness alone—not wickedness, not cruelty, not any error on our part—brings shame upon us, the ugly duckling and me. Other ducklings are cute, in the image of our mother. But we were hatched from a larger, vagrant egg—an odd beginning, producing an odd shape. Therefore, we are pecked and pushed and scorned. Our wonderful mother defends us; but we feel only pity for her that she should so unjustly suffer for our own troubles, which are not hers, after all, since she is a beautiful duck. Merely that she loves us is cause for pain. Oh, it is so complicated to be ugly!

She tries to comfort us by saying, "That is the way of the world," meaning that there shall be misery on earth. It doesn't comfort us.

For our own sakes she also says, "I wish you were far away"—from pain and teasing, she means. But we take her literally. We run away to other barnyards, never to see her again.

On our own we discover "the way of the world." It includes the death of the few who befriend us: hunters kill two kindly wild ganders. It includes a sneering judgment against all the things we cannot do: can't lay eggs like chickens, can't arch our backs like cats and make sparks. Do, do, do, cries society; but we can do nothing it likes and therefore are the uglier. We can't by taking thought save ourselves or add one cubit to our height.

It is utterly natural that in the end we wish to die. Sorrow drives us to such extremities, even though we are but a child and a duckling.

In the dead of a dreary winter we notice three swans moving in absolute elegance, nobility, and beauty. Surely, they too will despise our ugliness, and their spite will be as intense as their distant beauty. Surely, then, they will kill us. In fact, we desire to die by beauty rather than by any other means. It seems right. We honor the beautiful. We think to ourselves, *It is better to be killed by them than to be bitten by the other ducks.*

But here appears the outrageous grace that we never anticipated: all along, while we were ugly indeed, another mercy was working within us, uncaused by us but given to us purely as a gift. What was this mercy? What sort of gift is given now to us? Why, it is we ourselves, transfigured!

"Kill me," whispered the poor creature, and bent his head humbly while he waited for his death. So goes the story, and thus do we deny ourselves, surrender ourselves completely. "Humbly, . . ." writes Andersen. "Humbly," my father reads, and I more than hear it; I experience it: I feel fully such humility in my heart. I am the one who cannot run. But what does such humility reveal to me?

In Andersen's words: "But what was that he saw in the water? It was his own reflection; and he was no longer an awkward, clumsy, gray bird, so ungainly and so ugly. He was a swan! It does not matter that one is born in the henyard as long as one has lain in a swan's egg." And Andersen goes on to name the goodness that has existed in all our sorrow, the duckling's and mine. Andersen names the grace upon grace that we have received, and the graciousness that we shall show hereafter (which neither the chickens nor Ellery Yurchuck may ever be able to understand or to show): "He was thankful that he had known so much want, and gone through so much suffering, for it made him appreciate his present happiness and loveliness of everything about him all the more. . . . Everyone agreed that the new swan was the most beautiful of them all. The older swans bowed toward him."

But does sinful pride or vengeance then rear up in him, or in me? No, and that is much the point: for the suffering transfigures us even to the soul. Humility showed us our new selves; humility remains in our hearts to keep these selves both beautiful and virtuous: "He felt so shy that he hid his head beneath his wing. He was too happy, but not proud, for a kind heart can never be proud."

So then, there is hope—not only that there may emerge from my ugly self a beauty but also that the suffering which my ugliness has caused is ultimately valuable, making my beautiful self also a good and sympathetic self. In the end I shall love the world the more; and even the people who once did me dishonor, I shall honor.

Can any child receive a better impress on his person, a subtler, more spiritual shape than this, that he be taught grace and to be gracious?

And what is more fortified than the self-esteem that comes as a gift from God?

※

Night after night my father reads the stories from a thick book with pastel-colored pages, pink and blue and yellow. The book goes soft with so much reading. Night after night I live the adventures that order my turbulent days and shape my waking self, my instincts, my faith, my adulthood to come. Optimism grows in me, and hope in the midst of suffering, and this third thing, too, perhaps the most difficult thing of all: forgiveness for my own most self-centered and wretched sins. Not the doctrine of forgiveness. Not the concept. Forgiveness in fact, as a mold to my experience ever hereafter. Andersen's world is a dramatic enactment of theologies which the child simply cannot grasp in the abstract.

My father reads in a murmuring voice, so softly that the words resolve themselves into spaces and things around me. The north wind whistles at the eaves, an almost malevolent warning. This is a treacherous story. Everything is full of foreboding. The curtains stir at the attic window. Shadows twist in the corners. I would not listen if I did not trust the kinder heart of the storyteller. This story has a harmless title, but that's deceptive. The tale is frightening. It knows too well my secret faults and the evil imagination of the thoughts of my heart.

"This story," my father murmurs, the pipe gone dead beside him, "is called 'The Red Shoes.'"

A fatherless girl named Karen appears before me. She is not aware of me, but I am of her. I join her. We are one. And we are both very vain. We think that we are more than pretty: gorgeous. Our gorgeousness so consumes us that we grow hard to those around who love and serve us. On the other hand, we want everyone to notice how splendid we are; therefore, even at inappropriate times, we slip our little feet into a pair of patent leather shoes so red, so red, O Lord, that we shine!

This is how vain we are, and this is how the story begins: at the funeral of our mother we follow the coffin in red shoes. And we are noticed. A kindly old woman notices us. We think it's because of our red shoes and our gorgeousness, but it isn't. It is her love (of which we know nothing) that sees us; she is moved by the sight of a newly orphaned child. So by grace we are granted a second mother, for the old woman takes us in and raises us as her own.

Her eyes grow dim. Ours stay sharp for red adornments. When the time of our confirmation arrives, and when we must buy shoes for the holy occasion, the old woman thinks we've bought black; but it is red we carry home, and it is red we wear to church. Everyone notices our bright red feet. Even the paintings on the wall and the bishop who blesses us stare at our feet.

We are so proud! Our mind is scarcely on the words of our "covenant with God to be a good Christian." We are thinking of red shoes.

The old woman learns from others the error of our ways. She scolds us and warns us how improper are red shoes in church. But on the very next Sunday, when we will attend Holy Communion, we can't help ourselves. The red shoes cry out to us, and we put them on.

Just before we enter church an ancient figure steps into our path and stops us. We might be frightened if we would heed him, but we don't. He speaks directly to the shoes. "What pretty dancing shoes!" he says. "Remember to stay on her feet for the dance," he says. But we can think of nothing except the shoes themselves. Even when the golden cup of Communion is raised to our lips, we see nothing but the shoes, as though they were reflected in the wine.

And then it happens that the old woman, our second mother, grows sick as our first mother had. Once we were ignorant of the world, of the laws of God, and of our own wicked tendencies. But now we have been taught and scolded and warned. This time we ought to know better. Nevertheless, we do again exactly what we have done before.

On the very night when the doctors say that the old woman is dying, we contemplate the red shoes, the alluring red shoes, the bright red shoes so perfect for our gorgeousness. There is a dance tonight. Looking leads to touching, and touching leads to donning; and as soon as the shoes are on our feet, we have to go. We leave the dying woman behind and steal away to dance. And we do dance. We laugh and whirl and dance the whole night through; for once we have begun, we cannot stop. It is the shoes that are dancing now. The red shoes! Dancing and dancing wherever they wish, taking us with them, down the stairs and out the door. And while they are dancing, the old woman dies . . .

I know this only too well.

For I have divided my mother into two; and I have dealt with her as though she were only a stepmother, nothing to me. Me! I was then the center and significance of all my life. My mother the dim-eyed old woman, my mother the stepmother, who unjustly (so it seemed to me) punished me for many things, could easily be dismissed, all her wishes, all her scoldings and her disciplines, all her self! I have run out to play when (if I had thought about it) I knew she didn't want me to go. I have stayed gone too long, causing her (if I had stopped to consider it) anguish at my absence. And when she confronted me with my fault, I have whistled. I have presented her with a blank face and have whistled stupid tunes to prove I wasn't listening. I have reduced her, once or twice, to tears at my cold impertinence. Oh, I have made my mother cry, and she has gone into her bedroom and shut the door and grieved in a deep frustration— and I knew I did that by my stubbornness. Then I was burned by guilt to hear her hurt. She was ill in her bedroom, dying. She said so: Dying. "I am sick to death of your disobedience," she said. O Mama! Never again! I have vowed this in my heart: Never again! But always my demons have been too powerful for me, and I have done it again in spite of every resolution. I am Karen, surrendering to sin until my sin has taken me over completely—and even when I want to stop, I cannot. Even when my heart desires goodness, it has it not. Dancing and dancing, our shoes have taken us into the street. Oh, wretched children that we are! Is there no help for us, who cannot help ourselves?

We dance toward the church. Maybe there is help for us in church. But at the door an angel appears dressed in white, holding a shining sword.

"You shall dance," he declares, "dance in your red shoes until you become pale and thin. When you pass a house where proud and vain children live, there you shall knock on the door so that they will see you and fear your fate. Dance, you shall dance. Dance!"

"Mercy!" scream Karen and I together. But we cannot hear what the angel answers, because the red shoes carry us away and away, always dancing.

Dance we must, and dance we do. The shoes have fastened to our feet like skin.

One morning in a lonely place we dance past a solitary cottage. The man who comes out when we cry is the Executioner. "I am the one," he says, "who cuts off the heads of evil men."

"No," we plead, "for then I should not be able to repent. But cut off our feet instead."

We confess our sins (isn't this enough?), and the Executioner cuts off our feet, and the red shoes go dancing away into the forest. For us the kindly Executioner carves wooden feet. He teaches us the psalm that penitent people sing. We kiss his hand and go.

Now have we suffered enough?

We go again to the church. Is this what it takes? That we are severed of our sin? Will ritual and formality receive us now? No, no, this isn't enough. For when we come to the door, the red shoes arrive ahead of us and dance and dance to block our way. In horror we flee. O God! The sins keep coming back! What can we do to be free?

All week long we weep on account of our sins. We are so sorry. We do repent. And by week's end we think, *I'm as good as any who sit and pray in church right now.* This gives us courage, and we go a third time. But at the gate of the churchyard the red shoes meet us, dancing, dancing, dancing, and we flee.

So now we despair. Nothing we do can save us. Not true sorrow, which we have done. Not true goodness, which we have done. Do this, do that— we've done it all, and still the shoes, they mock us.

Therefore, let us live in misery till we die. We deserve no better.

We go to the minister's house and ask for work. In pity he takes us in, gives us his roof and food. The minister's wife, also in pity, gives us work, and we work very hard though hopelessly, for we know this changes nothing. Look: our feet are still wooden. In the evening the minister reads to his children from the Bible and we listen; but we make no great account of the listening, because we are wiser now and know this changes nothing.

On Sunday the minister's whole family goes to church. We are invited, too, but our eyes fill with tears. They go without us.

We take ourselves to a tiny room and there sit down to read a psalm-book. While we sit, the wind blows hither the music of the church organ. We hear it, and we weep. We lift our face and whisper simply: "O God, help me."

All at once the sunlight seems doubly bright in the room, and the angel of God is standing before us—in the tiny room of the minister's house, in the attic bedroom where my father is reading and the north wind whistles at the eaves. This is the very same angel who held a sword at the church's door—but now he holds a rose branch thick with flowers. He raises the branch and touches the ceiling above Karen and above my bed. The ceiling suddenly sails aloft, and where he touched it a golden star appears. He brushes the walls of my attic, and they widen. Lo, here is the church organ! All around me—even though this is my bedroom and my father is reading still—the congregation is sitting and holding their psalmbooks and singing. The church has come to us, to Karen and me! When the psalm is done, someone sees us and smiles and whispers, "It is good that you came, Karen." Good to see you, Wally.

And this is what Karen replies; so these are the words in my mouth, too, brilliant with significance: "This is the mercy of God."

Mercy! It never was what we might do that could save us. It never was our work, our penitence, our goodness that would forgive us and bring us back to God again. We can do nothing! It always was the pure love and mercy of God—God's doing, given us freely as a gift. When finally we quit trying, then God could take over. When we murmured in perfect helplessness the perfect truth of our relationship, "O God, help me," then God was no longer hindered by our spiritual pride. God was God, and not ourselves—and God was our God too.

Mercy. Mercy is the healing that had waited for us all along. Love. Pure, holy love, unpurchased, undeserved.

When my father reads the final sentences of this story, I am crying. I am tingling. For I am not learning, but rather I am experiencing the highest truth of our faith. Not in doctrine, but in fact it is releasing me from the sins against my mother, even as it is imprinting me for adulthood, to show in what I speak, to shine through what I write forever.

But I don't know that yet. I'm just a child, reshaped and borne outside to ride the north wind warmly to a home I shall never, never forget.

"The great organ played," my father reads, his dear head bowed above a tattered book of stories, "and the voices of the children in the choir mingled sweetly with it. The clear, warm sunshine streamed through the window. The sunshine filled Karen's heart till it so swelled with peace and happiness that it broke. Her soul flew on a sunbeam up to God; and up there no one asked her about the red shoes."

In the depths of my bones I know and believe in forgiveness, for I have lived it. By Andersen's stories I was shaped in it—and the shape remains, forever.

GETTING STARTED WITH ANDERSEN

My references to Andersen's tales come from Hans Christian Andersen, *The Complete Fairy Tales and Stories,* translated from the Danish by Erik Christian Haugaard (Garden City, N. Y.: Doubleday & Company, Inc., 1974). (This is not the book my father used. That has long since disappeared.)

I also recommend the foundational book on fairy tales by Bruno Bettelheim (from which my Bettelheim quotations are taken): *The Uses of Enchantment: The Meaning and Importance of Fairy Tales* (New York: Alfred A. Knopf, 1976).

11

GEORGE MACDONALD
Nourishment for a Private World

Madeleine L'Engle

I n other writings I have talked about my lonely childhood in a New York apartment. My parents were nearly old enough to be my grandparents. My father had been gassed in the First World War, and he coughed his lungs out until I was nearly eighteen. I was an unsuccessful, nonachieving child at school, unappreciated and unloved by teachers and peers alike. My real world was my solitary life in my little back bedroom that looked out onto a courtyard and the windows of other apartments. There I was free to do my own thinking, which didn't coincide with what I was expected to think at school, and to do my own reading, which was never anything assigned to me by teachers, for they, I had learned, weren't going to like what I said about the stories they asked me to respond to.

Certainly I had enough to eat as a child, but it was alone, on a tray in my room. My parents dined later, at eight. I mentioned this to someone

Madeleine L'Engle has written more than fifty books that cover many genres: fantasy *(A Swiftly Tilting Planet)*, poetry *(A Cry Like a Bell)*, essays *(Walking on Water)*, and biography *(Two-Part Invention* and others from *The Crosswick Journals)*. She has received numerous awards, including the Newbery Award for *A Wrinkle in Time*.

who exclaimed in horror, "How awful for you!" But it didn't seem awful at all. I ate with my feet on the desk and a book on my chest and was completely happy. On the one day I ate with my parents, Sunday, we didn't know what to say. I called them Mother, and Father, and assumed my private life, which was for me the real world, would not be interesting to them. I was probably wrong, but, regardless, we didn't know how to talk to each other.

At first I was in a good school where I enjoyed work and my teachers and my friends. After my third year in that little school, though, my mother, over my father's protests, put me in a private school for girls in New York. Thank heavens I had learned to read and write before third grade was over, because I learned nothing more in school until I got to high school. It quickly became apparent that I was not doing well in this new school, that I was, in fact, miserably unhappy. But my father insisted that because my mother had chosen the school for me against his wishes, I had to stay there. I was evidently a battleground for my parents; I'm not sure why, since I was a devoutly longed-for child, the first and last child my mother had been able to carry to term.

(Odd: I've only begun to understand some of my childhood in the last year or so, though I've written about it in stories all my life. Maybe it has taken me this long to allow my parents to be human, to have made terrible mistakes. And maybe it has taken me this long to understand that this in no way diminishes the fact that they were people of great integrity, whom I could trust implicitly despite their many mistakes in arguing over me and how I should be treated. I knew without understanding that the first Great War had totally dislocated their lives. I heard my father coughing, coughing. I read many books about that terrible war, and I would beg, "Father, there will never be another war, will there?" But my father knew that the First World War and the impending Second World War were all one war, and he did not try to console me with platitudes.)

Possibly as a defense against the troubled, everyday world of my childhood, for nourishment I learned to rely more and more on the private world that I discovered in books, and it was there that I met George MacDonald. I was blessed to have been given MacDonald's books for Christmases and birthdays from the time that I was a small child. At that time his books were not readily available in America, but my grandfather, who lived in London, fed me a steady stream of English children's books. If I was intellectually starved at school, and sometimes psychologically abused, I was nourished at home alone in my own little room.

I read indiscriminately, good and indifferent and even poor writing. But the books I returned to were the books where the writer revealed the darkness of the subconscious mind as well as the daylight of the so-called rational mind. I read whatever I could get my hands on by George

MacDonald, but since I was limited by the books I was given and the books in my parents' bookshelves, I mostly read his fairy tales. These are what he is primarily known for, although his books marketed for children are only a very small part of his prodigious output. (Let anyone be known as a children's writer, and that is what the person is known for, because, of course, if you're good enough to write for adults, you don't bother with children. That fallacy is still prevalent, and it is good for raising low blood pressure.)

A good book for a child is a book a child will read, a librarian friend once told me. When I went to my parents' bookshelves I looked for quotation marks, conversations. I tended not to try to read books with long paragraphs. But I read. Read. Reread.

I read *Gulliver's Travels*, another "children's book" that happens to be a very raunchy book and would probably horrify parents if they bothered to read it. I also loved my parents' copy of *An Arabian Night's Tales,* lavishly illustrated by Edmund DuLac, and was delighted by *Paradise Lost*, though I'm sure that Dore's pictures meant more to me at eight or ten than did the text. I also read my favorite poet, William Blake, particularly the *Songs of Innocence and of Experience,* and I devoured such books as *Five Little Peppers, Poppy Ott, Black Beauty, What Katy Did, Emily of New Moon* (my favorite), to name but a few. The important thing was that in my reading I was being guided into a world far more real than the one offered me at school—even had I been a good and successful student.

Jung says that we are a sick society because we have lost a valid myth to live by, and in my small back room I was absorbing a mythic view of the universe, a universe created by a power of love far too great to be understood or explained by tenets or dogmas. That power of love was offered me by those writers and artists whose imaginations took me beyond literalism. Long before Joseph Campbell and others popularized a mythic view of the universe, that was my view; and probably the most important influence in deepening my mythic understanding was George MacDonald. He comforted me, but not with cozy platitudes. The mythic world he offered me promised no easy solutions. Rather, it gave me solid ground under my feet, a place where I could stand in a world which was confusing and dangerous and unfriendly. I read the books in my small bookcase. I read the books on my parents' shelves. And the world widened.

※

The works of George MacDonald shook the writer C. S. Lewis to the core. He later said of MacDonald, "I know hardly any other writer who seems to be closer . . . to the Spirit of Christ himself."[1] When I went back to George MacDonald's stories after I was grown and had children of my own, I was amazed at his sermonizing. MacDonald was a preacher. Preaching was as natural to him as breathing; and in the nineteenth century works of fiction, particularly those marketed for children, were filled with sermons. Perhaps the preachers were so discouraged at the lack of response from the adults that they turned to the children. Regardless, what I remembered from MacDonald's books was the story. Although I must have read the sermons, his message came over to me much more clearly in the stories themselves.

My father was clean-shaven and George MacDonald was bearded, but to some extent they overlapped in my life. If I did not talk to my parents about the princess who lived in a castle with a strange, wise old woman up a staircase that was not always there, or about Curdie, who had to plunge his hands into a fire of burning roses—nevertheless, because my parents were both artists, the world in which I lived was a familiar world to them, and so they provided me with an atmosphere in which my imagination could flourish. They saw nothing incompatible with the world at the back of the North Wind and the world of Jacob who wrestled with an angel, or Mary of Magdala, who saw Jesus first after the resurrection.

George MacDonald's name sometimes brings up an image of easy comfort, of a world where everything is going to be beautiful as long as we are loving, of a kindly God who never chastises the beloved children. But that image is a false one. Although this prolific writer indeed had a loving heart, his fiction shows that he also had a realistic view of the complexity of human nature.

One reason why so many adults feel children should outgrow the world of story, myth, fantasy, and fairy tale as soon as possible is that it is too difficult and too complex a world for the adult to find comfortable. How many grown-ups really want to plunge their hands into a burning fire of roses? And yet, after Curdie had gone through the pain, whenever he shook hands with anyone he was able to feel what that person was really like. He could sense the slipperiness of a snake, or the talons of a bird of prey, or the trusting hand of a child. Shaking hands has never been the same for me since.[2]

And where did MacDonald's image of the fire of roses come from? How far back does it go? Such images as these are found throughout literature, and now I am coming across them in the work of serious scientists. (Dr. Anthony Zee, for example, takes the title of his book, *Fearful Symmetry,* from Blake's marvelous poem that begins "Tyger, tyger burning bright . . .") We find the fire of roses in Dante's *Divine Comedy,* but I suspect it is a primordial image that goes back almost as far as the time when lightning brought fire to our ancestors. It is not a "pretty" image. It is as fearful as lightning. Laughter is needed if we are to live with this fear, and George MacDonald also taught me about laughter, reminding me that, "It is the heart that is not sure of its God that is afraid to laugh in His Presence."[3]

George MacDonald lived in a world where man—or rather, half of man, the male half—was foremost. The image of God was a male image. When it was a good image it looked not unlike George MacDonald himself. When it was a bad image it looked like Moses in a bad temper. It was, at best, only a partial image, but we cannot rewrite history. And so the image of God that comes through MacDonald's writing is also a male image—the best possible male image, but male. A loving Father who knows that sometimes "No" is the only possible answer of Love, a Father who can be trusted, who understands laughter and tears, a Father who is nothing like the stern, Victorian image. The Father-God image is almost irrevocably stuck in the Victorian father image; but that is not a mythic image, and George MacDonald lived in a more expansive, mythic world, where everything is more than it is.

Despite living in a patriarchal society, George MacDonald nevertheless had a reverence for wise women. It was a woman—the North Wind—who understood death. It was wise women who understood the complexities of the human heart and did not try to iron out, smooth, limit. It was wise women who dared enter the darkness on the other side of reason, the darkness that is the largest part of the human psyche. It was the largest, hidden part of the iceberg that sank the *Titanic*. Just so, it is the hidden part of the iceberg that the wise woman is willing to look at, aware of the dangers but knowing that to ignore the underwater self is even more dangerous.[4]

When I read and reread MacDonald as a child, I did not think about his life or even wonder or ask questions about what he was like as a person. I knew that he had to be loving. And I knew even then that the work is more than the worker. Later, as I learned more about the man, I was grateful to know that he did not hesitate to ask the big theological questions, and that the loving, forgiving God of Scripture was often far from the punitive god taught in school and church.

The belief that the elect were the only focus of God's love was intolerable to MacDonald. "I did not care for God to love me if he did not love everybody," he writes.[5] How terrible that some people thought (then, and still do, now) that "hell is invariably the deepest truth, and the love of God is not so deep as hell."[6] That was not consistent with the God of love MacDonald found in Scripture. How can hell be stronger than God! The God who could not go as deep as hell, who was willing to mete out hell and damnation to more than half the people in the world, was not a God of love, George MacDonald declared. How can it be that a God of total love is more frightening to some of God's people than a God of punishment, vengeance, and retribution?

In another place, MacDonald prays, "Lord Jesus, let the heart of a child be given to us, that so we may arise from the grave of our dead selves and die no more, but see face to face the God of the living." MacDonald's God of love is seen with a child's heart, but not a childish one. The God of love is not sentimental, "for love loves into purity. Love has ever in view the absolute loveliness of that which it beholds. . . . There is nothing eternal but that which loves and can be loved, and love is ever climbing toward the consummation when such shalt be the universe, imperishable, divine. Therefore all that is not beautiful in the beloved, all that comes between and is not of love's kind, must be destroyed." Indeed, "Our God is a consuming fire," and I turn to the analogy of the burning bush, which flamed and yet was not consumed, the bush where everything that is dross must be burned away.[7]

There is no doubt that MacDonald believed in hell. And he felt we should not resist the consuming fire; but even more strongly he believed in the final victory of God. "But at length, O God, wilt thou not cast Death and Hell into the lake of Fire—even thine own consuming self? Death shall then die everlastingly. . . . But thou wilt burn us. And although thou seem to slay us, yet will we trust in thee."[8]

How ironic it is that those writers and theologians who proclaim God's loving forgiveness should so often be accused of heresy! MacDonald was no exception. He had to resign from his church, and he managed to make a meager living for himself and his family with a little substitute preaching, some lectures, and with his writing. Ultimately what had begun as only a few small jobs here and there expanded until he had as much work as he could manage and he was able to support his family comfortably. But charges of heresy left their mark on him.

Because I was so much alone, left to work out my own theology with the stories I read and the stories I wrote, and with long conversations with God, I avoided a lot of the misconceptions of God which MacDonald fought against so fiercely. My father's painful lungs breathed most easily in the afternoon and evening, so my parents slept late, and on Sunday mornings there was no one to take me to Sunday school. That was a great blessing. How many adults I have met who have never been able to shake off the Victorian punitive god they were taught on Sunday mornings!

In the late afternoons my parents and I went to Evensong, in a day when most Episcopal churches in New York still had that beautiful service. I learned to love church because of the great words of Cranmer and Coverdale and the King James translation of the Bible, and to love the great harmonies of liturgical music. Later, when my parents obviously felt they had to make the effort to rise in time to take me to the eleven o'clock service, I felt differently. The church was large and cold and so were the sermons—cold, that is; not large. It was a church filled with people who epitomized for me the epithet, "God's frozen chosen."

Something in the marble and the cold light was destructive for me. Our church had been a small church of warm dark wood which held only a few hundred people, but it had been sold and in its place rose this new, large, rich church which for me epitomized snobbishness, selfishness, and elitism. Maybe it wasn't that way at all in reality, but this was how it was for me. It was everything that made me feel rejected and inadequate at school. It had nothing to do with George MacDonald and Hans Christian Andersen and Pallas Athene and the wine dark sea, or the grandmother who lived at the top of a flight of interminable stairs and "who got a large silver basin and, having poured some water into it, made Irene sit on the chair and washed her feet."[9]

Not long after the new church was built—the church we went to in the morning instead of in the kinder light of late afternoon and Evensong—we moved to Europe, to find Alpine air, which Father could breathe with less pain. The doctors had advised him to go to Saranac, which at that time was where patients with lung problems were sent, but Saranac was expensive. The Depression had hit the United States, and the standard of living in France was lower than in New York. I was twelve when we moved, so I took for granted no running water or indoor plumbing. I took with me a few of my favorite books, and I continued to live in a world where there were winding stone stairs with wise old grandmothers weaving spiderwebs and moonlight at the top.

Ultimately I was sent to boarding school, which continued the hell that school had been for me. It was, in fact, an even deeper hell because I had no small private room to come home to at the end of the school day. I was twelve, but a very young twelve, so I managed to wrap my mythic world around me and so escape the worst of the school.

I learned little at that school. I did discover a much mutilated Malory's story of King Arthur and his dream of a round table. Somehow or other I came across a copy of Kenneth Grahame's *The Wind in the Wil - lows* and gloried in the world of Mole and Rat and Toad and Badger and fell breathlessly into one of the great pieces of religious writing: the scene in which Mole and Rat go to the Island with the great god Pan. (This, I am told, is now being labeled as "unChristian." Such blindness is sad indeed, and comes from a literalism which is unscriptural and judgmental and unloving. And am I being judgmental and unloving? I don't want to be, but I think there is a difference between judgment and judgmentalism, and I don't want fear of metaphor to deprive children of the awe and wonder with which we must all approach God.)

It was an Anglican school, with mandatory Morning and Evening Prayer, badly read by one of the mistresses. But they couldn't quite ruin the language of the great poets of the sixteenth and seventeenth centuries. The chapel was in the basement, lit by lights high up on the walls, and I got into the habit of slipping away from the sound and fury of the common room and going into the chapel to pray. One day one of the mistresses found me there and dragged me out by the ear, as though going to be alone with God was something obscene and perverse.

As far as the Christian faith was concerned, I learned nothing in that school which I did not learn from my own illicit reading—for of course fairy tales were forbidden. I do remember a visiting English clergyman coming in to lecture the whole school and talking about the legalism of the pharisaical world surrounding Jesus, a marvelous lecture in a school completely based on legalism, and that is the one thing that has stayed clearly in my mind from my time there.

We were taught Latin, at least a little. I'm not sure where or when I came across these words of Hugo of St. Victor: *Sumpta sunt vocabula, ut intellegi aliquatenus posset quod comprehendi non poterat.* "These words were chosen so that that which could not be comprehended might yet in some measure be understood." Hugo of St. Victor spoke of the way in which I "understood" Kenneth Grahame and George MacDonald and the Brothers Grimm.

We came back to the United States when I was fourteen and I was still a child, with my hair in braids, and my lips devoid of lipstick. The only boy I knew during our time in the Alps was a Canadian boy my own age, and when we were together during the holidays we played games of make-believe and let's pretend. His body was, like mine, still a child's, and our games were about princesses and gentle knights. I was totally unprepared for a world in which girls wore bras and makeup and conversation was about dates.

In a way I was saved by being sent to another boarding school, another girls' school. Although many of the other girls thought of nothing but dances and boys and kisses, there were enough students who were backwards, like me, and lived in a slightly different fairy-tale world—for we loved Shakespeare and had the opportunity of acting in *The Tempest* and *Twelfth Night* and read deeply in Shakespeare's wonderfully mythic world. And I am sure MacDonald knew Shakespeare's works, knew them well.

I was wonderfully happy in this school where I could grow up at my own slow rate. Life at home during the holidays was less happy. My father was still coughing his lungs out, in constant pain. My grandmother's heart was slowly giving out. We were living at her cottage on the beach in north Florida, a wonderful, drafty, rambly old building perched high on the dunes. First thing in the morning we would put on bathing suits, walk along a long, coquina ramp which ran over the jungle beneath, a jungle full of Spanish bayonets and poisonous snakes and tarantulas, but which I could completely ignore as I ran down the ramp and onto the sand, and then across the wide white beach and into the ocean.

The ocean. The primordial waters which once covered the entire planet. The playground of dolphins who, when they cavorted on the horizon, assured me that it was safe to swim out beyond the breakers. George MacDonald's mythic world made real.

There came a sunny, hot, Sunday afternoon. We sat out on the wide verandah which wrapped itself all the way around the house. We cooled ourselves with lemonade and palm leaf fans. Various members of the family dropped by to visit, to sit and chat. Ultimately everybody left except my parents and my grandmother, and we prepared for bed.

I knelt by my bed to say my prayers, and I was overwhelmed with a sense of pressure and fear. Something terrible was going to happen. At first the fear was a vague fog. I was afraid there might be a fire. Then the fear narrowed in, centering on my grandmother. I knew my grandmother was going to die that night. I knelt by my bed and I prayed and I prayed to God to take away the fear, to take away the death, not to let it happen. And God's answer was NO.

Finally I got into bed, but I did not go to sleep. I drifted in and out of the shallows of sleep, but always with one ear open to my grandmother's room, which was next to mine. My parents' room was beyond that. Just before dawn I got up and went to my parents and woke them and said, "Please go in to Dearma." Dear Ma. That was what my grandmother was called. My parents responded without question to the urgency of my voice and the three of us went in to my grandmother's room. She was propped up on pillows, and she gave several shuddering breaths and died.

"God!" I cried later that day, after the doctor had come, after there was no denying that death had come. "God! Don't do this to me! I don't want to know! Don't let it happen again!" God has been kind, though not totally. On occasion I have known things I have not wanted to know. I do not believe that this "prevision," as it is sometimes called, influences or changes the future. It simply makes one aware of something that is already happening.

When I last said good-bye to my father, the autumn of my senior year at boarding school, in the dusty light of a great railroad station as he put me on the train to go back to school, I knew I was saying good-bye forever.

When I "knew" that my husband was dying, before he ever became ill, I am convinced the cancer that killed him was already within him, that my "knowing" did not come before but after death had already marked him, after God had already called him.

Lucy Maud Montgomery's character, Emily of New Moon, had this kind of prevision.[10] The Scots call it Second Sight. It is not a gentle gift. I am not sure why it comes to some of us and not others. But it is entirely consistent with the loving God shown me by MacDonald. For him, even death, that which we most fear, was no final defeat of love. While grieving for those closest to him, he was able to write to his parents, "But, dear father and mother, death is only the outward form of birth. . . . Surely if we are sure of God, we are sure of everything. He never gave a good gift like a child to take it back again."[11] As a friend of mine wrote in the margin beside those words, "What God gives, He gives eternally."

MacDonald's own health was precarious. His lungs hemorrhaged—and not for the first time—and everything seemed dark. He wrote:

> My harvest withers. Health, my means to live—
> All things seem rushing straight into the dark.
> But the dark still is God. . . .
> . . . Am I not a spark
> Of him who is the light?[12]

And then, late in life, he began to write his fantasies, those extraordinary books which bewilder those whose faith is not as firmly grounded in God and Christ as was MacDonald's. Above all, it was these fantasies that opened up for me a wider world, a world I first glimpsed as a small child, and which I am still sometimes allowed to see. The curtain is often pulled aside when things are most difficult or painful, for it is during these times, I have learned, that Christ is closest to us. "The Son of God suffered unto death," MacDonald wrote, "not that men might not suffer, but that their sufferings might be like his."[13] (Men, of course, is meant generically: man, male and female. God made man in El's own image, male and female.)

As always, the wise woman is prominent in his work. North Wind (in *At the Back of the North Wind*) has to sink a ship and explains to young Diamond, "I will tell you how I am able to bear it, Diamond: I am always hearing, through every noise, through all the noise I am making myself, even, the noise of a far-off song. I do not exactly know where it is, or what it means; and I don't hear much of it, only the odor of its music, as it were, flitting across the great hollows of the ocean outside this air in which I make such a storm; but what I do hear, is quite enough to make me able to bear the cry from the drowning ship."[14]

I cannot understand this strange mercy except in the language which George MacDonald introduced to me when I was a child. Indeed, it is a strange language, and so it is fearful. And to some people what is fearful should be shunned, slandered, even assumed to be from Satan. Yet Scripture itself, Scripture in which George MacDonald is grounded, is full of this strange language. Ezekiel, with his extraordinary wheels (echoed in John's Revelation), with his dry bones crying out to God to be enfleshed; Daniel, again echoed in Revelation; even hilarious Jonah— all offer us a world of radiant wildness, where we see brilliance in the forests of the night.

Meeting George MacDonald's writing when I was very young was a blessing to my understanding of God and creation and our own small but potentially beautiful place in it. As MacDonald makes clear all through his writing, God promises us joy, but not safety; a full life, but not a painless one; the laughter that comes with full faith in God's loving purpose, but also tears. He promises us a broad road with a narrow gate, with lions and other wild beasts ready to attack unless Love speaks first and angels are standing by. There are, indeed, manifestations of energies, both good and evil, which we human beings are seldom able to see because we have rejected the world of fantasy and faerie as untrue.

What accounts for all the anger and horror in the world around us? Where are the angels? Can they come if we refuse to believe in them? What accounts for the darkness in human hearts as the world becomes more and more secular? Why are people turning to drugs for comfort rather than to the Light of Love? I don't know the answers to these questions. But I do know that wherever the light is, the darkness tries to snuff it out. Perhaps all the terrible things that are happening are, indeed, a sign that the Spirit of Love is abroad, that more and more of us are turning to this forbearing and yet ferocious power who pushes us into doing what we don't think we can do, who gives us courage we never dreamed we had.

I take the devil and his machinations seriously indeed. One thing which we can count on the devil to do is to take the original good which God created, and try to make something ugly out of it. Sometimes he succeeds—though that does not make the original good any less good. There are people today who play with the powers of love, who take them trivially, who seek easy answers.

There are no easy answers, but I think we need to be aware that if we deny the world beyond the world of technology and provable fact, we do so to our peril. George MacDonald said, "The miracles of Jesus were the ordinary works of His Father, wrought small and swift that we might take them in."[15] Jesus walked on water and refused to turn the stones into bread for Satan. But he multiplied the loaves (the things of his own creation) for love of the hungry people. He healed, laughed, wept, was transfigured, rose from the dead. He was completely human and he was completely divine.

MacDonald answers an accusation that he has lost his faith with brilliant words of faith, concluding,

> I cannot say I never doubt, nor until I hold the very heart of good as my very own in him, can I wish not to doubt. For doubt is the hammer that breaks the windows clouded with human fancies, and lets in the pure light. But I do say that all my hope, all my joy, all my strength are in the Lord Christ and his Father; that all my theories of life and growth are rooted in him; that his truth is gradually clearing up all the mysteries of this world. . . . To him I belong heart and soul and body, and he may do with me as he will—nay, nay—I pray him to do with me as he wills: for that is my only well being and freedom.[16]

GETTING STARTED WITH MACDONALD

The Complete Fairy Tales includes all of George MacDonald's beloved fairy tales. Bethany House Publishers has been gradually releasing newly edited versions of his longer novels as well. And Harold Shaw Publishers has brought out editions of MacDonald's sermons; of these, *Life Essential: The Hope of the Gospel* provides the best introduction to his thought. C. S. Lewis compiled an anthology of daily devotional readings from his mentor, published as *George MacDonald: An Anthology,* and MacDonald's own *Diary of an Old Soul* gives much more in this genre. Finally, the biography, *George MacDonald* by William Raeper fills in fascinating details of the Scotsman's life.

12

J. R. R. TOLKIEN
Master of Middle-Earth

Stephen R. Lawhead

I discovered J. R. R. Tolkien in exactly the same way as millions of other admirers: through the pages of *Lord of the Rings*. I was a college student at the time, teaching an eighth-grade art class, when I noticed one of my students—a shy, overweight kid with an intellectual bent—coming to school early to pore over these thick paperbacks.

At the time, I was only dimly aware of this fantasy trilogy or its author, but they had already won legions of devoted fans around the world. Certainly, the devotion that boy lavished on those books bordered on the fanatical. Every spare moment he labored over reams of the most intricate and exotic script: runes, he told me. Or he practiced one of the eleven languages he'd learned from the books—he was so enthralled with the story he even taught himself to speak elf!

Stephen R. Lawhead is a writer of mythic history and imaginative fiction. He has authored children's books as well as science fiction and fantasy novels, the most recent being *Byzantium* and the *Celtic Crusades Series,* which begins with *The Iron Lance.* Originally from Nebraska, since 1990 he has made his home in Oxford, England, with his wife, author Alice Slaikeu Lawhead, and two sons.

"You should read these books, Mr. Lawhead," he'd say when he came to show me his latest runic epistle. "J. R. R. Tolkien is the greatest author who ever lived."

To be honest, his endorsement steered me away from the books for a good long time. I am contrary that way. Let anyone praise a thing too highly and I make tracks in the opposite direction.

It wasn't until seminary a few years later that I picked up a copy of *Fellowship of the Ring*. Probably I was supposed to be reading homiletics or hermeneutics or something of similar weight, but boredom and curiosity finally got the better of me. In fact, my head was so full of the massive profundity of seminary study that ol' J. R. R. came across as a gulp of fresh air to a man drowning in mud.

His tale of hobbits and magic rings and a world inhabited by orcs, elves, dwarfs, wizards, and dragons proved a perfect antidote to the arid drear of Old Testament hagiography. Within the pages of his remarkable book real "people" lived and struggled and died. An entire universe of them!

The Tolkien Trilogy quickly became my bedtime reading, doled out in carefully measured nightly doses. I savored each and every syllable of that shining prose.

I have always been an avid reader—some of my best friends are books. But until I cracked the cover of Professor Tolkien's classic, I had never encountered a book of such splendid magnitude, such grace, such scope and wholeness of vision. And all of it was seamless, unforced, genuine, and extremely entertaining.

Well, it made an impact. Although I was never moved to communicate in runes or begin babbling in High Elf, I learned a lasting lesson about the nature of storytelling. Through the long, elegant movements of *Lord of the Rings* I grasped the structure of the epic, and something of the interplay of story elements, and the force of narrative.

More, I began to understand the enormous power of fiction to speak to the heart and soul of the reader, to lift the spirit, to ennoble and challenge and inspire.

These things I learned, and the learning went deep, I think. At least, it went underground for a season. For the next years saw me at *Campus Life* magazine, mastering what I could of the writing craft. I rarely thought about Tolkien's books during that time, nor did I think seriously about fiction; and hobbits hardly ever entered my conversation. But the seed that Tolkien's books had sown was germinating. There in the moist, fertile darkness of my subconscious (or wherever these things sprout), the first notions of writing the sort of books I loved reading began to take root.

About this same time, I discovered the Inklings—quite by accident, as it happens. While researching an article about Tolkien for *Campus Life,* I picked up a copy of Humphrey Carpenter's biography of the professor. The author described the importance in Tolkien's life of his literary friends, a fairly informal group of Oxford academics of one sort or another who went by the name of the Inklings.[1]

Having enjoyed Tolkien's books, I tracked down and read some of the work of some of the other Inklings—C. S. Lewis and Charles Williams especially. I enjoyed the books, but in the end it wasn't the Inklings' work that moved me. It was the informing spirit of their work, a spirit which I began to sense they all shared.

What was this peculiar spirit? I was content to wonder about this in my own slow way, gathering bits and pieces of it whenever and wherever they popped up, salting them away in my private cache.

Then one day, a few years later, I sat down at the typewriter to write a book. I was, for the first time in my life, completely free to write whatever I liked. (That is to say, I was unemployed.)

It was the worst possible time to undertake such a venture from any practical point of view. No job, few prospects, living in a strange city, a mortgage to feed and family to care for: a two-year-old child and a baby on the way. Putting the best face on it, one could say that the needs of a burgeoning family life motivated me to new heights of industry. It was like that, and yet it wasn't. It is a quirk of my nature that I can, with patience and perseverance, overlook hardship and adversity. My wife cynically calls it shortsighted self-involvement. I prefer to think of it as sublimating my suffering: rendering the dross of travail, as it were, into pure, golden art.

However it was, when I settled at my desk that day I felt the heady exhilaration of the freelance artist. It is the same thrill I imagine jungle explorers feel—striking off into uncharted territory with only your instincts to protect you from certain disaster. It's high adventure. While you might not be eaten by a cannibal or fall prey to a hideous tropical disease, the peculiar risks of freelance life are real enough.

For example, there is the very ominous and ever present danger that one's creation will fail and be repudiated, that the beautiful child of one's artistic devotion will fall flat on its chubby little face. There is potential discouragement, rejection, loss. Artistic sensibilities are tender, creative egos fragile. They bruise more easily than bananas.

So, what did I write when I settled before the keyboard that day?

The answer is obvious: I said to myself, "I shall write a masterwork of heroic fiction after the style of *The Hobbit!* Indeed, I shall swathe myself in the mantle of the Beloved Tolkien and become an author of massive fantasy novels. What is more, the example of the Inklings will become my constant inspiration and my guiding light."

As much as I might like to remember it that way, the truth is a good deal less high-flown. Utterly mundane, in fact. I really had no idea what I would do that first day. I simply went into my bedroom office and sat down at the desk, rolled a piece of yellow paper into the typewriter, and began typing. If I gave thought at all to what I wanted to do, it was simply to write the best and most entertaining story I could. That is, to write a book that I myself would like to read. I figured that if I liked the book, then I'd have pleased at least one person.

I did not think in terms of fantasy. I did not think in terms of Great Literature. I did not think in terms of Tolkien. I set out to please myself—Tolkien didn't enter into it.

Now, many people find that extremely odd. I know because I run into these people all the time. They approach me assuming that since I have written a fantasy book or two, I must have a Tolkien shrine in my living room before which I prostrate myself daily. They assume I carry photos of C. S. Lewis in my wallet, and that I've named my children Clive and Bilbo. I must, they think, have committed to memory whole passages of *The Hobbit* and can recite the entire *Chronicles of Narnia* upon request.

It disappoints them to learn the shabby truth: I keep no shrine, I own no autographed first editions, my children do not have a Frodo or Staples between them. I couldn't repeat a scrap of *Dawn Treader* to save my scalp. I have never smoked a pipe.

Yet, the lessons I learned from Lewis and Tolkien penetrated deep into my psyche—deeper than emulation, deeper than imitation. In short, it was not Tolkien's style or subject matter that influenced me; it was the integrity of the work itself.

I found this same integrity in Lewis's space tales. Taken together, these books possessed an inner worth that far exceeded the narrative skirts of their authors. *Perelandra* and *Lord of the Rings* seemed to me more in total than the simple sum of their parts. These books, I concluded, derived their value chiefly from this inner worth, this integrity that lay behind the stories themselves. But what was it?

It was, of course, the Christian faith of the authors shining through the fabric of their work. I saw that faith informed the story, and infused it with value and meaning, lifting the tale above the ordinary expressions of the genre. Even though the stories of Lewis, Tolkien, or other Inklings like Charles Williams, were not explicitly promoting Christianity, nevertheless the books were ripe with it.

What an extraordinary thing, I thought; though Tolkien makes never so much as a glancing reference to Jesus Christ in a single paragraph of all *The Lord of the Rings'* thick volumes, his face is glimpsed on virtually every page. *The Lion, the Witch, and the Wardrobe* is the furthest thing from a religious tract, yet it proclaims a clear and winning gospel. In my narrow experience, I had never before encountered such a thing. How did the authors do that?

That is what I set out to discover. And here is where I had my first surprise: they did not do it on purpose. At least, not as I defined the word. I had assumed that when Christian writers wrote, they entered a process that went something like this:

"Well," the writer says, "I have this burning message I must at all costs communicate to a lost and dying world. How shall I then write? I have it! Yes! I shall compose an engaging work of fiction which will subtly, yet ingeniously deliver my life-changing message to the fallen masses who shall read my masterpiece and turn as one to the Light of salvation."

As an American Christian I come out of a long tradition of nuts-and-bolts pragmatism, a sort of holy practicality that looks upon all things as possible conduits for the Good News. I had it drummed into my head that when it came to the propagation of the gospel, virtually any medium of communication could, and should, become a tool.

I figured this was universally recognized and patently self-evident. I had been taught that if you were a Christian, your first duty was spreading the Good News. Whether you were a banker or a bricklayer, your solitary goal and ambition should be to further the faith by spreading the gospel message in your sphere of life. Certainly, if you were an artist of any sort, then your path was fairly well determined: you must use your art.

After all, the logic goes, if tea bags and T-shirts can be pressed into the service of completing the Great Commission, then certainly art ought to be. And if communicating the gospel is the primary goal of a Christian, then writing, the most directly communicative form of art, should communicate the gospel most directly.

Relentlessly utilitarian though it may be, that is the evangelical tradition. Perhaps I am perverse. But words like "ought" and "should" always make me uncomfortable. They seem to suggest a stern, probably puritanical disapproval of what is. Equally discomforting are words like "art," which always seems to connote some sort of immense, fogbound philosophical abstract of interest only to fatuous snobs and the eggheaded effete.

Yet what I discovered in the pages of Tolkien's *Return of the King,* and Lewis's *Perelandra,* was no mere argument for eggheads but a very powerful and persuasive proposition for us all. Put in the smallest nutshell, the proposition, as I understand it, goes like this: art is a holy entity unto itself and therefore requires no explicit religious imprimatur to warrant its existence. Art, as the saying goes, needs no justification.

Now, I know this is not a new idea. But I cannot tell you how revolutionary this notion was, and is, to me. I heard in it the thunder of locks exploding and the whine of long-rusted gates swinging open. Ah, freedom!

Freedom, because for me the idea of art as an inherently godly enterprise meant that I did not have to make of my work a disguised sermon, or somehow include the Four Spiritual Laws of Salvation in my story outline, or fuss about right doctrine, or evangelism, or any other parochial religious concern. I was free to pursue my artistic vision wherever it led me, no apologies, no looking fearfully over my shoulder to some imagined arbiter of ecclesiastical approval.

In pretty short order, however, I came to see that this freedom also carried a responsibility (wouldn't you know it?) to practice my art at the highest level of my abilities, to strive for excellence, to make it true. Still, as long as I held true art as my aim, I was free to write as I pleased. The proof was sitting squarely on my bookshelf in four fat volumes by J. R.R. Tolkien.

As I have become persuaded, the most important part of what art does is search for, capture, and offer up to view the three verities: Goodness, Beauty, and Truth. This is the High Quest of art, and Tolkien taught me—no, he showed me—how this quest could be successfully undertaken. I came away convinced that as an artist I had a distinct responsibility, a duty to conduct the quest in my own work.

(That much of modern artistic endeavor has chosen to abandon its duty to the High Quest does not mean that the duty has been revoked. The marching orders have not been rescinded merely because the soldiers have lost their way. That, frankly, is their problem. Mine is to pursue the High Quest to my utmost ability, to search for, capture, and offer up to view Goodness, Beauty, and Truth. This is my calling, yes, but it is the same for anyone else who dares pick up pen or brush or leotard.)

Struggling after Goodness, Beauty, and Truth is, I believe, the only legitimate business of art and artists. If our art tries to do anything else—such as preach or evangelize—it devalues itself and thus falls prey to the same fate awaiting other works whose creators have abandoned the Quest.

So many Christian artists find themselves hung out to dry on the twin horns of that age-old artistic dilemma: pure art versus propaganda. The purists dig in at the art-for-art's-sake pole and erect their elitist totems. They declare that art, to be true, must reject all constraints and duties, especially, it seems, the duty of providing a moral message. Meanwhile, half a world away, the propagandists set up camp in the art-as-means-to-an-end arena. They maintain that the pursuit of pure art is futile because once art has loosed all bonds of duty—such as providing a moral message—it ceases to be true.

I have learned that the path into the heart of that debate is old and thorny, with plenty of pitfalls on either side. The more I worked at threading my way through the conflict, the more treacherous the path became. Better hunters with bigger guns than mine have set out in high hopes of bagging a solution only to come dragging back in dismal defeat.

It was J. R. R. Tolkien who came to my rescue. He showed me a way out of the morass that allowed me to retain my artistic integrity and continue the High Quest without getting impaled on either horn of the unruly dilemma. In the pages of *Lord of the Rings,* I saw that a judicious balance could be maintained which allowed the artist the cherished freedom to work—without becoming a dreary moralist drudge on the one hand, or a slave to soulless purism on the other.

Tolkien's middle way might be called the Freedom of Implicity. The way I came to see it, the Freedom of Implicity slogan goes something like this: Art, when conscientiously following the High Quest, reveals more of God implicitly than it could any other way—even more than if it had set out to reveal God in the first place!

There is a paradox of sorts at work here. How to explain it? Perhaps it is like a painter who sets out to paint a portrait of God. "After all," says he, "what could be more inspiring and winning than God's beatific image? It will move entire nations to worship and adoration. What more godly purpose for my work could I ask?" So he begins to paint with great religious fervor and zeal.

But he doesn't get very far before he discovers that since no one alive has ever seen the face of the Almighty there are no suitable references— no photographs, no sketches, no graven images of any kind. How then does he paint a portrait of a subject who refuses to give a studio sitting? That is the question: How does one illustrate the invisible?

It cannot be done. At least, it cannot be done explicitly. But an artist can achieve a satisfactory, even extraordinary, result with an implicit approach. That is, he does not paint God directly. Instead, the artist paints the Creator's reflected glory—paints the objects God has touched, the visible trail of his passing, the footprints he leaves behind.

That is precisely what I saw in *Lord of the Rings:* the visible trail of God's passing, the hallowed glow of his lingering presence. In his massive fantasy epic, Tolkien paints a convincing portrait of Goodness, Beauty, and Truth. His art is true. And insofar as it is true, it is godly. The story of furry-footed hobbits and men struggling to save the world of Middle-earth from the ravages of creeping evil reveals much of God and his redemptive work in this world. Tolkien's creation is a powerful and revealing portrait of the Creator.

What is more, I am convinced that this revelation was no happy accident. Tolkien meant to do it. He worked intentionally and purposefully to that end. Now, on the face of it, this would seem to contradict what I wrote earlier about "freedom" and "not doing it on purpose." Not really. The apparent contradiction is the result of confusing the purpose of the work with the effect achieved.

When I turned the last page of *Lord of the Rings,* I little guessed that such a stunning and stirring portrait of godliness could be achieved in any way other than by cold-blooded calculation on the part of the author. But I had confused the effect of the work with the purpose of the artist.

And the more I learned about Tolkien, the more I learned that his primary aim as a writer had been to tell an entertaining story—not to preach godliness. This I discovered through his letters.

I lived in Oxford for a time, working on the first volumes of my Pendragon Cycle. During that time Blackwells, the ancient and honorable bookstore in the university precinct, hosted a fiftieth anniversary celebration of the publication of *The Hobbit.* As part of the festivities Blackwells put on an exhibit of Tolkien memorabilia, including a sampling of Tolkien's correspondence. I read those letters, and they provided me a firsthand look.

One letter was especially telling. It was written to his publisher following the release of *The Hobbit,* a book greeted with fair success. Naturally, the publisher had inquired whether Professor Tolkien had any more stories about hobbits lying about—if so, they would like to see them, yes they would.

Apparently, Tolkien took his time responding and in the end was forced to write back with a negative answer, saying, "All the same I am a little perturbed. I cannot think of anything more to say about hobbits." In another place he wondered, "What more can hobbits do?" In the end, however, he conceded, "But if it is true that *The Hobbit* has come to stay and that more will be wanted, I will start the process of thought, and try to get some idea of a theme drawn from this material. . . ." He goes on to express his "faint hope" that his writing will begin to loosen the financial constraints he has labored under for many years so that he can devote more time to his work.

There was no mention of purpose or message, no hint of any explicit didactic purpose at all. This letter and others I have read reveal Tolkien's primary concern: to find and tell a good story. Indeed, *The Hobbit* began as a bedtime tale for his children's entertainment. Likewise, on evidence of the letters, *Lord of the Rings* began as a simple response to supply the publisher with another book—more from a financial motive than any other, as I read it.

Don't blanch at such a pragmatic motive. What matters isn't what motivates a writer to sit down at his desk; it is what the writer does once he gets there. What Tolkien actually did when he put pen to paper was nothing less than to create a whole new class of literature: heroic fantasy.

Say the word "fantasy" in a crowded room and alarm bells go off. I know, because I get letters from these alarmed individuals all the time by virtue of my work. For them, the words fiction and lies are synonymous, with not a nickel's worth of difference between them. Since by definition *fiction* is not factual documentary, *fiction* is therefore false. Anything false is a lie. All lies are evil. Ergo: *fiction* is evil. And the most suspicious fiction of all is (snarl, snarl) escapist fantasy.

Escape! To many people the term "escapist fantasy" connotes frivolity, sensuality, idleness, and unreality—hardly healthy involvements for hardheaded, feet-on-the-solid-ground, no-nonsense, just-the-facts Christians.

Tolkien had to face this same attitude; in his day, he was accused of writing escapist literature which would lead people to abandon reality in favor of an impossibly rich and exciting imaginary life. Tolkien's response was unequivocal: "I have claimed that Escape is one of the main functions of fairy-stories, and since I do not disapprove of them, it is plain that I do not accept the tone of scorn or pity with which 'Escape' is now so often used: a tone for which the uses of the word outside literary criticism give no warrant at all. In what the misusers are fond of calling Real Life, Escape is evidently as a rule very practical, and may even be heroic. . . . Why should a man be scorned, if, finding himself in prison, he tries to get out and go home?"[2]

In that pithy pronouncement I heard once again the sound of those prison doors swinging open. Tolkien brilliantly deflects the objection by admitting the truth of the observation. And he goes on to say that since fantasy is escapist, it makes little difference what you are escaping from, but a very great deal of difference what you are escaping to. For the best of fantasy offers not an escape away from reality but an escape to a heightened reality—a world at once more vivid and intense and real, where happiness and sorrow exist in double measure, where good and evil war in epic conflict, where joy is made more potent by the possibility of universal tragedy and defeat.

In the very best fantasy literature, like *Lord of the Rings,* we escape into an ideal world where ideal heroes and heroines (who are really only parts of our truer selves) behave ideally. The work describes human life as it might be lived, perhaps ought to be lived, against a backdrop, not of all happiness and light but of crushing difficulty and overwhelming distress. It is this modeling of behavior which nourishes and strengthens the inner child in all of us. And, unless I am very much mistaken, this same inner child is who we will become when the mortal flesh melts away, and we enter the life eternal.

Yes, fantasy is escapist. The spiritual journey of the soul is not easily rendered in terms of the ultrarational, ultrarealistic. But it is natural to the escapist medium of fantasy, Tolkien maintained. And he might have added as an aside to well-intentioned Christians that Christianity itself is a venture founded on the conviction that escape is good for the soul. What is salvation, if not escape?

We hope, through our faith in Christ, to escape the death penalty which sin has decreed. It seems to me that fantasy literature actually mirrors this great hope in its fundamental design. Perhaps it is enough that it does so. But, when the mirror of fantasy is polished bright by a master storyteller engaged in the High Quest, it becomes, like Alice in Wonderland's mirror, not a mirror only, but also a window to another world. A world which is really our own world lovingly created anew.

The world of the author's creation is offered up to the delight of the reader, and because he delights he entertains. And because he entertains, all sorts of things become possible. An entertained person is a receptive person, open to the unfolding experience, open to taking in something of the artist's vision. It is all to the good if that vision is true and godly.

Tolkien demonstrates this process absolutely. In his tale of Frodo, Strider, Gandalf, and their beautiful, magical world of Middle-earth, Professor Tolkien masterfully illustrates the tremendous power of true art to inspire, enlighten, ennoble, challenge, and persuade, not to mention entertain—which was, after all, Tolkien's primary purpose.

Back at my desk, toiling away to master the power of implicity in my work, I began to get a grip on it at last. As I wrestled my way through the Dragon King Trilogy and then Empyrion I and II and on into the Pendragon Cycle, I learned that there was a greater force at work here than I first realized. I mentioned before that I thought Tolkien had set out to make his work godly on purpose. As usual, I had it backwards. He set out purposefully to make his art true. And because he succeeded, it became godly.

Stating it like that may make the process sound a bit random or haphazard, but there is nothing at all arbitrary about it. Tolkien worked at his art in a very exacting, methodical way, according to a philosophy of literature which he had developed—a philosophy his friend C. S. Lewis called the "Tolkienian Theory of Sub-creation."[3] According to this theory, the artist is a creator working in exactly the same way as God the Creator works; the artist becomes a mini-creator, his world a sub-created world reflecting God's creation.

In the final analysis, that is precisely what fantasy literature is: a celebration of life in all its myriad elements. It is nothing less than a praise hymn to creation, and its melody runs through all fantasy literature. Even the shabbiest fantasy pulp novel contains strains of it. No other entertainment form that I know of is so constructed on this premise, this fundamental recognition of the holiness of creation. It is basic to the enterprise. In fact, the fundamental act of writing the fantasy novel requires a strict acknowledgment of the basic beauty and immanent goodness of God's creation by the author. The sub-created world becomes an extension of the Divine Presence.

I do not suggest that every writer of fantasy consciously conceives his work in just this way. I suppose many, perhaps most, do not. Tolkien himself worked blindly much of the time. The agonizing process by which his masterwork came to be written is detailed in the collection of his letters, where, after twelve years of difficult gestation, he writes to the publisher in utter shock and dismay at what he has created. "I am, I fear, a most unsatisfactory person," Tolkien announced bleakly. "Now I look at it, the magnitude of the disaster is apparent to me. My work has escaped from my control, and I have produced a monster: an immensely long, complex, rather bitter, and very terrifying romance, quite unfit for children (if fit for anybody)."[4]

Tolkien was happily mistaken. The author is quite often the last to know what has transpired through him. Certainly, many writers with far less integrity than Tolkien remain blissfully oblivious to the High Quest all their lives. But that does not change the level of their participation in this holy scheme. A God who is capable of wringing shouts of joy from the rocks beneath our feet ought to be able to move a few myopic fantasy hacks to hum a snatch of harmony.

In the very best of fantasy literature the hymn of praise can achieve quite astonishing heights—something on the order of a psalm become symphony. Certainly, in *Lord of the Rings* we glimpse such a transformation. Tolkien was a master and worked very hard at his art; he also worked from a detailed understanding of his craft. For Tolkien, the creation and exploration of fantasy worlds were a way of examining the image of the Maker as revealed in his creation and in his creatures. It was also a way of probing the nature of the fall and the tremendous grace and power manifest in the incarnation and redemption. Fantasy, like all true art, becomes a kind of extended parable by which hidden facets of the multidimensional reality of life are illumined.

That it often does so in an extremely entertaining manner is, some would say, something of a plus, a serendipitous extra. But I disagree. In fact, it is much the other way around. Entertainment, you will remember, was for Tolkien the original intent and purpose.

Tolkien set out to entertain with his stories—his own children first, and then others. But in the telling, the stories grew into something far grander than anything he himself imagined when he began. That is always the best way. The writer begins with little more than the thread of an idea and the desire to follow it and see where it will go. But as he works at his creation, his labor becomes a sacrifice, of his time if nothing else (but most often, of much else besides). And if he is faithful to the High Quest, God, I believe, accepts the sacrifice and enters into it in ways unforeseen by even the author himself.

Though I make no claim to Tolkien's mantle, I have written enough imaginative fiction to know something of how it was for him. For I have seen the same things happen in my own work. My main purpose as a writer of popular fiction has always been to entertain. That is, after all, the reason people read popular fiction in the first place. But, as I have struggled to remain true to the High Quest, I have seen the narrative take some very surprising twists: events and characters resonating with deeper meaning; nuances of relevance highlighted; Truth, Beauty, and Goodness startlingly revealed. And all in ways that I could not have contrived with all my might, even on a very good day.

But then, is that not God's job? It is God who takes our meager sacrifices and transforms them into blessings—a few loaves and fishes into a feast for thousands! My job, I keep reminding myself, is to follow the High Quest to the best of my ability, to make the daily sacrifice, and let God take it from there. Tolkien has taught me that. And if I never write anything remotely approaching his monumental achievement, still I will have done my part.

GETTING STARTED WITH TOLKIEN

Tolkien's most famous works are available in paperback editions at any major bookstore, and usually come in a boxed set. *The Hobbit* serves as the introduction to three books known collectively as *The Ring Trilogy;* they are *The Fellowship of the Ring, The Two Towers,* and *The Return of the King*. A warning: some readers find *The Hobbit* less captivating than *The Ring Trilogy,* so don't make final judgment if you bog down in the first book. True Tolkien fans progress to *The Silmarillion,* a more difficult work which has not the same popular appeal. Readers interested in Tolkien's life can study *Tolkien* by Humphrey Carpenter or *Tolkien and the Silmarillion* by Clyde Kilby.

13

FYODOR DOSTOEVSKY
God and Passion

Eugene H. Peterson

I was in crisis and went looking for a priest, a pastor, a guide—someone who could help me work out my calling in a most uncongenial setting. I felt beleaguered. I needed help.

I made several attempts at finding a mentor among the living, without success. Then I found Fyodor Dostoevsky. I cannot now remember how I hit on him, for I had no previous acquaintance. An inspired hunch, maybe. A whim that turned lucky.

I took my appointments calendar and wrote in two-hour meetings with "FD" three afternoons a week. Over the next seven months I read through the entire corpus, some of it twice. From three to five o'clock on Tuesday, Thursday, and Friday, I met with FD in my study and had leisurely conversations through *Crime and Punishment, Notes from the*

Eugene H. Peterson is professor emeritus of spiritual theology at Regent College, Vancouver, British Columbia. He was the organizing pastor of Christ Our King Presbyterian Church in Bel Air, Maryland, and continued as pastor there for twenty-nine years. He has written twenty-seven books, among them *Reversed Thunder, Leap Over a Wall,* and *Answering God.* He recently completed *The Message,* a contemporary rendering of the Bible from the original languages.

Underground, The Idiot, A Raw Youth, The Devils, and *The Brothers Karamazov.* All winter long, through the spring, and a month or two into the summer I hid away in my study reading Penguin paperbacks. I spent those afternoons with a man for whom God and passion were integral—and integrated.

My crisis had come when I realized that I was living in a place where God and passion were only marginal, and I sensed subtle but insistent pressures to displace them in myself. But if God and passion became marginal, I would not be myself: I would not be a writer; I would not be a pastor. Writer and Pastor were the twin strands of a vocational identity that had been formed by God and passion.

The crisis took place in a Maryland cornfield fast being overlaid with asphalt: classic American suburbia. Sent there to organize a new church, I was a pastor without a congregation. I was also a writer but unpublished. I found to my surprise that God and passion, far from being assets in publishing and parish ministry, as I had naively supposed, were impediments. There was no market for who I was, no job that fit my vocation.

And then the crisis was over. Thanks to Dostoevsky, God and passion would never again be at risk, at least vocationally. The God-passionate lives of Sonja, Prince Myshkin, Alyosha, and Father Zossima furnished my imagination with living images.

My first real find in Dostoevsky was Prince Myshkin, "The Idiot." At the time I was looking for something that I later learned to name "vocational holiness," and the prince enlarged my imagination to grasp what it might be.

How do I make a difference? The world is a mess, in need of massive overhaul. People are living in spiritual impoverishment and moral squalor and material confusion. Somebody has to *do* something. I have to do something. Where do I start?

What does it mean to represent the kingdom of God in a culture devoted to the kingdom of self? How do delicate, vulnerable, fragile words survive in competition with money and guns and bulldozers? How do pastors, who don't make anything happen, maintain a robust identity in a society that pays its top dollar to country singers, drug lords, oil barons? All around me I saw men and women hammering together a vocational identity from models given to them from the "principalities and powers." The models all were strong on power (making things happen) and image (appearing important). But none of them seemed congruent with the calling I sensed forming within myself. But what actually should this unformed aspiration look like, vocationally? Prince Myshkin was Dostoevsky's contribution to my quest.

In *The Idiot,* Prince Myshkin strikes everyone who meets him as simple and naive. He gives the impression of not knowing how the world works. People assume that he has no experience of the complexities of society. He is innocent of the "real world." An idiot.

The St. Petersburg society he enters, as portrayed by Dostoevsky, is trivial and superficial. Pretense and pose are epidemic among these people, who rate each other by how much money they possess, what kind of family they come from, who they know: "empty headed people who, in their smugness, did not realize themselves that much of their excellence was just a veneer, for which they were not responsible, for they acquired it unconsciously and by inheritance."[1] The Prince is admitted into their drawing rooms, cautiously, only because of the possibility that he might be connected with nobility. But he is suspect from the start. Ignorant of the importance of names and station, he obviously doesn't fit.

And then gradually, without anyone knowing quite how it happens, the Prince becomes the central person for these empty-headed, obsessive lives, mad for recognition or sex or money. Although he associates easily with them, he stays curiously free of their obsessions. Various characters latch on to him in order to use him. But he is not "usable." He simply is. He is not good for anything; he is simply good. In the midst of the furious machinations by which men and women are striving to get their own way, he emerges as one who is significant simply in his humanity. People find themselves approaching him for counsel, attracted to this strange man, hardly knowing why they are pulled to him like filings to a magnet. They have no vocabulary for the phenomenon.

The silent source of the Prince's detachment is that he has no personal agenda. The most powerful emotional figure in the novel, Nastasya Fillipovna, excites powerful emotions—ranging darkly from vituperative scorn to animalistic lust—in all who meet her. All except Prince Myshkin. He simply loves her, respects her, maybe even understands her. His own needs don't clog up the relationship. Nastasya is a Mary Magdalene figure, a devil-afflicted, society-exploited woman who gets a chance at love and salvation through the person of Prince Myshkin. She doesn't, in the end, embrace it; but she has her chance, and even in rejection she is accepted and loved by the Prince.

I began to realize what Dostoevsky was doing in the person of Prince Myshkin. The society in which Dostoevsky lived was superficial, its values shaped by pettiness and social obsession. None of these people did real work; they were parasites on the vast peasantry who worked the fields. But on the edge were small pockets of intellectuals seething with energies for reform—young intellectuals who wanted to tear down the rotten structure of czar and bureaucracy and church and build a pure and just society. The rebels, comprising both anarchists and socialists, sometimes disagreed on methods, but were united in the conviction that God was best left out, and that any means, even murder, was justified in order to achieve the new order.

For anyone sickened by the complacent, corrupt society of nineteenth-century Russia, the attraction of the radical revolutionaries was powerful. And Dostoevsky himself had once been attracted. He dabbled with their ideas; he joined their groups. Finally, he was arrested and sent to Siberian exile.

The labor camp, which should have radicalized him forever, did not. Or rather, it radicalized him in a counterradical way. In the early days of imprisonment he was visited by a remarkable woman, Natalya Fonvizina, who made the sign of the cross over him and gave him a New Testament. Dostoevsky spoke later of having read and reread the New Testament in his Siberian prison camp. "It lay under my pillow for four years during penal servitude. I read it sometimes, and read it to others. With it, I taught one convict to read."[2] Instead of pursuing the anarchist and socialist utopias that were all the rage, he dug to the root, to the cross of Christ.

He returned from ten years of Siberian exile and, instead of pouring himself into atheistic and social engineering endeavors, spent the rest of his life creating characters who would enter society and change it by means of holiness. The vocational question for anyone disgusted with society and wanting to do something about it for the better centers on means—*how* do I go about it? Is it to be guns or grace? Dostoevsky created a series of characters, fools for Christ like Prince Myshkin and Alyosha (of *The Brothers Karamazov*) who chose grace.

Being in the company of Prince Myshkin has little to do with morality—doing and saying what is right. It has to do with beauty and goodness. These cannot be known in abstraction, for they only occur in living, loving persons. They cannot be observed, only encountered. The Prince provides *encounter*.

For most of us, the desire for beauty and the good proves infinitely frustrating, for we are mainly aware of what we are not. When we *do* things well, we get satisfaction. When we *are* well (holy) we are unconscious of it and so get no satisfaction, at least not in the sense of ego gratification. And since mostly we are *not* well (unholy), we live with a deep sense of inadequacy. The only reason we continue to aspire to holiness is that the alternative is so insipid.

A few people in every generation are prepared to enter into society with the intent of healing or reforming or instructing. I certainly thought I was. I came out of a faith which encouraged this approach. I worked from a text that promised that all things could be made new, and that introduced such life-altering words as "repent," "be baptized," and "take up your cross."

As a young pastor, I had little patience with pietism—fussy devotional practices that separated its practitioners into conclaves of self-righteousness. I was bored with moralism—bromidic *Reader's Digest* counsels on how to live safe and sound.

But what vocational shape should these energies take on? All the models I had were either managerial or messianic. Prince Myshkin offered a different model. Such a vocation equips one not so much for getting things done as for submitting to reality. "You know," said Prince Myshkin, "in my opinion, it's sometimes quite a good thing to be absurd. Indeed, it's much better; it makes it so much easier to forgive each other and to humble ourselves. One can't start straight with perfection! To attain perfection, one must first of all be able not to understand many things. For if we understand things too quickly, we may perhaps fail to understand them well enough."[3]

I now reflect, Who are the people who have made a difference in my life? Answer: the ones who weren't trying to make a difference. Prince Myshkin alerted me to notice other persons who communicated a love, a beauty, a holiness. In their presence it would occur to me, "That's the way I want to live. I wonder if it might be possible to be that kind of person. And I wonder if this could be worked out not only personally but vocationally?"

❈

Being a writer and being a pastor are virtually the same thing for me: an entrance into chaos, the *mess* of things, and then the slow mysterious work of making something out of it, something good, something blessed—poem, prayer, conversation, sermon, a sighting of grace, a recognition of love, a shaping of virtue. This is the *Yeshua* of the Hebrew faithful, the *soteria* of the Greek Christians. Salvation. The recovery by creation and re-creation of the image of God. Writing is not a literary act but spiritual. And pastoring is not managing a religious business but a spiritual quest.

Prayer, the intensity of spirit in attention before God, lies at the heart of both writing and pastoring. In writing, I work with words; in pastoring, I work with people. But not mere words or mere people but words and people as carriers of spirit/Spirit. The moment words are used prayerlessly and people are treated prayerlessly, something essential begins to leak out of life. It was this realization of a slow leakage, a spirit-loss, that had produced my sense of crisis. And Dostoevsky is nothing if not *spirited:* God-intoxicated and word-drunk.

My writer-crisis came when I was asked to write something that would appear as if written by someone else, someone well known. I had been submitting articles, poems, and manuscripts to publishers for several years and getting them returned with rejection slips. This reprieve from uninterrupted rejections seemed providential. I accepted the assignment without thinking much about what I was doing, except that I was being appreciated, and paid well.

The article was published by a firm that had rejected several far better written manuscripts that I had submitted under my own name. I knew then that I could continue to be published and paid for it if I continued to write this way. It would be honest and useful work. But I also knew that what I had just written, while being factual (except for the attributed authorship) was not *true* in any living way. Such work was a job, not a vocation. I remembered Truman Capote's sneer, "That's not writing, it's typing."

My pastor-crisis was concurrent. In the course of organizing a new congregation in the suburbs, I felt pressure to get a lot of people together as quickly as possible in such a way that they would provide the financial resources to build an adequate sanctuary for the worship of God. I found that gathering a religious crowd was pretty easy, provided I didn't get too involved with God. My ecclesiastical superiors sent me to workshops that showed me how to do it. I observed the success of other pastors who did it. Religious consumers, like all other consumers, respond to packaging and bargains. But I also knew that to follow this route I would have to abandon the very thing that gave the life of a pastor its worth: a passion for God.

Crisis. Decision time. I wanted to be published; I wanted to have a large congregation. But I couldn't be a writer and be published. And I couldn't be a pastor and get a large congregation. Not on the terms that were being offered to me at that time.

The world then was redolent with narcissism (it was the decade of the sixties). The story of Narcissus has long endured as a warning against the dangers of self-absorption, and a most useful warning it has been. But something different was happening here: Narcissus, instead of being used to warn, was being held up as patron. Human potential was all the rage in the parish; spiritual confessionals were best-sellers in the bookstores. *Self* was front and center.

On one level, this all seemed plausible. The aspirations of the human-potential psychologists mirrored the Christian aspiration to the abundant life. As for confession, hadn't confession always been a Christian staple? Making it into a religious literary genre didn't seem that far out of line. But something wasn't right. I felt confused. Dostoevsky unconfused me.

Dostoevsky helped me to discern that this sudden enthusiasm for the Self was not at all the same thing as the historic Christian concern for the Soul, that the Self, in fact, was a devilish distortion of Soul. What people were calling the Self was similar to what Christianity has always named the Soul, but with all the God-hunger, the righteousness-thirst excised. Dostoevsky taught me that not by arguing but by creating— creating characters who demonstrated the dehumanized desiccation of an unGodded life and, in contrast and comparison, the terrible beauties of a pursuit after God.

The modern zeal to explain human nature, to eliminate suffering and discontent and to make us comfortable in the world—this obsessive *self-*interest, Dostoevsky demonstrated, was a reduction of vast, mysterious creatures with raging thirsts for God and insatiable hungers for holiness into what he dismissed as "Euclidean"—something that could be accounted for by lines and angles, measurements, and numbers. "Man is not an arithmetical expression; he is a mysterious and puzzling being, and his nature is extreme and contradictory all through."[4] I began copying out these Soul-recovering sentences:

"People are people and not the keys of a piano."[5]

"Man's whole business is to prove to himself that he is a man and not a cog-wheel."[6]

"For 2 and 2 make 4 is not a part of life but the beginning of death."[7]

In his Russia and in my America, interest in God had been elbowed to the sidelines by a pushy interest in the Self. Writer after writer and pastor after pastor were engaged in the titillating business of unpacking emotional suitcases and holding up the various items for view. It was bra-and-panty voyeurism: guilt and innocence, anger and affection, lust and love—the undergarments of the soul—all exclaimed over and handled, but with no passion for God himself, no pineal embrace in the nightlong struggle for identity through suffering and prayer with the God who suffers and prays with and for us in Christ.

The voyeurism developed into fetishism. The reduction of Soul to Self, and displacement of God from the center, had made it possible to diagnose Self (bereft of mystery) and fabricate a religion precisely suited to the satisfaction of Self needs, but with all the intricacy of God and human relationship removed. "The fetish," as Ernest Becker put it so succinctly in *The Denial of Death,* "is the manageable miracle, which the partner is not." I edited Becker's sentence: "fetish spirituality is the manageable miracle, which God is not."[8]

The culture in which I was trying to work out my vocation was hellbent on partializing (Otto Rank's term) the unmanageable largeness of life.[9] Dostoevsky's large-spirited, extravagant, and reckless immersion in the depths of evil and suffering, love and redemption, recovered God and passion for me. Stavrogin was not a man who could be dissuaded from his evil life and educated into salvation with a newly revised church school curriculum. Alyosha did not become holy by attending a therapy group.

Unlike his great contemporary, Tolstoy, who was forever drawing up educational programs and reform plans to eliminate poverty and suffering and injustice, Dostoevsky entered into the sufferings, into the mysterious crucible of faith and doubt, and looked around for the miracle, the rising from the dead. He would have nothing to do with a future in which people were made good and comfortable at the expense of their freedom, at the cost of God.

But the vocational culture in which I was trying to find my way was definitely Tolstoyan. The so-called "spiritual" leaders of my time were putting enormous pressure upon people to conform, adjust, and fit in—to submit to explanations and be reduced to functions. My own denomination had what was called a "program agency," which published a "program calendar." "Program" was the chief vehicle of ministry. I remember being startled by a statement from a pastor whose reputation was high in those years. His athletic energy was topped off with a good smile, which he used to great effect. After serving one congregation for five years, he was moving to another, three times its size. His readiness to move surprised me, and in my naivete I asked why he was leaving so soon. "I have accomplished what I came to do; I have my program in place and working."

Program? What has program got to do with spirituality, with creativity? Programs are fine for Euclidean minds and spirits, I suppose. And they are always useful for peripheral matters. But at the center? Program? I reached for another Dostoevsky novel, *The Devils* this time, and used it to maintain a healthy distance from the program mentality with its reformist ancestry, and settled in to stubbornly endure mystery with Shatov.

A writer discovers a workable plot and writes the same book over and over all his life to the immense satisfaction of his readers. The readers can feel literary without thinking or dealing with truth. Prostitute writer.

A pastor discovers a workable program and repeats it in congregation after congregation to the immense satisfaction of his or her parishioners. The church members can be religious without praying or dealing with God. Prostitute pastor.

My most frightening encounter came with Raskolnikov in *Crime and Punishment*. Raskolnikov had selected a socially worthless person to run an experiment upon, an experiment in murder. It could matter to no one whether the old woman, a pawnbroker, was dead or alive, for she had absolutely no usefulness to anyone or anything. She was a parasite, he thought, living off the poor. Raskolnikov killed her. And then, to his great surprise, he was shaken to the core of his existence: it *did* matter. This worthless old woman had a spiritual power simply by being human. Bare human existence contains enough glory to stagger any one of us into bewildered awe. Raskolnikov was awakened to an awareness of spiritual heights and depths that he had never dreamed of.

Suddenly, with a shock of recognition, I saw myself as Raskolnikov. Not murdering, exactly, but experimenting with words on paper and parishioners in the congregation, manipulating them in godlike ways to see what I could make happen. Pushing words around on paper to see what effect they might have. Pushing people around in the pews, working for the best combination. Reducing words to their dictionary sense. Reducing people to the value of their pledge. Facility with words and facility with people carry a common danger: the hubris of contemptuous disrespect. One of Raskolnikov's successors, Joseph Stalin, once said, "Paper will put up with anything written on it." So will fetish-ridden, idol-addicted congregations.

I retraced my steps. How had I arrived in the world of Raskolnikov? How had I come to think so irreverently of these people around me?

I was living in classic suburbia, and not liking it very much. The cornfield into which I had moved was daily being covered over with tract homes and asphalt. The people who gathered to worship God under my leadership were rootless and cultureless, only marginally Christian. They didn't read books. They didn't discuss ideas. All spirit seemed to have seeped out of their lives, replaced by a garage sale clutter of clichés and stereotypes, securities and fashions. Dostoevsky's sentence hit the target: the "people seem to be watered down ... [they are] darting and rushing about before us every day, but in a sort of diluted state."[10] It was a marshmallow culture, spongy and without substance. No hard ideas to push against. No fiery spirit to excite. Soggy suburbia.

This scene was new to me. I had grown up in a small Montana town and went to schools in the seaport cities of Seattle, New York, and Baltimore. In the small western town virtually everyone had a three-dimensional character around which anecdotes clustered like barnacles. In the cities I encountered the cross-cultural fertilization of Asians, Europeans, Africans. But now everyone was, or was fast becoming, the same. I was thirty years old and had never experienced this blandness, this willingness to be homogenized into passive consumerism.

I had no idea that an entire society could be shaped by the images of advertising. I had lived, it seems, a sheltered life. The experiments of Pavlov accounted for the condition of these people far better than anything in the four Gospels. They were conditioned to respond to the stimulus of the sale price quite apart from need, as effectively as Pavlov's dogs were trained to salivate at the bell's signal, quite apart from hunger. These were the people for whom I was praying and for whom I was writing, these people whose spirits had taken early retirement, whose minds had been checked at the door. Suburbia lobotomized spirituality.

In the flatness and boredom I lost respect for these anemic lives. These people who assembled in worship with me each week had such *puny* ideas of themselves. In a fast-food culture they came to church for fast religion help. Hanging around them all week long, I was in danger of reducing my idea of them to their self-concepts. And then Dostoevsky, who lived in an almost identical society, rebuked me. While showing the greatest aversion to the culture itself, he refused to take the evidence the people presented of themselves as the truth, and dove beneath the surface of their lives; there he discovered in the depths fire and passion and God.

Dostoevsky made them appear large again, vast in their aspirations, their sins, their glories. The Karamazovs for instance—so large, so *Russian*. He showed me how to look long and carefully at these families until I saw Karamazovs in every home. He trained my antennae to pick up the suppressed signals of spirituality in the denatured language of their conversations. I discovered tragic plots and comic episodes, works-in-progress all around me. I was living in a world redolent with spirituality. There were no ordinary people.

My task now was to pray and write, aware of these torrential energies and capabilities among the people who were unaware of them in themselves. I had been tricked into taking these peoples' version of themselves as the true version. But it was not true. Their lives had been leveled and overlaid with asphalt in a way similar to the grading and platting of these so recently green and rolling hills. But that visible surface was a two-inch-thick lie. If I worked on the surface of what they showed me, I would end up committing Raskolnikovian crimes out of ignorant disrespect for these glorious beings who had been created in the image of God. I was sobered, and I became repentant.

Now when I came across dull people, I began to insert them into one of the novels to see what Dostoevsky would make of them. Before long the deeper dimensions came into view: the eternal hungers and thirsts— and, in the background, God. I started finding Mozartian creativity in adolescents and Sophoclean tragedies in the middle-aged. The banality was a cover. If I looked hard and long enough, there was drama enough in this vanishing cornfield to carry me for a lifetime.

One day I came across a sentence in Karl Barth that compared the methods of the Book of Genesis with the novels of Dostoevsky.[11] They both, Barth noted, cavalierly ignore conventional valuations and honors and approach the lives of men and women by unearthing the underground and unsuspected depths of God in their conventional-appearing lives. Dostoevsky and Genesis do not respect the masks of men but judge their secrets; they see beyond what men and women present themselves to be and perceive what they are from what they are not; they see, in Paul's terms, their righteousness *reckoned* as the divine "nevertheless" and not as a divine "therefore," as forgiveness and not as an imprimatur upon what they think they are.

Dostoevsky had the good fortune, which becomes an inherited good fortune for all who read him, of getting it all together in his final novel, *The Brothers Karamazov*. By no means a polished work—nothing Dostoevsky either wrote or lived was polished—it is, nevertheless, exuberant with the large potentialities of the soul. Frederick Buechner, writer and minister, called it "that great seething bouillabaisse of a book. It's digressive and sprawling, many too many characters in it, much too long, and yet it's a book which, just because Dostoevsky leaves room in it for whatever comes up to enter, is entered here and there by maybe nothing less than the Holy Spirit itself, thereby becoming, as far as I'm concerned . . . a novel less *about* the religious experience than a novel the reading of which *is* a religious experience: of God, both in his subterranean presence and in his appalling absence."[12]

There is a shining moment in this valedictory book when Alyosha experiences a kind of integrating benediction:

His soul, overflowing with rapture, was craving for freedom and unlimited space. The vault of heaven, studded with softly shining stars, stretched wide and vast over him. From the zenith of the horizon the Milky Way stretched its two arms dimly across the sky. The fresh, motionless, still night enfolded the earth. The white towers and golden domes of the cathedral gleamed against the sapphire sky. The gorgeous autumn flowers in the beds near the house went to sleep till morning. The silence of the earth seemed to merge into the silence of the heavens. The mystery of the earth came into contact with the mystery of the stars. Alyosha stood, gazed and suddenly he threw himself down upon the earth. He did not know why he was embracing it. He could not have explained to himself why he longed so irresistibly to kiss it, to kiss it all, but he kissed it weeping, sobbing, and drenching it with his tears and vowed frenziedly to love it, to love it forever and ever. "Water the earth with the tears of your gladness and love those tears," it rang in his soul. What was he weeping over? Oh, he was weeping in a rapture even more over those stars which were shining for him from the abyss of space and he was not ashamed of that ecstasy. It was as though the threads from all those innumerable worlds of God met all at once in his soul and it was trembling all over as it came in contact with other worlds.[13]

To anyone who has moved through an apprenticeship in all those earlier novels, each of them seeking but not quite arriving at this sense of God's integration, Alyosha's blessing puts together what the devil puts asunder. But even a short apprenticeship in words and/or the Word—trying to write words honestly, trying to address people reverently—is sufficient qualification to appreciate the rapture.

Dostoevsky had intended to write a sequel. He planned to develop the life of Alyosha, Prince Myshkin's successor in the "fool for Christ" line, through an adulthood of vocational holiness. But he didn't write it. He died two months after completing *Brothers*. Maybe it is just as well. This kind of work is never complete. At best, we plant seeds. And die. And wait for resurrection. The scriptural epigraph to *The Brothers Kara - mazov* is, "Verily, verily, I say unto you, except a corn of wheat fall into the ground and die, it abideth alone: but if it die, it bringeth forth much fruit" (John 12:24 KJV).

Seed-planting Dostoevsky: six seed-novels sit on a shelf in my study, all that is left of his life still making a difference in my life. God and passion. He spurned the trivial and went for the jugular. He didn't fit. He made a mess of his marriage and was tortured in his love. He gambled compulsively. His epilepsy crippled his writing. But he created. He lived immersed in passion. He lived expectant of God. And he did this *voca - tionally*, making a calling out of passion and God.

Father Zossima explicated John's text in a homily:

> Many things on earth are hidden from us, but in return for that we have been given a mysterious inward sense of our living bond with the other world, with the higher, heavenly world and the roots of our thoughts and feelings are not here but in other worlds. That is why philosophers say that it is impossible to comprehend the essential nature of things of earth. God took seeds from other worlds and sowed them on this earth and made his garden grow, and everything that could come up came up, but whatever grows is alive and lives only through the feeling of its contact with other mysterious worlds: if that feeling grows weak or is destroyed in you then what has grown up in you will also die. Then you will become indifferent to life and even grow to hate it.[14]

I have listened to that sermon many times. It continues to do its work by returning me to the pencil-and-parish soil of my vocation—to my writing table as I try to put one word after the other honestly, to my parish rounds as I determine to set one foot after the other prayerfully.

GETTING STARTED WITH DOSTOEVSKY

Crime and Punishment, I think, is the place to start. It has the cleanest plot and fewest characters, which makes it most accessible to new readers. And then straight on to the heights, *The Brothers Karamazov,* which is chaotic and sprawling, but simply seethes with spiritual creativity. Dostoevsky's life is not nearly as interesting as his novels, but if you want to explore the person behind the books, my choice is the biography by Norwegian scholar Geir Kyetsaa: *Fyodor Dostoevsky, A Writer's Life* (Viking, 1987). Also, in 1988 Plough Publishing, an arm of the Hutterian Brethren, brought out *The Gospel in Dostoevsky,* a sampling of passages from Dostoevsky with an explicitly Christian emphasis.

14

CHARLES DICKENS
Love to See Things As They Are

Tim Stafford

One of the funniest, darkest sequences I know in English literature involves Tony Last, Evelyn Waugh's nonhero in *A Handful
of Dust*. Tony has escaped England and his ruined marriage to
seek a Lost City in the jungles of Brazil. Unfortunately he is stricken
with malarial fever, his Indian guides run off after being terrified by a
mechanical mouse, and his adventuring companion canoes over a waterfall to his death. The delirious Tony wanders through the jungle until,
by sheer luck, he happens on the remote camp of Mr. Todd, who doses
him with herbs and tenderly nurses him back to health.

Tony's return to health becomes a fate worse than death. Mr. Todd
is illiterate and lives in a hut, but he possesses a complete set of Dickens—well, nearly complete, for some volumes have been eaten by insects.
Mr. Todd fondly remembers his father reading aloud from these books,
and he is quite intent that Tony read to him from them as well. At first

Tim Stafford is senior writer for *Christianity Today* and the author of many books, including
Knowing the Face of God, The Stamp of Glory, Sisters, and *The Law of Love.*

Tony finds this enjoyable as he recovers from his illness. Gradually he grows restless and then discovers the truth. Mr. Todd is interested in Tony's health only so that Tony can read Dickens aloud. The book ends as we realize that Tony Last will complete his days in the Brazilian jungles, held more or less by force, reading aloud from an endless cycle of Dickens. For Mr. Todd wants nothing more from life than to be able to hear Charles Dickens's endlessly interesting works endlessly repeated.

Many little jokes lie embedded in Waugh's death-by-Dickens, the greatest being, of course, that the reading of the beloved English novelist, Mr. Dickens of *The Christmas Carol,* of *Oliver Twist,* becomes an instrument of torture in Brazil. (It should be noted that Tony is an Anglophile of the purest, most sentimental nature.) Then there is the fact that Dickens's most sincere fan is an illiterate, mixed-race maniac. And finally, one can hardly avoid noticing that Mr. Todd, in his lucid, calm madness, could very easily be a character in one of Dickens's novels—one of those wonderful inventions come, oh horrors, to life.

To my mind, Waugh makes in this passage a most touching tribute to Dickens. He manages somehow both to touch the genius of Dickens, and to laugh at it. Or, I should say, to laugh at himself, because the joke is really about *reading* Dickens, and the helpless, ever astonished addiction that Dickens brings out in those who love him. Sometimes it seems like a form of self-torture. So much is bad in Dickens's work, so much is maudlin and sentimental, moralistic and insincere, so much made up from bad serial adventures or cheap romances, that when you have finished a novel and wake up from its spell, you cannot help wondering how you read past all those imperfections hardly noticing. Somehow for all his faults Dickens is endlessly interesting, and not just to Mr. Todd, because a light shines out of his pages, something no one has ever imitated. I like George Orwell's comment very much: "Rotten architecture, but what gargoyles."

Someone once asked G. K. Chesterton what book beside the Bible he would want if stranded on a desert island. His answer was something like, *Boyle's Guide to Practical Shipbuilding.* I would say, contrariwise, that I would choose a complete set of Dickens. And that, I suppose, makes me as crazy as Mr. Todd.

✳

When I first got this wonderful assignment, to write about an author you love, I thought of William Faulkner, though not for long. As soon as I realized that Dickens was unchosen by my peers—indeed, that the other great Victorian novelists, George Eliot and Jane Austen, as well as Anthony Trollope and Thomas Hardy, were unchosen—I knew that I had to write about one of them. (I did also begin to doubt, I admit, the quality of the Society.) Those novelists are to me the pinnacle of literature, the best flowering of genius and delight in English. I understand that many readers find it difficult to read books from almost two hundred years ago, and I can still remember how it was for me at one time, when reading Victorian novels was real work. But once you are accustomed to the slower pacing and the more ornate and polished sentences, you would never consider it difficult. These are books for the beach.

One mistake people make, when they are unfamiliar with Victorian novels, is to think that they are all more or less the same. But this is wildly untrue. And of no one is it more untrue than of Dickens. He is utterly unlike anyone, including his fellow Victorians. It is difficult to imagine him and Jane Austen even in the same room together, making conversation. Their habits of mind, their style, their idea of what makes a novel (or a life), had nothing in common. Dickens was a wild man, an untamed, undereducated character more like a modern rock star, perhaps, than like his intelligent, civilized, sharply observant female counterparts Eliot and Austen. One sign of the unparalleled greatness of the nineteenth-century English novel is that it managed to be great in such startlingly different ways.

Which brings me back to Faulkner. While Faulkner and Dickens are worlds apart—different centuries, different continents, utterly different prose style—one *can* imagine them in the same room, making very interesting conversation. Both grew in unlikely soil: Faulkner in the rural South, Dickens in commercial, middle-class London. Living in societies that didn't greatly value literature, both learned how to write on their own, without much tutoring, and therefore both have a style that is eccentric and flawed. Both offer a corpus of unified literature, a large number of books that are recognizably related to each other, so that you can describe literature that is Faulknerian or Dickensian and be immediately understood. And if you ask what unites their respective corpora, it is the same thing: geography. Faulkner wrote of Yoknapatawpha County in Mississippi. Faulkner country, it is now sometimes called, the most important character in his novels—a brooding, seductive, primal force that presses on all the lives that inhabit it.

For Dickens, the seductive and primal force is the great city of London. Dickens is not terribly interested in landscapes or buildings, and he offers few passages of vivid physical description. The little physical description he does offer is intended mainly to evoke experience and feeling. Consider the beginning of *Bleak House:*

London. Michaelmas Term lately over, and the Lord Chancellor sitting in Lincoln's Inn Hall. Implacable November weather. As much mud in the streets, as if the waters had but newly retired from the face of the earth, and it would not be wonderful to meet a Megalosaurus, forty feet long or so, waddling like an elephantine lizard up Holborn Hill. Smoke lowering down from chimney-pots, making a soft black drizzle, with flakes of soot in it as big as full-grown snow-flakes—gone into mourning, one might imagine, for the death of the sun. Dogs, undistinguishable in mire. Horses, scarcely better; splashed to their very blinkers. Foot passengers, jostling one another's umbrellas, in a general infection of ill-temper, and losing their foothold at street-corners, where tens of thousands of other foot passengers have been slipping and sliding since the day broke (if the day ever broke), adding new deposits to the crust upon crust of mud, sticking at those points tenaciously to the pavement, and accumulating at compound interest.[1]

What Dickens describes is mud and bad weather. What we feel is London. London in common experience is a powerful presence in nearly all Dickens's novels. If his characters are not physically in London, they are leaving it, going toward it, remembering it, moving in its orbit like moons. London's chaotic energy, wretched poverty and restless ambition, withering traffic, quiet squares, all the sights and sounds that must have mesmerized Dickens and thousands of talented middle-class young men and women like him who came to the city—these you feel more than you see. Take Faulkner out of Yoknapatawpha, and you have a very mediocre novelist. Take Dickens out of London and you have cut off both his legs.

I began to read Faulkner avidly when I was in high school, but I never saw Mississippi until, ten years later, I married a woman from the deep South. I remember being struck then at what ordinary materials Faulkner had used to build his mythology. The brooding forests, the fanatical characters were there all right but easily missed. The landscape looked unexceptional, unless you learned to see it the way Faulkner did. I imagine that is how Dickens's London must have seemed to his peers. When you read about London in other novelists of Dickens's period, it is just a place, a location with many buildings, much commotion, but little personality. Dickens gave the dirty streets a living force, and made them a breeding ground for his eccentric characters.

If London is Dickens's center of gravity, these characters are his endlessly interesting subject matter. Dickens created basketfuls of unforgettable personalities—gargoyles and grotesques, sharp, funny, true, and unique. They are more memorable than anything else about his books. Dickens could, as I say, write very badly, and some of his books are not particularly good by usual literary standards; but not one of them lacks these astonishing creations, which is why all his novels are worth reading.

Take, for example, Sam Weller of *Pickwick Papers,* Dickens's first novel. Sam is a manservant, the kind of character many novelists of the period hardly notice, but clearly (by his own lights) the master of all that he surveys.

Sam inquired, with a countenance of great anxiety, whether [a surly horse groom's] master's name was not Walker.

"No, it ain't," said the groom.

"Nor Brown, I s'pose?" said Sam.

"No, it ain't."

"Nor Vilson?"

"No; nor that neither," said the groom.

"Vell," replied Sam, "then I'm mistaken, and he hasn't got the honour of my acquaintance, which I thought he had. Don't vait here out o' compliment to me," said Sam, as the groom wheeled in the barrow, and prepared to shut the gate. "Ease afore ceremony, old boy; I'll excuse you."

"I'd knock your head off for half-a-crown," said the surly groom, bolting one half of the gate.

"Couldn't afford to have it done on those terms," rejoined Sam. "It 'ud be vurth a life's board vages, at least, to you, and 'ud be cheap at that. Make my compliments in-doors. Tell 'em not to vait dinner for me, and say they needn't mind puttin' any by, for it'll be cold afore I come in."

In reply to this, the Groom waxing very wroth, muttered a desire to damage somebody's head; but disappeared without carrying it into execution, slamming the door angrily after him, and wholly unheeding Sam's affectionate request, that he would leave him a lock of his hair, before he went.[2]

Or consider Quilp, a dwarf, who has got Mr. Brass drunk in *The Old Curiosity Shop.*

Mr. Brass's first impression [upon regaining consciousness] was, that his host was gone and had left him there alone—perhaps locked him in for the night. A strong smell of tobacco, however, suggested a new train of ideas, he looked upwards, and saw that the dwarf was smoking in his hammock.

"Good bye, Sir," cried Brass faintly. "Good bye, Sir."

"Won't you stop all night?" said the dwarf. "Do stop all night."

"I couldn't indeed, Sir," replied Brass, who was almost dead from nausea and the closeness of the room. "If you'd have the goodness to show me a light, so that I may see my way across the yard, Sir—"

Quilp was out in an instant; not with his legs first, or his head first, or his arms first, but bodily—altogether.

"To be sure," he said, taking up a lantern, which was now the only light in the place. "Be careful how you go, my dear friend. Be sure to pick your way among the timber, for all the rusty nails are upwards. There's a dog in the lane. He bit a man last night, and a woman the night before, and last Tuesday he killed a child—but that was in play. Don't go too near him."

"Which side of the road is he, Sir?" asked Brass, in great dismay.

"He lives on the right hand," said Quilp, "but sometimes he hides on the left, ready for a spring. He's uncertain in that respect. Mind you take care of yourself. I'll never forgive you if you don't. There's the light out— never mind—you know the way—straight on!"

Quilp had slily shaded the light by holding it against his breast, and now stood chuckling and shaking from head to foot in a rapture of delight, as he heard the lawyer stumbling up the yard, and now and then falling heavily down. At length, however, he got quit of the place, and was out of hearing.[3]

Quilp is the sort of horrible character you hate to meet in life but eagerly anticipate in the novel. And so it is for so many of Dickens's grotesques—of which there are dozens and dozens.

It must be said that characters were hit and miss for Dickens. In particular, he had no idea how to write about women, especially good women of the kind that a middle-class man like himself might marry. He writes about them so badly that I can only think he was terrified of them. His good women are so perfect, so pliant and sentimental, so clinging and delicate that it makes you want to throw up. At the same time, it is quite obvious that Dickens knew and admired other kinds of women, models for Betsey Trotwood and Nurse Peggotty and Mrs. Micawber, to name three absolutely amazing and wonderfully strong characters in *David Copperfield* alone. But when he tries to pull our heartstrings, as he did with Little Nell in *The Old Curiosity Shop,* or Emily in *David Copper - field,* when he tries to write about a conventionally lovely woman, he is almost too sentimental to bear.

It is a puzzle. Dickens writing about a conventionally good woman is invariably inert, like the most wooden beginner. For example, Little Nell:

"Dear grandfather," cried the girl with an energy which shone in her flushed face, trembling voice, and impassioned gesture, "I am not a child in that I think, but even if I am, oh hear me pray that we may beg, or work in open roads or fields, to earn a scanty living, rather than live as we do now."

"Nell!" said the old man.

"Yes, yes, rather than live as we do now," the child repeated, more earnestly than before. "If you are sorrowful, let me know why and be sorrowful too; if you waste away and are paler and weaker every day, let me be your nurse and try to comfort you. If you are poor, let us be poor together, but let me be with you, do let me be with you, do not let me see such change and not know why, or I shall break my heart and die. Dear grandfather, let us leave this sad place to-morrow, and beg our way from door to door."[4]

Who would want to read any of this? Yet regarding other women, Dickens is compellingly observant. The tightly wrapped Miss Murdstone, for example, in *David Copperfield:*

She looked at me, and said: "Is that your boy, sister-in-law?"

My mother acknowledged me.

"Generally speaking," said Miss Murdstone, "I don't like boys. How d'ye do, boy?"[5]

Then, shortly thereafter, speaking to David's girlish mother:

"Now, Clara, my dear, I am come here, you know, to relieve you of all the trouble I can. You're much too pretty and thoughtless"—my mother blushed but laughed, and seemed not to dislike this character—"to have any duties imposed upon you that can be undertaken by me. If you'll be so good as give me your keys, my dear, I'll attend to all this sort of thing in future."

From that time, Miss Murdstone kept the keys in her own little jail all day, and under her pillow all night, and my mother had no more to do with them than I had.[6]

Most of Dickens's best characters are humorous; some are villains (like the 'umble Uriah Heep); all are exaggerated. They have a cartoonish nature, not to be confused with real life. And yet, they are real life, with a core reality pulled out and lit up, turned at an angle and made to dance. These are not real people yet we recognize them. They are crushing bores that never bore us; pests that we turn the page eagerly to get more of; oddballs and eccentrics that we somehow associate with the dear comforts of home and hometown. If you think it is easy to take ordinary people and exaggerate their qualities like this, try it. Like a magician who pulls rabbit after rabbit out of his hat, Dickens could reach down into the ordinary people you might see on a bus or sit next to in a doctor's waiting room, and draw out, not rabbits but hippos, camels, and ostriches. And yet—and here he is a real magician—his audience can see quite clearly that these odd creatures were there all along. Dickens had a fantastic imagination, not to make things up but to see what is there. When we read Dickens, a little of this current of imagination flows through to us. Life seems brighter, more various, more interesting, because it seemed so bright, various, and interesting to Charles Dickens.

Dickens left a will commending his soul to God and to the mercy of Jesus Christ, and there is no reason to doubt his sincerity. There is, however, plenty of reason to doubt the depth of his confession. Dickens had a very conventional side which may never have thought to doubt the truths he was raised on. He seems to have believed in God in about the same way that he believed in the queen. She exists, she deserves our respect, but she does not intersect with ordinary life at all.

His novels occasionally bring in religious sentiments, but always in such a conventional way that you sense absolutely no commitment, not even any curiosity. He must have known real Christians, and the effects of Wesleyan revivals surely were visible on the streets of London, but they seem to have made no impression on him. Perhaps by his day the revivals had fossilized into predictability. Dickens's only noticeable religious interest is, just occasionally, to skewer some hypocrite, most notably Mrs. Jellyby, one of his gargoyles who is so devoted to the souls of Africans that she neglects her own children.

For anyone who sees God as the center of life, Dickens's neglect of him presents a problem. It is hard to appreciate modern novels where God is treated as a cause for hardened disgust. Nineteenth-century literature frequently offers a more difficult challenge: a God who exists but simply does not matter. That is certainly the case with Dickens. Yet even so Dickens has taught me a very Christian lesson.

In Dickens you find what is left of religion after God has left the building: you find morality. It is not, however, what you might expect from middle-class Victorian morality. Dickens's sense of right and wrong is not fussy, nor preoccupied with codes. It is not an us-over-them morality. He cares about truthfulness and honor, and seems genuinely shocked that one person might betray another. (Think of Steerforth and his treatment of Little Emily in *David Copperfield*.) Primarily, however, he shows concern for the poor and the weak. This is because he never forgot his own vivid experiences in childhood.

One of my favorite passages has David Copperfield unknowingly under the influence of his widowed mother's suitor, who entertains David for a day:

> "And who's this shaver?" said one of the gentlemen, taking hold of me.
>
> "That's Davy," returned Mr. Murdstone.
>
> "Davy who?" said the gentleman. "Jones?"
>
> "Copperfield," said Mr. Murdstone.
>
> "What! Bewitching Mrs. Copperfield's incumbrance?" cried the gentleman. "The pretty little widow?"
>
> "Quinion," said Mr. Murdstone, "take care, if you please. Somebody's sharp."
>
> "Who is?" asked the gentleman, laughing.
>
> I looked up, quickly; being curious to know.
>
> "Only Brooks of Sheffield," said Mr. Murdstone.
>
> I was quite relieved to find that it was only Brooks of Sheffield; for, at first, I really thought it was I.
>
> There seemed to be something very comical in the reputation of Mr. Brooks of Sheffield, for both the gentlemen laughed heartily when he was mentioned, and Mr. Murdstone was a good deal amused also. After some

laughing, the gentleman whom he had called Quinion said—"And what is the opinion of Brooks of Sheffield, in reference to the projected business?"

"Why, I don't know that Brooks understands much about it at present," replied Mr. Murdstone; "but he is not generally favorable, I believe."

There was much laughter at this, and Mr. Quinion said he would ring the bell for some sherry in which to drink to Brooks. This he did; and when the wine came, he made me have a little, with a biscuit, and, before I drank it, stand up and say, "Confusion to Brooks of Sheffield!" The toast was received with great applause, and such hearty laughter that it made me laugh too; at which they laughed the more. In short, we quite enjoyed ourselves.[7]

Mr. Murdstone's approach becomes quite different once he has married David's mother.

"David," he said, making his lips thin, by pressing them together, "if I have an obstinate horse or dog to deal with, what do you think I do?"

"I don't know."

"I beat him."

I had answered in a kind of breathless whisper, but I felt, in my silence, that my breath was shorter now.

"I make him wince, and smart. I say to myself, 'I'll conquer that fellow;' and if it were to cost him all the blood he had, I should do it. What is that upon your face?"

"Dirt," I said.

He knew it was the mark of tears as well as I. But if he had asked the question twenty times, each time with twenty blows, I believe my baby heart would have burst before I would have told him so.[8]

Dickens remembered the suffering of children at the hands of unaccountable authority. He remembered the feeling of poverty, of being filled with ambition yet holding little hope.

Dickens went beyond this, moreover, to sympathize with people and causes with which he could hardly identify. Sometimes this comes out as conventional radicalism (if those two words can be put together). Dickens seems to have sometimes fancied himself, as many writers do, a champion of the oppressed. Much more often, though, he acts as a free agent, without any ideology to tell him who deserves concern and who does not. He shows a genuine disturbance with, and a sharp eye for, any social system whereby somebody makes hay at another's expense. He writes about debtor's prison (*David Copperfield*) and the court system (*Bleak House*), and the catch-22 bureaucracies that do nobody any good except the bureaucrats and warders. He writes about schools and the bullies who run them to wring money out of children whose parents do not believe their complaints. He writes about the poorhouse. He writes about thieves and cheats, both rich and poor, who prey on the foolish and defenseless. He writes of the unfairness whereby the rich can avoid any responsibility for their deeds. By every sign Dickens seemed to genuinely feel for the underdog.

Sympathy for the poor and the oppressed, however, is not what makes Dickens's morality finally attractive. England was a Christian country, and plenty of people could say they were concerned for the plight of the poor. No, what makes Dickens's morality most powerful is that he not only pities the poor, he is interested in them. When he writes of pickpockets he portrays them as fascinating human beings. He has not closed off his imagination to the poor any more than he has closed it off to the oddities of chancery court or rich old ladies. They are all fully alive.

The making of Dickens's characters, rich and poor alike, was more than the creative work of a great imaginative artist. It was an act of love. His delight in God's creation—in things as they are, not as they might be—made it possible for him to see clearly, without prejudice. (Chesterton once wrote that whoever thinks love is blind was never married.)

As a Christian I could wish to see more of redemption. I could wish to see bad people made good, enemies reconciled, peace restored. But that is not Dickens's theme. He seems to have had no imagination for it. (And perhaps that is why he had no imagination for Christianity.) Whenever he tried to write of redemption he grew sentimental and maudlin. Other writers of his century came closer to that mark—George Eliot, or Leo Tolstoy. Charles Dickens, for all his many faults as a man and as a writer, had the eyes of love for human beings as they are—real people, with all their oddities and faults. Because he loved the world so desperately, Dickens makes us see it so much more plainly, and love it too. That is why the best word to use when describing the effect of Dickens on the heart is joy.

GETTING STARTED WITH DICKENS

A warning: don't start with *A Christmas Carol.* Its brevity and fame may appeal, but it is a low-watt bulb. I'd also avoid beginning with *A Tale of Two Cities* or *Great Expectations.* They're both wonderful books, but neither one offers much of the classic Dickens appeal. For that, look to Dickens's own favorite (and mine), *David Copperfield.* The cast of characters is simply brilliant. If you don't like *David,* you won't like Dickens.

15

EVELYN WAUGH
Savage Indignation
Gregory Wolfe

Both in his own lifetime and in the quarter century since his death, Evelyn Waugh has triggered violent emotional reactions, ranging from adulation to revulsion, in those who encounter his writings. He is in fact one of those rare figures who manages to evoke positive and negative responses within the same individual. He has been called a fascist, a snob, a reactionary Catholic, and "one of the three nastiest writers in the twentieth century." When his *Diaries* were published ten years after his death, the reviewer in the London *Sunday Times* concluded that the books constituted "a portrait of the artist as a bad man." Yet he

Gregory Wolfe is the publisher and editor of *Image: A Journal of the Arts and Religion,* and writer-in-residence at Seattle Pacific University. He has published essays, reviews, and articles in numerous journals, including *First Things, National Review, Crisis, Modern Age,* and *Chronicles.* Among his books are *Malcolm Muggeridge: A Biography* and *Sacred Passion: The Art of William Schickel.* Wolfe is also the editor of *The New Religious Humanists: A Reader* and the coauthor of *Books That Build Character; Climb High, Climb Far; The Family New Media Guide;* and *Circle of Grace.* He received his B.A., summa cum laude, from Hillsdale College, and his M.A. in English literature from Oxford University. Wolfe is currently writing a book on religious humanism.

monly acknowledged to be a comic genius and one of the masters of English prose style. All but one or two of his thirty books remain in print, and two films made from his novels have appeared to critical acclaim *(Brideshead Revisited* and *A Handful of Dust).*

Of course, as you may already suspect, Waugh relished controversy and is undoubtedly looking down on the ruckus which attends his literary reputation with the deepest satisfaction. Waugh's taste for provocation went beyond his outrageously funny satires upon a veritable rogue's gallery of imbecilic aristocrats, petty African dictators, and social climbers. According to his most recent biographer, Waugh would, in his later years, attend public functions dressed in loudly checked suits, sporting "a Victorian ear trumpet which he would raise when talking and lower when spoken to." He was not averse to making a scene.[1]

This same biographer, Martin Stannard, recounts an incident which typifies Waugh's flair for offensiveness. In 1960 the BBC got Waugh to agree to a rare television interview. His interlocutor was a man named John Freeman, whose skills at probing intimate personal matters would easily rival those of Phil Donahue or Geraldo Rivera.

> Soberly dressed, a carnation in his buttonhole, with the inevitable cigar and a quizzical glare of amused condescension, [Waugh] answered all the questions designed to reveal psychological instability with devastating brevity. When pushed for details, he mixed fantasy and truth at just the right pitch of levity to confuse and deflate his inquisitor. At last, somewhat desperate, Freeman managed to pin Waugh to a definite statement. The novelist agreed that the best he could hope for was that people should ignore him. "You like that when it happens, do you?" "Yes." "Why are you appearing on this programme?" "Poverty," came the reply. "We've both been hired to talk in this deliriously happy way."[2]

Perhaps one more anecdote cuts closer to the heart of Waugh's personality. In the early 1930s, Waugh, his reputation already established, had the opportunity to meet Hilaire Belloc, the aging, crusty Catholic controversialist. When the meeting took place, Waugh remained uncharacteristically shy and reticent: a recent convert to the Catholic Church, he felt awed in Belloc's presence. After Waugh had left, Belloc was asked about his impression of the young man. His answer was not what Waugh's friends had expected. "He is possessed," Belloc said.[3]

Belloc did not mean by that mysterious comment that Waugh was—literally speaking—a hostage to the devil. Rather, the old man was paying tribute to Waugh's capacity not so much to outrage others as to be outraged by the sins and follies of his time. Waugh felt himself to be plagued by the demons of the modern world; his writings were to become acts of exorcism which would cast out the things that so thoroughly galled him.

As I reflect on my personal debt to Waugh's literary and spiritual vision, I realize that it is this fierce inner struggle that accounts for his greatness and the fascination he holds for me. The figure in literary history to which he seems closest is Jonathan Swift, the eighteenth-century wit who also blended venom and comic inventiveness into a potent satirical mix. Like Waugh, Swift was accused of snobbery, reactionary politics, and, above all, of hatred of his fellow man. But critics have rarely understood—particularly when they have felt the lash of the satirist's wit themselves—that compassion and principle can coexist with stinging ridicule.

Perhaps those who place themselves in the role of prophet suffer from the occupational hazard of confusing righteous wrath with wrath pure and simple. Swift's epitaph, which he composed himself, read *"Ubi saeva indignatio ulterius cor lacerare nequit"* (Where savage indignation can no longer tear his heart). The prophet and the satirist inevitably appear as naysayers—they are always calling down the thunderbolts upon the wicked. But in fact the true satirist is not a pure cynic but one whose idealism has been wounded by awareness of how far men fall short of their potential.

In the crucible of their art, great writers like Swift and Waugh refine away personal grudges and vendettas; their savage indignation is, in the end, the bitter herb intended to violently purge the sickness of a world which is truly "fallen." To put it another way, the surgeon's knife may seem menacing, but it is used to restore health. And without a notion of what constitutes a sound body, there can be no healing.

What I discovered, in time, was that Evelyn Waugh's "possessed" quality was precisely his greatest gift. The more of his fiction I read, the more clearly I saw that behind his satirical wit, the source of my delight and attraction at first, there also lay a profoundly coherent worldview. Waugh's public persona may have been marked by exhibitionism and querulousness, but his fiction spoke to me with the force of prophetic insight.

I began to read Waugh in graduate school, during what proved to be a turning point in my life. My adolescence had been both rocky and lonely: the experience of living through my parents' separation and divorce deepened a natural tendency toward nonconformism and isolation. Going off to college, I felt not only the normal exhilaration of independence but also the sense of joining a cause. I had chosen a school with a national reputation for its ties to the conservative intellectual movement.

The late 1970s were bracing times for conservatives, who were advancing toward the political victory of Ronald Reagan's election to the presidency. "Bliss was it in that dawn to be alive, / But to be young was very heaven"—Wordsworth's famous lines of enthusiasm for the fledgling French Revolution perfectly describe my mood at that time. As a budding conservative, I felt on a deep emotional level that I belonged to a community, a new family.

But as I progressed through my undergraduate years, while most conservatives grew more euphoric, I became troubled and divided. Many of my professors had introduced me to classic works of history and literature which, far from supporting political triumphalism, spoke of the "tragic sense of life," original sin, and the limitations of partisan politics. The strain of American conservatism embraced by Ronald Reagan—a form of messianism going back to the Puritan conviction that America was the "shining city on a hill" that would lead the world to peace and prosperity—struck me as arrogant, unhistorical, and downright dangerous.

I had even more misgivings as I became involved with the public institutions of the conservative movement. I found them riddled with hypocrisy, corruption, and greed. At the foundation where I worked immediately after graduating, the phones seemed to be ringing off the hook with conservatives desperate for high-level positions in executive branch bureaucracies they had been committed, "in principle," to abolishing. (These same conservatives soon began talking about their departments as "agents for constructive change.") In one sense, of course, my youthful idealism was getting its inevitable battering; I was growing up. But it was no longer possible for me to seek comfort in an ideological "family." I went off to Oxford for graduate work in English literature, once again relieved to be away from a painful environment but no longer so anxious to "belong."

In the long vacations between grueling eight-week Oxford terms, I read through the entire Waugh canon, starting with the early romps, *Decline and Fall and Vile Bodies,* and ending with his much-underrated World War II trilogy, *Sword of Honour*. What these novels gave me—apart from sheer delight, which is, after all, the one prerequisite for good art—was a way to organize my experience. As a Christian in the late twentieth century, I needed to find a way to address the spiritual crisis of the modern West without falling into either apathy or the ready-made answers of ideology. I found it, in part, in Waugh's tragicomic vision. That vision, with all of its stylistic brilliance and complex ironies, was fueled not by personal malice or childhood trauma but by an unshakable conviction that civilization could only be held together by religious faith.

Waugh's novels are excruciatingly funny—in the most literal sense. The essence of Waugh's comic genius is his ability to cause the reader to feel *both* pleasure and pain. No sooner are you laughing at some bizarre caricature or piece of knockabout farce than Waugh suddenly inserts the stiletto between your ribs. In *Black Mischief,* an early satire of the crumbling British Empire, set in an African nation, the young innocent abroad shares a meal with some natives only to find that he has just digested his girlfriend. Rather than an isolated piece of grotesquerie, an episode like this fits into a tautly constructed whole. As Waugh explained:

> *[Black Mischief]* deals with the conflict of civilization, with all its attendant and deplorable ills, and barbarism. The plan of my book throughout was to keep the darker aspects of barbarism continually and unobtrusively present, a black and mischievous background against which the civilized and semi-civilized characters performed their parts: I wished it to be like the continuous, remote throbbing of those hand drums, constantly audible, never visible, which every traveller in Africa will remember as one of his most haunting impressions.[4]

Waugh's deft constructions and thematic seriousness set him above the mere humorist and put him in the same class as the two most devastating satirists in our literature: Juvenal and Swift.

The key to Waugh's irony is *absence.* What is missing from the world he depicts is religious faith, with its attendant stress on moral and cultural standards. There are, to be sure, regular church attenders and even American revivalists in his novels, but religion has become nothing more than a social habit. For Waugh, civilization is a precarious artifact, not a natural condition. Without the inner ordering which a living faith in a transcendent Creator entails, he believed, the external ordering of society would become brittle and collapse into fragments.

Interestingly, many of Waugh's early readers were unaware that his novels had any serious "point." In some ways, they can hardly be blamed. There is in his fiction none of the direct castigation of society's ills such as can be found in Juvenal's philippics. Most readers follow the anarchic whirl of events in these stories in a state of breathless exhilaration. As Martin Stannard puts it, Waugh's art was "an anarchic defence of order."

Human institutions, like anything under the sun, inexorably decay; as William Butler Yeats put it, "The centre cannot hold." In 1935, before Auschwitz and the Gulag Archipelago, Waugh published a manifesto which contained these lines: "Civilization has no force of its own beyond what is given it from within. It is under constant assault and it takes most of the energies of civilized man to keep going at all. . . . . Barbarism is never finally defeated; given propitious circumstances, men and women who seem quite orderly will commit every conceivable atrocity. The danger does not come merely from habitual hooligans; we are all potential recruits for anarchy."[5]

Yet the greatest danger, Waugh continues, is not anarchy itself but the establishment of tyranny to fill the vacuum of disorder. "Anarchy is the nearer to right order, for something that has not developed may reach the right end, while something which has developed wrongly cannot. . . . The disillusioned Marxist becomes a Fascist; the disillusioned anarchist, a Christian."[6]

Waugh was himself a disillusioned anarchist. At the height of the roaring twenties he had gone about with the decadents and aesthetes at Oxford, and later with the riotous young aristocrats in London known as the Bright Young Things. He married quickly and thoughtlessly, and was divorced in little over a year. And while his novels unquestionably capture some of the thrill of the anarchic social and moral conditions of the post–World War I years, they all contain the retracted stiletto blade, which eventually springs out to remind us that we are all potential recruits for barbarism.

Nowhere is Waugh's irony more lethal than in *A Handful of Dust,* arguably Waugh's greatest work, which has been made, incidentally, into a film. Tony and Brenda Last live in a decaying country house called Hetton. The house, though on the site of the ancient family seat, is a neo-Gothic monstrosity built in the Victorian era. Tony, as his surname implies, is the last of civilized men. His love for Hetton is genuine, but his weak aesthetics are the clue to his fatal flaw. He is unaware that this vulgar Victorian imitation of the integrated medieval order is not grounded in the vigorous faith of that earlier age. Tony is a romantic in an age of cold, hard calculation and barbarous passions.

Brenda loathes Hetton and pines for the social life of London. She meets John Beaver, an amoral sponger, and soon moves into a London flat in order to carry on an affair with him. Tony, who potters about Hetton in the role of country gentleman, remains ignorant of the affair. Beaver's mother is an interior decorator much in demand in London high society. When Mrs. Beaver visits Hetton, she concludes that various rooms should be remodeled in chrome and sheepskin. She, like her son, lives parasitically off the rot of the English ruling class. In her barbarism, she would enclose the remnants of Western art in abstract, antiseptic metal.

Tony's Sunday church attendance is nothing more than a social ritual. "Occasionally some arresting phrase in the liturgy would recall him to his surroundings, but for the most part that morning he occupied himself with the question of bathrooms and lavatories, and of how more of them could be introduced without disturbing the character of his house."[7] But the vicar, the Reverend Tendril, isn't really "there" either. An elderly man, he has spent most of his life as a missionary in the far-flung British Empire. He continues to preach as if to a military garrison in Afghanistan or India. His Christmas sermon provides an example: "Instead of the glowing log fire and windows tight shuttered against the drifting snow, we have only the harsh glare of the alien sun. . . . Instead of the placid ox and ass of Bethlehem . . . we have for companions the ravening tiger and the exotic camel, the furtive jackal and the ponderous elephant... ."[8]

The Reverend Tendril's sermon returns us to the theme of the perennial conflict between civilization and barbarism. Waugh makes this explicit in the novel's conclusion. Tony, the last to learn of Brenda's infidelity, emerges from his passivity (too late, of course), deciding to file for divorce as the injured party and thus refuse Brenda any financial settlement. On impulse, he agrees to accompany a crackpot explorer, Dr. Messinger, on an expedition into the South American jungle to find a mythical city, a lost paradise. Dr. Messinger, who utterly fails to comprehend the natives, meets an untimely end, while Tony comes down with a nearly fatal fever. In Tony's delirium, Waugh presents a richly suggestive phantasmagoria. At first Tony thinks he has seen the mythical city; it is a glorified but sentimentalized version of Hetton, all Gothic turrets and banners. Later he thinks he is addressing John Beaver:

> You would hear better and it would be more polite if you stood still when I addressed you instead of walking around in a circle. . . . I know you are friends of my wife and that is why you will not listen to me. But be careful. She will say nothing cruel, she will not raise her voice, there will be no hard words. She hopes you will be great friends afterwards as before. But she will leave you. She will go away quietly during the night. She will take her hammock and her rations of farine. . . . Listen to me. I know I am not clever but that is no reason why we should forget courtesy. Let us kill in the gentlest manner. I will tell you what I have learned in the forest, where time is different. There is no City. Mrs. Beaver has covered it with chromium plating and converted it into flats. . . .[9]

Instead of the City of God, glimpsed through the highest achievements of Western art and civilization, there is only the jungle. But the new jungle in London will be more inhospitable to man than the Amazon for the simple reason that it denies the essence of humanity itself. As Waugh said on more than one occasion, man without God is less than man.

Nowhere in *A Handful of Dust* is there any representative of traditional Christian faith. Waugh requires the reader to follow the lines of his irony back to the missing element in the equation. In this use of absence, Waugh is actually close to the aesthetic techniques of the modernist writers—T. S. Eliot, Ezra Pound, and James Joyce. In works like Eliot's *The Waste Land* and Joyce's *Ulysses,* the reader is set down in a bewildering world where he must make his own way, taking his bearings from the relationship of the parts to an unstated whole. The challenge of this style of writing is that it requires the reader to weigh various interpretations and make his own judgments. Though few readers will be able or willing to engage in this process of discovering meaning, an encounter with modernist literature can be exciting—the opposite of passive reception. Waugh's fiction cunningly allies modernist technique with a Christian vision of the world.

The realization that Waugh, for all his public stuffiness about modern art, had mastered some of the stylistic achievements of literary modernism, was important to me. It has become increasingly clear to me that today the Christian writer cannot merely hearken back to happier ages when the faith was publicly endorsed. We cannot "ring the bell backward. . . . Or follow an antique drum," Eliot reminds us in *Four Quartets*.[10] That would be an exercise in sentimentality and irrelevance. No, the modern Christian artist has to speak to his age in the language and forms of his time. With breathtaking artistic genius, Waugh managed to use the anarchic and frenetic state of modern society to reflect the poverty of a culture severed from its roots in the *cultus,* the Christian faith.

In reading Waugh, I had started where any good reader of fiction should begin: I tried to take in the unique flavor of his style. I had, in short, accustomed myself to the particular kind of aesthetic lens, with its specific tint and magnification, through which the author wanted me to see the world. But two questions soon obtruded themselves. There was, in the first place, the problem of standards; the satirist has to launch his salvos from a fixed position, the only alternative being a thoroughgoing nihilism. What was the source of the norms against which Waugh measured human folly and evil? The second question involved my curiosity about Waugh's theological background. What strand of Christianity did he find the most satisfying?

As it turned out, both questions had the same answer: the Roman Catholic Church, to which Waugh had converted in 1930. These were not academic questions for me but urgent, burning issues. Like many young Christian writers in the 1970s, I had come from one of the "Low" churches to embrace the Episcopal Church, or what I preferred to call the "Anglican Communion." My literary heroes, C. S. Lewis and T. S. Eliot, had been Anglicans, and my immediate Christian mentors, Thomas Howard and Sheldon Vanauken, were shining beacons along what has been called "the Canterbury trail." I was intoxicated by the language of the King James Version and the Book of Common Prayer; Evensong with an Anglican boys' choir was, I felt certain, a direct preview of the heavenly consort. Sacraments, ritual, priesthood—all these elements of "Catholic" Christianity became like richly colored stained glass through which I basked in the light of God's grace.

But there was soon trouble in paradise. When I looked to the Episcopal Church for clear and unambiguous teaching on the crucial moral issues of the day—marriage and divorce, abortion, homosexuality—I found a Babel of conflicting voices. It was impossible for me simply to "transcend" these problems which centered around the family, the one institution that most clearly stood between civilization and anarchy. Nor could I accept that these were private matters, part of a legitimate "pluralism" within the church. So the question of the teaching authority of the church became paramount. As I stood on the step of a beautiful neo-Gothic Episcopal church, I gazed across the street to a hideous roller-rink style Catholic church, envying not the aesthetics of its parishioners but the force and clarity of their church's teachings.

Because my childhood experiences of Christianity had been in what I call the "Transcendentalist" tradition—Christian Science and liberal Congregationalism—I never had the dogmatic frame of mind that relied on elaborate logical and biblical proofs. For me, the measures of truth were much more concrete and specific: hence my interest in art and morals. In my own search for a home within the Christian community, therefore, works of the imagination, such as paintings or novels—Waugh's among them—served as essential guides.

Evelyn Waugh's early novels, such as *A Handful of Dust,* do not confront the experience of faith directly. But his most famous novel, *Brideshead Revisited,* is about the Catholic Church and the way it shapes and affects its communicants. *Brideshead* marked a new phase in Waugh's fiction. His conversion in 1930 had been a relatively intellectual affair, primarily an assent to the dogma of the church. But during World War II Waugh came to believe that in his personal life and in his art he ought to make the church an active force. The ambitious goal he set for himself in *Brideshead* was to show "the operation of divine grace on a group of diverse but closely connected characters."[11]

Ironically, the reaction of many readers, including a good number of Catholics, to *Brideshead* can be summarized by a letter received from an American reader soon after its publication: "Your *Brideshead Revisited* is a strange way to show that Catholicism is an answer to anything. Seems more like the kiss of Death."[12] A plot summary would certainly seem to support that contention. The agnostic painter, Charles Ryder, witnesses one member after another of the Catholic, aristocratic Flyte family die or fade away in lives which appear largely futile. Early in the novel, Ryder's intimate friend, Sebastian Flyte, explains:

> So you see we're a mixed family religiously. Brideshead and Cordelia are both fervent Catholics; he's miserable, she's bird-happy; Julia and I are half-heathen; I am happy, I rather think Julia isn't; Mummy is popularly believed to be a saint and Papa is excommunicated—and I wouldn't know which of them was happy. Anyway, however you look at it, happiness doesn't seem to have much to do with it, and that's all I want. . . . I wish I liked Catholics more.[13]

By the end of the novel, Sebastian and Cordelia are also living stunted and sad lives. But, as happens so often in the fiction of Evelyn Waugh, a throwaway phrase contains the core of the novel's meaning: "happiness doesn't seem to have much to do with it."[14]

For Waugh, the common notion that the life of faith ought to lead inevitably to worldly prosperity and what the pop psychologists call "wellness" is both unrealistic and dangerous. In a fallen world, afflicted by evil and stupidity, happiness can never be a gauge of fidelity to God. To think otherwise is to confuse happiness, with its bourgeois connotations of comfort and freedom from any burdens, with *blessedness,* or what Catholics call the "state of grace." Waugh's depiction of the mysterious presence of grace in the midst of suffering and adversity was not unique; I had found it in the other major Catholic novelists of the twentieth century: Graham Greene, François Mauriac, Georges Bernanos, Flannery O'Connor, and Shusaku Endo.

People of faith, Waugh believed, have always clung to the foot of the cross, profoundly and intuitively aware of what the Spanish philosopher Unamuno called "the tragic sense of life." When Julia Flyte, one of the "half-heathens," reaches a moment of crisis in *Brideshead Revisited,* it is the unexpected memory of the crucifix on the wall of her nursery that shocks her into a recognition of how far she has drifted from God.

As the characters in *Brideshead* enact their "fierce little human tragedy," it becomes clear that they are all in some fashion struggling against God and his church, symbolized by Brideshead Castle, that magnificent baroque backdrop to the novel's action. Thomas Howard has spoken of the church as the "unseen" character in the novel.[15] Even the fervent adherents to the church, such as Lady Marchmain, can't avoid abusing their faith. Lady Marchmain's spiritual intensity and manipulativeness drive both her husband and her son Sebastian to drink and exile. When Charles falls in love with Sebastian's sister Julia, the lovers awaken in each other a passion for life that they felt they had lost. After failed marriages, Charles and Julia seem at last to be on the verge of happiness. But when Lord Marchmain returns home to Brideshead, and to the church, on his deathbed, Julia realizes that in denying the church (by remarrying after divorce) and trying to seek out happiness on her own terms, she is condemning herself and Charles to a life of alienation from God.

I'm convinced that Waugh *intended* the church to look like the "kiss of death," not out of perversity, but because he understood it to be a "sign of contradiction." The sufferings that it seemingly inflicts, because of its laws and absolute claims, are the bitter herbs through which the disease of sin is purged. On closer inspection, the lives which the characters lead at the end of the novel, while not "happy," are in many ways "blessed."

Sebastian, for example, is a holy fool, a drunken porter for a monastery in North Africa. Charles asks Cordelia about him, "I suppose he doesn't suffer?"

"Oh yes, I think he does. One can have no idea what the suffering might be, to be maimed as he is—no dignity, no power of will. No one is ever holy without suffering. It's taken that form with him. . . . I've seen so much suffering in the last few years; there's so much of it coming for everybody soon. It's the spring of love. . . ."[16]

Cordelia, who has worked for an ambulance service in the Spanish Civil War, returns to this work with her sister Julia in World War II. They and their brother Brideshead are all stationed in the Holy Land. Symbolically, they become true aristocrats, who go to the Holy Land not for the ambiguous aims of a crusade but to suffer with and for others and to defend the remnants of Christendom. The novel ends with Charles Ryder's hesitant first steps to embrace the faith he has for so long misunderstood.

One of the key themes in *Brideshead* is that the church has the power to actually form one's identity, to stamp it in an indelible way. For the Flyte family, the church had impressed its archetypes in childhood, as even the half-heathens, Julia and Sebastian, discover. Indeed, the Flyte family itself, though its members cause each other enormous pain, is intended by Waugh as a metaphor for the church. The church, like the family, is foundational: you can never really leave it, wherever you go.

This "stamp" of the church was difficult for me to fathom, coming as I did from the Protestant tradition, where there is so much shopping in the religious supermarket for the right denomination, church, and set of theological propositions. The very notion of Protestant implies that the association of believers is voluntary, and can be dissolved or divided when members disagree.

At one point in the novel, Lady Marchmain reads from a Father Brown story by G.K. Chesterton, in which the priest detective says of the thief:

"I caught him with an unseen hook and an invisible line which is long enough to let him wander to the ends of the world and still to bring him back with a twitch upon the thread."[17] This is a metaphor for the church, which is a family, not a voluntary association; one's relationship to it has nothing to do with the will. Hence its inexorable claims.

While I was studying at Oxford, I soon had an unexpected confirmation of the Catholic Church's ability to form not only the conscience but the whole person. My English girlfriend (now my wife) had begun to return to Christianity through my influence. She had been, in her words, a "collapsed Catholic." She began willingly attending Anglican services with me and never once attempted to proselytize for the Church of Rome. But as her faith strengthened, I watched in amazement as her Catholicism emerged naturally and unself-consciously. Soon she realized that she was outside of her home, that she needed to be reconciled and to get inside where it was warm and where she would be fed. It was the same process that Charles Ryder had witnessed in Julia Flyte—only for them it led to a tragic parting.

Brideshead Revisited is a work of fiction, not a tract. It is a dramatic rendering of "the operation of divine grace on a group of diverse but closely connected characters."[18] Its cumulative effect on me was to suggest that the church, far from being an external, bureaucratic, and oppressive structure, is a channel of grace, the living and undivided body of Christ. Once again, Waugh was forcing his readers to supply the missing answer. If the Church appears as an arbitrary and demanding mother, it is because the characters have been wayward and ill disposed toward their parent.

The church is the bride, sullied at times and often unworthy of Christ, its Bridegroom and Head. At least, this is what Waugh believed and what his novel implies. I came to agree with him. On the Feast of Corpus Christi, 1983, I was received into the Catholic Church, a family to which I could belong without tensions or regrets. Evelyn Waugh had played a role in that decision. To celebrate the event, we went off to a pub outside of Oxford, situated in a charming Cotswold village. Later I found out that the pub was once a favorite haunt of the outrageous Mr. Waugh.

GETTING STARTED WITH WAUGH

Happily, almost everything Evelyn Waugh ever wrote is still in print and readily available. For sheer delight, and to get a sense of "vintage Waugh," I suggest beginning with the early satires: *Decline and Fall, Vile Bodies, and Black Mischief,* but the later novella, *The Loved One,* is also a good place to start. *A Handful of Dust,* the *Sword of Honour* trilogy, and *Brideshead Revisited* are the classics. For those who are interested in Waugh's life and opinions, there are *Diaries, Letters,* and a hefty but rewarding tome, *The Essays, Articles and Reviews of Evelyn Waugh.*

16

SHERWOOD ANDERSON
Back Home to *Winesburg*

James Calvin Schaap

A number of years ago, after four years of college teaching in Iowa, I took a leave from my position to do graduate work at the University of Wisconsin in Milwaukee, but I didn't move into the city. Instead, my family and I moved our belongings into a small frame home in a town about fifty miles north of Milwaukee, along the Lake Michigan shoreline, the village where I grew up, Oostburg, Wisconsin.

My father made us an offer we couldn't refuse. He bought a little old house, secured my wife a part-time job in the bank where he worked himself, then waited for us to move in. The commute to Milwaukee was only forty-five minutes.

James Calvin Schaap is the author of five novels, *Home Free, In the Silence There Are Ghosts, The Secrets of Barneveld Calvary, Romey's Place,* and most recently *Things Hoped For, Things Not Seen,* as well as three collections of short stories, *Paternity, The Privacy of Storm,* and *Still Life.* In addition, he has written a number of devotional books for families and a variety of nonfiction works. He has frequently won Evangelical Press Association and Associated Religious Press awards for his short fiction.

Even though the village was twice as big (two thousand souls) as it had been when I had grown up there fifteen years before, I may well have been the only full-time, thirty-year-old, male graduate student in town. On Mondays, Wednesdays, and Fridays, I was almost certainly the only stay-at-home dad. No matter. Those behaviors were hardly public. In 1980, my eccentricity in Oostburg was most obvious when I took early morning jogs down village streets. I think I was the only male in town who ran.

I felt a bit uncomfortable, even vulnerable, in sweats and sneakers, lugging my not inconsiderable bulk along Oostburg sidewalks. Jogging is necessary, after all, only for those men who don't get exercise otherwise. The town where I grew up sits in the lap of lakeshore farm country, but by the 1960s already the place had lost its agrarian soul when making a living on an Old MacDonald farm became impossible. Farming began to turn into "agriculture," and agribusiness swept up dozens of farm families, replacing them with corporations.

Ever since the early seventies, with the completion of a new interstate up the lakeshore, the business with real legs has been real estate. Most men in Oostburg, then and now, make their living in construction, because the whole shoreline from Chicago to Green Bay is becoming one loop suburb. Still today, there's lots of construction work along the lakeshore, and most men, then as now, work with their hands—laying concrete, nailing shingles, hanging drywall. Most of the men don't jog. They don't have to.

But I loved running in Oostburg—which is not to say I loved running. Never have, never will. What I loved was jogging past places I remembered vividly from my childhood on streets that were daily transformed into an open-air museum when I plodded down their sidewalks. I remember thinking I could write a story about almost every house on Main, every one. Even though I felt slightly less than wholly masculine when I'd meet some of my old masonry-dusted, T-shirted friends going to work in their Dodge Ram pickups, I wouldn't have missed those daily treks for the world—they were as full of memory and meaning as the morning air was thick with lakeshore humidity.

I'd leave the house and run west to the old bank corner, then south, past the First Reformed Church parking lot, a spot where, as a kid, I'd played hours and hours of home-run derby, swinging at a hard rubber ball with a taped-up wooden bat we'd salvaged from the barrel in the dugout at the village park, where the high school team did its proud thing before a throng of loyal fans.

Then I'd keep going south past Cold Storage (where some summer nights we'd hike up on the roof and look down on the town) and then Gilson (where my father had once worked), then down the sidewalk past

Te Ronde's pond (rafting), past Triphan's house (where we kept guinea pigs), and out to Davis's corner. Then east, towards the lake, past the culvert where one of my best high school friends ended his life when the Corvette he was driving pinwheeled into the embankment and shattered like a windowpane. When I'd reach the top of the hill, Lake Michigan lay like a broad blue blanket beneath the open sky horizon; but I'd keep running, past the old De Smith barn and then down to De Master's Service Garage, a place that once healed the ills of cars that broke down along busy old highway 141 from Milwaukee to Green Bay, but, with the new interstate, had long since gone out of business.

There, I'd turn north and start a return trip, jogging past an old fieldstone house with its 1850s birth date scripted in black metal that's set into the stone over the front windows; past a tree farm where the owner once tried, unsuccessfully, to put in a miniature golf course; and finally to the corner of the road coming straight east out of town, to Meerdink's farm, the corner place, now barnless, on the road we used to call, strangely enough, "straight down" simply because it ran straight out of town to Lake Michigan.

From there I'd turn west, back into town, and come up Main Street, past one old house after another, each of them evoking a story from little more than a window, a side door, a front porch, or a shady garage. My kindergarten girlfriend lived in the stone house on a corner lot, next door to a hairdresser with an ebullient personality, a widow who boarded schoolteachers who, as outsiders, were always worth watching. My mother's friend lived just up the block. She and her husband had a troubled son who scared the dickens out of me as a kid and eventually took his own life somewhere far away from the town I'd loved and I suppose he'd hated.

I'm not telling you all the stories either. There were more, tons more. Some of them I've told elsewhere, under cover. Some still reside in my heart and soul and may never be told, too hurtful they are to those who suffered them, people whom I know and who know me.

No one else in the world knows the Oostburg landscape in exactly the same way I did then or do today. There are those, of course, who would recognize all of the places I've listed and who likely know something of the stories I've already mentioned. But the path I ran back then—and remember today—is really a collection of stories which belongs only to me because the memories and impressions I have exist only in my mind and heart. The very same houses speak wholly different tales to hundreds of others. Of the billions of human beings in the world today, only the tiniest fraction have ever heard of Oostburg, Wisconsin, much less lived there; and none of those few—not one—remembers exactly the same stories as I did, or do. About Oostburg itself, the town where I grew up, nobody knows exactly what I do.

Good writing, or so it seems to me, is always set in time and place, grounded in the specific manners of locale, setting, backdrop. Faulkner wouldn't be Faulkner if he'd written about southern California. Try to put Flannery O'Connor's stories in small-town Minnesota, or Garrison Keillor's delightful monologues in rural Georgia, and the music goes horrendously off-key. James Joyce is Irish, not Italian. Willa Cather tried on other settings for size, but her best work is set in an isolated prairie town named Red Cloud, where, as a child, she watched her own singular production of the American ethnic pageant staged on the red hills of what seemed an eternal Nebraska prairie.

As improbable as it may seem, an irrefutable paradox of the literary endeavor is that, oddly enough, those experiences most personal to us carry emotional truth somehow capable of communicating universally. Our most intimate experience belongs to everyone else. Our secrets are often the same; our most private feelings are, strangely enough, quite common. The mind has a strange compass. If I did my work well, the little tour of the parameters of the town of Oostburg, Wisconsin, I just offered, may have prompted your imagination to visualize not only the images I attempted to create but also the shadowy outlines of your own childhood's landscape. Stories live, not only because they open us up to other worlds but also because they reveal our own. What is most us, strangely enough, is often most everyone.

And that's how it is, I suppose, I've come to claim Sherwood Anderson's *Winesburg, Ohio,* as the single piece of literature most significant to my development as a writer. I've never been to Clyde, Ohio, the place everyone understands to be Winesburg's prototype. I've never even seen pictures of the place. But I know Winesburg, Ohio, because I know Oostburg, Wisconsin. Punctuationally, I know Winesburg, Ohio, a town which doesn't exist, because I know *Winesburg, Ohio,* a town which does.

Once in a while in teaching, I've used a long passage at the beginning of one of the stories in *Winesburg,* the story titled "Nobody Knows," to try to prompt students to get some mileage out of setting. Here's the passage:

Looking cautiously about, George Willard arose from his desk in the office of the Winesburg *Eagle* and went hurriedly out at the back door. The night was warm and cloudy and although it was not yet eight o'clock, the alleyway back of the *Eagle* office was pitch dark. A team of horses tied to a post somewhere in the darkness stamped on the hard-baked ground. A cat sprang from under George Willard's feet and ran away into the night. The young man was nervous. All day he had gone about his work like one dazed by a blow. In the alleyway he trembled as though with fright.

In the darkness George Willard walked along the alleyway, going carefully and cautiously. The back doors of the Winesburg stores were open and he could see men sitting about under the store lamps. In Myerbaum's Notion Store Mrs. Willy the saloon keeper's wife stood by the counter with a basket on her arm. Sid Green the clerk was waiting on her. He leaned over the counter and talked earnestly.

George Willard crouched and then jumped through the path of light that came out at the door. He began to run forward in the darkness. Behind Ed Griffith's saloon old Jerry Bird the town drunkard lay asleep on the ground. The runner stumbled over the sprawling legs. He laughed brokenly.

George Willard had set forth upon an adventure.[1]

Here's the assignment: Mimic that passage with one created from your own neighborhood, the place you remember best as a kid.

It's really a simple, paint-by-number exercise to anyone blessed with a fair-to-middlin' imagination and a small-town childhood—but then, even a small-town childhood isn't required. Even though kids today don't remember a time when horses standing downtown "stamped on the hard-baked ground," they all remember what it looks like to peek into those mysterious nooks and corners where adults talk furtively to each other, out of the earshot of kids. What makes the passage work is the yeasty mix of George Willard's anxiety about what he is about to do (engage in his first sexual adventure) in the middle of an adult world oblivious to what is really going on. Good writing is always visual, and, in this short passage, one *sees* the story begin.

In settings like this one, Anderson showed me what was memorable about good writing, and when he did, he allowed me to believe that the storefronts I knew as a boy, like the houses I remember along Main, were inestimably precious places. Jesus Christ redeems me from my sin, but Sherwood Anderson's *Winesburg,* oddly enough, redeemed the odd little town where I grew up, made it valuable to me, helped me to realize that what I'd experienced as a boy in a small Dutch-American burg on the Wisconsin shore of Lake Michigan was something worth exploring for myself and others, even if it wasn't Madagascar, the African veld, or a tenement in the Bronx. Anderson taught me that if Winesburg had stories worth telling, so did Oostburg. Anderson is my greatest enabler.

For those who don't count themselves among the citizens of *Wines -burg,* who've never walked its streets with George Willard, the novel's protagonist, let me head up the chamber of commerce for a moment. Anderson's *Winesburg, Ohio* is a collection of rather oddly shaped tales which are linked by the eccentricity of the town's characters (Anderson himself calls them "grotesques"), by the town itself (a single small Ohio town), and by the slowly developing maturity of a young man who emerges frequently in the stories—cub reporter George Willard. Willard is a kid, an innocent, a subject of considerable interest to the town's caseload of odd birds, who somewhat mysteriously understand him to be singularly capable of understanding them.

In "Hands," the unforgettable opening story, Wing Biddlebaum, a one-time teacher who was prematurely retired by ugly innuendoes about his relationship with a student, regales young George to get out of town before he himself becomes just another Winesburg character. Like many of the other eccentrics in the book, Wing Biddlebaum, whose nervous hands make him the best berry-picker in town but are so hyperactive as not to be trusted, is drawn to George's ample innocence.

Each of the grotesques—a sexually repressed preacher, a devoted lover long ago abandoned, a childlike artist, to name just a few—each of them somehow enlist George to listen to their stories and their plight, and often ask him to untangle the mess they've become both to themselves and to everyone else in town. They come to believe that George Willard can be the sole recipient of their personal dignity, a dignity they otherwise cannot and will never attain in town. He becomes their champion after a fashion—something of a savior—not because he frees them from their neurosis or psychosis but because he holds their stories in his possession.

But to call the narratives of *Winesburg* "stories" is to risk misunderstanding. Sherwood Anderson, writing from the Chicago of the 1920s, found himself rather joyfully fallen into the literary vanguard. He despised conventional narrative forms, wished that every writer would avoid what he considered to be the yawning tedium of O. Henry's stiffly patterned plotlines—exposition, then complication, then surprise conclusion. Very few of the little stories in *Winesburg, Ohio* are actually traditional stories of the type Anderson despised. Many seem barely not to end in ways stories traditionally do.

The best of Anderson's individual sketches are the profoundly mysterious actions done by deeply passionate souls. In "The Teacher," for instance, Kate Swift, one of George's boyhood teachers, is adamant about her former student learning to take life and human character much more seriously than he does. She begs George to take on a calling and task that's far above being a "mere peddler of words." "The thing to learn," she tells him—passionately—"is to know what people are thinking about, not what they say."[2]

Anderson tells us that among the Winesburg populace, Kate Swift is "the most eagerly passionate soul"; but there's little opportunity for passion in the arduous boredom of day-to-day life in Winesburg, so there's no outlet for the yearning incarcerated in Kate's soul. When it finds a release, it tumbles out, despite her own fears. She speaks to George Willard, reminds him of what he has, of what he can do someday if he focuses on a higher calling and task, and then loses control of her otherwise rigidly attended emotions. "In the newspaper office," Anderson says, "a confusion arose." Kate Swift confounds her own mission.

> She was a teacher but she was also a woman. As she looked at George Willard, the passionate desire to be loved by a man, that had a thousand times before swept like a storm over her body, took possession of her. In the lamplight George Willard looked no longer a boy, but a man ready to play the part of a man.[3]

Like Wing Biddlebaum, she is incapable of negotiating the line between teacher and ex-student, and when she feels the confluence threatening her, she runs away, deeply afraid of herself and what's been seemingly unleashed from inside. That kind of moment Anderson calls "an adventure." Throughout the novel, those "adventures" are never really sustained narratives. Instead, they seem more like explosions of emotion and feeling that do far less to change characters than define them. Anderson wouldn't have wanted to change his grotesques into something more, well, normal; in fact, there are few dynamic characters in the entire collection, characters who achieve wholeness by any means in the stories. In *Winesburg,* Anderson is obsessed with mystery, especially the mystery of the human character.

When I read the book for the first time, I liked that. Still do, in fact, because—at least in part—I've long ago accepted the premise that each of us is a mystery of cause and effect, of nature and nurture, of the image of God each of us carries, and the frightful remnant artifact of our fall into sin in the Garden. We are, at once, cabbages and kings. We're capable of extraordinary heroism and stupendous silliness. In the 2000 presidential race George W. Bush won the office by the thinnest of margins in an election that will be second-guessed for years to come. His lack of mandate seemed sure to plague his presidency, as did his established reputation as a beer-swilling no-mind; his gaffes often grabbed the best headlines. Yet, after the terrorist attacks on the World Trade Center, the man who seemed a spoiled frat-boy president turned miraculously into a determined, powerful leader, the kind of leader few would have guessed him capable of becoming. Anderson's characters are similarly complex and rich—and richly human, even if they are eccentrics.

I liked *Winesburg* because it brought me to a small Midwestern town, the terrain I already knew well, and showed me characters I thought totally real. But I liked the book also because I could feel for its characters, even though so many of them seem terribly distressed, weakened, and incapable of changing themselves or their worlds.

In one of the final stories, George Willard's mother, herself a "grotesque," a woman who has been kept silent about her own dreams, comes to the office of the eccentric Doctor Reefy. Reefy senses her need for being loved, holds her in his arms, and for a moment it seems as if at least one of Anderson's grotesques may escape the confines of her own psychic death; but then "heavy feet" rise up the stairwell and, without a word, they quickly and fearfully break away. "The thing which had come to life in her died suddenly," Anderson says, and George's mother goes to her grave in the stoic, thwarted silence that had characterized most of her life.[4]

Together, the tales become a dog-eared scrapbook of eccentrics, "a few gnarled apples the pickers have rejected," as Anderson's narrative voice explains in the story "Paper Pills."[5] A few stories seem rather misplaced among the others, but most of them feature strange characters who've been so troubled throughout their lives that they've literally lost their souls, not so much given them up as simply and completely misplaced them.

Anderson may well have considered himself a quintessential modern, for to him the Christian faith was simply passé, the means by which people of an earlier, unsophisticated time sometimes ordered their lives, acquiescing to the stiff moral authority created by what he likely considered biblical superstition or myth. In the longest single narrative in the volume, "Godliness," Anderson pokes around in what he assumed to be the last, late nineteenth-century vestiges of religious devotion. "Godliness" is not Anderson at his best, but passages in that story offer his sense of the Christian faith. The central character of four tales which comprise "Godliness" is Jesse Bentley, a man who, as a boy, wanted to become a preacher, but instead becomes a visionary leader of new American business enterprise—a huge landowner, an agribusinessman, something of a tycoon. But Bentley's youthful religious enthusiasm never disappears completely; it smolders instead beneath his business acumen, so that when certain odd occasions arise, those old passions flare suddenly and uncontrollably. For an instant, he envisions himself Abraham and sets forth to sacrifice his own grandson, as if the boy were Isaac. In "Godliness," Anderson examines the death throes of the old Christian faith, a death Anderson himself undoubtedly accepted as gospel truth.

It certainly wasn't Anderson's Christianity that captivated me when I opened the book and walked into that town. Little real faith abides anywhere in the neighborhood.

In fact, there were and are lots of reasons for me to dislike *Winesburg, Ohio*. All told, Anderson's collection of emotionally infirm characters sometimes resembles a midway freak show. Many of his characters are truly pitiable, decidedly incapable of taking in a breath without gasping back fear. Most of the adventures are set in semidarkness, the only time of day such people can steal away without risking danger from others or themselves. Most of the folks described are abject failures, so psychically deformed they create a village landscape that, we can be assured, will never get a mention on *Money* magazine's list of sweet places to live.

Winesburg is not an asylum, but when, in the final pages of the book, George leaves town, we don't doubt his smarts. Wing Biddlebaum's advice has some currency. Clearing out of town, thereby escaping the fate of becoming one of the grotesques himself, seems very much the right thing to do. Life exists elsewhere, especially for one as young and soft as George Willard.

I wouldn't care to live in Winesburg, not just because so many of its residents would make strange neighbors but because, in part, Winesburg has played no small part in sculpting those folks into the eccentrics they have become. Winesburg is certainly a long way from paradise.

There's no accounting for taste, I suppose, and maybe there is no single good reason for my deep and long-held admiration for the novel. But I know very well that upon my first reading I was hooked in appreciation.

And there are reasons, in addition to the ones I've already alluded to. *Winesburg* may well seem a literary freak show, but finally it is not. For while the characters are misshapen apples, the ones the pickers left behind, they are much, much more than mutants. "One nibbles at them and they are delicious," Anderson tells us. "Into a little round place at the side of the apple has been gathered all of its sweetness. One runs from tree to tree over the frosted ground picking the gnarled, twisted apples and filling his pockets with them. Only the few know the sweetness of the twisted apples."[6]

. Clearly, Anderson loves his grotesques, not simply because they are so pathetically photogenic but because they are, finally, sweet—maybe even more so than the bushels of perfectly round fruit the pickers take to market. Anderson gives humanity to characters some might otherwise easily cast aside, and in writing the stories of those people he offers them the dignity which every lost soul under heaven deserves. It seems that Anderson himself wouldn't have given a dime for the Christian faith, but in offering the grotesques their moment in the sun, he bestows upon them the humanity so many of us would simply have neglected and do neglect to impart to others like them. I'm not about to baptize Sherwood Anderson here, but I am going to make a claim that in his regard for and even appreciation of Winesburg's "least of these," he's exercising something of the most noble task of the writer, to give meaning—and even hope—to the existence of all of us.

Despite the painful conditions of most of the town's inhabitants, there is hope in the novel, and that hope is realized in George Willard, whose progress is slowly but not always smoothly charted through the succession of tales. When Wing Biddlebaum takes him aside in the first story and implores him to make something more of himself, to "forget all you have learned" and "learn to dream," young George is dumbfounded.[7] He has little idea what this eccentric ex-schoolteacher and champion berry-picker really means. When Wing anxiously ambles away, crossed up by his own strangely convoluted desires, he leaves George "perplexed and frightened on the grassy slope."[8] George has much to learn.

A few stories later, in "Nobody Knows," a story whose introduction I've already quoted at length, we watch Willard grope blindly into one of his own "adventures," a sexual tryst with Louise Trunnion, a desperate young woman whose social and economic circumstance marks her as someone of significantly less power and standing than he is. In a note to George, she scribbles, "I'm yours if you want me," a line which he reads, in the pounding surf of his adolescent passion, as forthright solicitation.[9] What he doesn't read in the note or see in Miss Trunnion is a young woman with her own sad but precious story. When their tryst is over, George feels that he's come of age, having conquered. But his adolescence—and his outright bigotry—are manifestly clear when he says, "She hasn't got anything on me. Nobody knows."[10] The indictment against the boy is never quite as strong as it is here, early in the book. Louise, by his reckoning, is nobody. George Willard has much to learn about human beings.

In "Respectability," Anderson describes Wash Williams, Winesburg's telegraph operator, as "the ugliest thing in town. His girth was immense, his legs feeble. He was dirty. Everything about him was unclean. Even the whites of his eyes looked soiled."[11] But Wash Williams has a story, and George, here as elsewhere, seems to know that Williams has a tale to tell. Whenever he looks at the man, he is "consumed with curiosity."[12] What he senses is that something must have happened to Wash Williams to make him what he has become: "A thing had happened to him that made him hate life, and he hated it whole-heartedly, with the abandon of a poet," Anderson says.[13] When Williams tells George that story, a story of abuse at the hands of two women, his wife and his mother-in-law, George is physically moved: "The boy's body shook as from a chill." Later on, Anderson says, "The young reporter felt ill and weak," and then he adds this line: "In imagination, he also became old and shapeless."[14] With the ugly Wash Williams, Willard's ability to empathize grows. He's slowly learning to appreciate the grotesqueness of characters who have their own varieties of sweetness.

Farther along in *Winesburg,* in a story titled "Loneliness," George Willard meets Enoch Robinson, an artist, a man of ideas who is totally disenfranchised in a world of business concerns. Although during some periods of his life he attempts to become part of the commercial world he despises, he seems destined to failure there. When his marriage fails, Anderson says, Robinson's wife's departure "takes him out of the world of men altogether."[15] But Enoch Robinson recognizes a kind of cosmic sadness in George Willard, a kid whose mother has been sick and who has been worried about his own sense of purpose, and when he tells George his story, once again George is deeply moved: "He wanted to put his arms about the little old man. In the half darkness, the man talked and the boy listened, filled with sadness."[16]

Throughout the stories Anderson assembles in *Winesburg, Ohio,* George matures, slowly comes of age as he grows in his appreciation of what human beings really are and where it was they have been. By the end of the book, his empathy grows, finally, into respect for the humanity of those he meets, to those to whom he listens, no matter how grotesque or unseemly.

He suffers his final "adventure" at the death of his mother, an event which seems not to affect him greatly until he sits alone at her bedside, her spirit already departed. The child in him resents his mother's passing because her death came, for him, at such an inopportune time, at the moment when he was to visit a girlfriend, Helen White. He sits beside his mother's corpse, and "then something happened," Anderson says. "He looked at the figure of the dead woman under the sheets and shame for his thoughts swept over him so he began to weep. A new notion came into his mind and he turned and looked guiltily about as though afraid he would be observed."[17]

A flurry of conflicting ideas and emotions suddenly advances, and he steps out of the room, leaves his mother's side. For a moment he loses sense of reality until his aunt stands beside him, and he tells her, first and finally, "My mother is dead." There's a paroxysm of grief and sadness and even joy in him, all of it coming very suddenly, and he repeats a phrase his mother had frequently used of others—"the dear, the dear, the lovely dear," speaking of her.[18] What has occurred here is a wonderful moment of certitude, George accepting the death of his mother by affirming the humanity of her life.

That event enables him to achieve a mature relationship with Helen White. Instead of treating her as if she were Louise Trunnion, George Willard now looks for something deeper than sex or even passion with Helen White, and she offers him what he needs, something crucial to his own maturing self: "In the darkness under the roof of the grandstand, George Willard sat beside Helen White and felt very keenly his own insignificance in the scheme of things." What he comes to understand is not his own importance but his unimportance; and that lesson in humility serves him well. "He began to think of the people in the town where he'd always lived with something like reverence. He had a reverence for Helen."[19]

But by the end of the novel, and by way of the string of folks who talk to him, plead with him, and even beat on him, George Willard has a stronger sense of the meaning somehow hidden amid the chaos. While he leaves Winesburg behind at the end of the book, he leaves carrying neither regret or relief but shouldering the heritage of the very human world of Winesburg. When he looks out of the window of the train that is bringing him to the city, "the town of Winesburg had disappeared and his life there had become but a background on which to paint the dreams of his manhood."[20] *But* is an interesting word in that sentence; it redefines what might otherwise have been a more, well, positive leave-taking.

In that one word, one feels the very ambivalence Anderson might well have felt toward the town he'd created. Like so many other early twentieth-century writers who, for good reasons, found the small town stifling, Anderson knows—and he knew from the beginning—that George had to leave; but also, in the process of writing and by way of the treasury of humanity he's created both on the streets of town and in its dark corners, George Willard, like Anderson himself, has grown in appreciation of the sweetness of every one of those folks he's brought onstage.

The fact is, George won't shake the dust off his feet as he leaves Winesburg because what's there behind him is a heritage—it is a "background." What's behind him is the raw material from which he will fashion his dreams. The George embarking now on manhood wouldn't be the same man without that raw material. There's value there on the streets of Winesburg, value that will carry him into his own artistic future. George takes Wing's advice and leaves town, but the final line is indication of the fact that no city will ever quite scour what's there of Winesburg from the boy's dreams.

It may well be a very simple story after all, this strange little novel *Winesburg, Ohio*—George Willard coming to grasp a sense of his humanity by accepting those whom society itself has rejected as grotesque. Some people like to say that there are only a few stories in the world, just thousands of variations; if they're right, then Anderson's novel offers a tale of growing up that may well be more tidy and moral than he'd ever intended, but no less true than the greatest of Sunday school lessons he'd ever rejected: we become more loving by loving.

I've used the book for years in my college classroom, at that point where students are where I was when I first read the novel—just eighteen or nineteen years old. At the beginning of their reading, they find *Wines - burg* strange; some of the more pious frown at the sexual nature of so many of the tales. But when we've completed our reading, most students find the stories remarkably true to the experience they are themselves going through, away from home for the first time, the pageant of their own childhoods now recurring to them in ways that it couldn't have had they never left. For the first time in their lives they find themselves meeting people and ideas that they wouldn't have appreciated a year ago in childhood. They recognize themselves in George Willard, and they find some strength in the nature of his resolution to grow, but not at the expense of the place and character of where he'd grown up.

There's hope in this novel. Life has meaning, even when it's peopled by freaks, the likes of which one finds emerging from almost every story both George and the reader encounter in *Winesburg, Ohio*. You won't find that kind of meaning or that kind of appreciation in, say, Sinclair Lewis, an American writer of Anderson's era, also known for portraying small-town life on the canvas of his work.

Even today, years later, when I walk—not run—down the streets of my hometown, I remember stories that are made memorable by the actions of people who once lived in the houses on Main, on Cedar, on Superior, and Lake Drive. Sherwood Anderson taught me to believe that those stories were worth telling, not simply because of their eccentricity or their potential for maudlin or prurient interest but because those stories feature us, humanity itself, in its sadness *and* its sweetness.

Anderson's *Winesburg* made my Oostburg a legitimate world for my own work, and for that I thank him.

GETTING STARTED WITH ANDERSON

If it can be said that some writers have only one good book in them, Sherwood Anderson might well be an example. Although Anderson wrote other books and many other short stories, nothing else he ever wrote comes close to the achievement of *Winesburg, Ohio*. As a result, very little of his other work is read anymore, except by those graduate students busily dissertating. For years, high school anthologies of American literature contained wonderful short stories like "I Want to Know Why" or "I'm a Fool," other Anderson stories about growing up in small-town America. Thousands of boomers probably read those selections twenty or more years ago. Today, those stories are largely gone.

But *Winesburg, Ohio* lives on in a variety of inexpensive paperback editions (Norton Critical Editions, Penguin Classics), most of which come with friendly introductions and a smattering of helpful academic essays.

One really doesn't need help getting into *Winesburg;* one only needs to go. When you meet the strange folks on the streets of this small Ohio town, just remember that their stories may well seem a little unfinished at first, lacking the firm conclusion most readers come to expect of short stories. But watch George Willard listen to them and grow, and you will too.

17

NATIVE PERSPECTIVES ON THE WRITTEN WORD
Diane Glancy

※

For Lewis Hall (1908–1972)

I do not remember my father reading to me, nor my mother. A neighbor gave me a book when I was old enough to read, but I don't remember reading it either. What was it about my father, who kept his words to himself, that he would be such an influence? Maybe he didn't know any story. Maybe he had not been told any, nor read to. Maybe he just didn't tell the stories he knew. Maybe they were too painful, and his own journey away from them had been too hard. He came from a mixed background. His mother, a Cherokee, married a country doctor when she was twenty-six and the doctor was in his fifties. He

Diane Glancy teaches Native American literature and creative writing at Macalaster College in St. Paul, Minnesota. She has published several novels, including *Pushing the Bear: The 1838 Cherokee Trail of Tears, The Only Piece of Furniture in the House, Flutie,* and *The Closets of Heaven.* In addition, she has published several collections of essays, including *The Cold-and-Hunger Dance,* as well as several collections of short stories and poetry. Glancy received the Native American Prose Award, an American Book Award, and a National Endowment for the Arts grant.

was a strong fundamentalist Christian; most of his family were, I heard someone say. My father pulled away from his father's overt religion and his mother's Indianness. I wonder what it was like for him to be born in that cross-world of two cultures. I don't remember anything he ever said about his childhood. I don't remember him mentioning his father, even once. His father's name was William Jasper Hall. He was killed from a fall from a horse before my father was sixteen. I think my Grandfather Hall was a stern man, though I don't know why I think that. I don't know his heritage, except that he was white. I wonder what it was like for him and my Indian grandmother, Orvezene Lewis Hall. What did they have in common? She was his third wife. His other children were grown.

In the Civil War records in the National Archives, I found some of my Grandfather Hall's notes. One of his patients, Woods Lewis, had suffered scurvy while in the Union army. The doctor was explaining his problems; there were drawings showing where he had rheumatism, etc., and he was requesting compensation for him, Woods Lewis, my great-grandfather, a full-blood Cherokee. According to Army records, he was five feet eight inches, had olive skin, black hair, brown eyes, and checked his race as white. I also know that he had fled Indian Territory and ended up in Tennessee at the beginning of the Civil War. He was covering his tracks. Did my Grandfather Hall meet my grandmother when he was treating Woods Lewis, her father? What was it about this Indian woman in the backwoods of Arkansas that made him want to marry her? In an old photograph, circa 1910, taken of William and Orvezene in their yard, my first thought, on looking at my grandmother was, how dark she is. What attracted him? They had two children—my father and his sister, Effie.

My father has been dead since 1972, my mother since 1986. Why do I still wonder who they were? And who were their people? We made trips back to my mother's parents and their farm on the Missouri-Kansas border. We made no more than a few trips back to see my Grandmother Orvezene. Why did my parents live without stories, without books, without meaningful language? Why had they packed it away, stored it somewhere I could never find? Left it unsaid. Moved on. What is it about my father, to this day, when he would have been ninety-two, that he is the one I look to, the one I remember as a holy man? Yet there was nothing holy about him, except commitment; when a man across the street abandoned his family, I knew my father would not do that. I trusted him, his steadfastness, his dependability, his presence in the house and in my life. He was the hunter. The provider. He would be there. He also pointed a place to me where he couldn't go. I don't remember him saying that, but somehow the idea was transferred to me. Maybe it was his first love of me that showed me the way to my own story.

I have evidence that others admired my father too. It wasn't just me. When my father died, a man came to the funeral whom my father had worked with, and told me my father was a moral man. It was something he wanted me to know. He told me in that way. I knew my father didn't drink nor smoke. He always came home. He took us to church, but there were no prayers in the home. Not much love between my parents. My father was hard on my brother. My father had a temper. I often heard him curse. I could list his shortcomings and contradictions easier than I could his strengths. Yet to this day, I have not lost the overwhelming admiration I have for him.

We went to a church that preached a social gospel. There was no Christ-centered worship as there is in churches I have attended as an adult, worship I sought out myself. I guess he was a Christian who didn't want too much to do with the church. He must have been put off by something. A strict father, I would guess. My father didn't finish school, not even grade school. He never would say how far he went. When I looked up the 1910 census in the courthouse in Little Rock, the man helping me said, "Your grandfather was a doctor." If he impressed the man at the courthouse, why was my grandfather never mentioned by my father? I wanted to know more, but that information was not recorded.

I knew none of my father's family—half brothers, half sisters, whoever they were. It was all long ago, but I hear their voices when I read Native novels in the Native American Literature course I teach. Grandfather Hall's side of the family, of course, was white. But it's the loss of family, of the past, I feel; it's the theme of disenfranchisement in the novels, the having to live in something other than one's natural world. I also have some general idea of the cause of the anger my father carried all his life. And maybe some of the heaviness my parents carried was from spending the early years of their marriage in the Depression.

If I had to say which Native writings as a whole have been meaningful, none stand out to me as complete; it takes the group, the community, to get across the significance and diversity of Native life, which is interesting becauseidentity isonly what you are in relationship to others. The individual is not an option in Native life. Maybe survival counted on group effort. Maybe community is natural, tribal; and the American way of the individual is unnatural. But the irony is this: what the many voices in Native literature does is to lead you to your own self, your own voice.

It does take many Native writers to tell the story of Native life. Not one voice could say all. There is diversity between Indian tribes. There is diversity within Indian tribes also. Not only am I a stranger to the Dakota and Chippewa in the northern plains where I live now, I am a stranger to the Cherokee in Oklahoma and Arkansas because I grew up outside that community. My father went to Kansas City to work in the stockyards. The loss of traditional heritage is the story with many Natives.

My brother does not share my romantic view of my father. I suppose to him, it was my mother who helped him—another cross-structure, this one of family instead of culture. My mother's family had come from the Black Forest of Germany two centuries earlier. She was a tormented woman, not happy with a family but not having opportunity to do anything about it. She felt an obligation to be a wife and mother, yet found it not to her liking once she got there. In those days, it was a trip from which you didn't return.

My father left his people and went out on his own because of economic necessity. He supported his mother and sister also, before she married and sometimes even after. He had his vision of an acculturated life; he was a father and husband, and he worked in the stockyards as a traveling superintendent from Kansas City to Indianapolis and back to Missouri several times, then Denver, Chicago, and Sioux City, where he died.

Maybe he was a disappointment to his father. Maybe in the way my father picked on my brother, I can see how his father treated him. He mocked him about his grades, maybe in the same way my father's father mocked him. For some reason, my father protected me. Later, my husband could not match an image I formed of a man from my father, and the marriage ended in divorce. There were other reasons also. I have not found another man I wanted to be with. Well, Christ, I suppose.

Where did my God-hunger come from? It's the first thing I picked up out of Native writing. The importance of Indian literature is its spirituality, the way it points out that direction as the answer. Again, there is diversity in voice, but there is also always the presence of the other world, the unseen world, the world behind our own.

I present these books not so much as literature as insight into the history of this country, because there is no completion until you know what can be known. One has to go back sometimes to go forward.

Indian Oratory: Famous Speeches by Noted Indian Chieftains, compiled by W. C. Vanderwerth

The Civilization of the American Indian Series (Norman, Okla.: University of Oklahoma Press, 1971). The series is now called *American Indian Literature and Critical Studies Series.* The authors are Indian. It is a book filled with particular bitterness.

To follow are only a few of the speeches, and only a part of each of them. The fatalism of Washakie, Shoshone, 1798–1900, to the Mormon missionaries:

The white man can make this (picking up a Colt revolver), and a little thing that he carries in his pocket, so that he can tell where the sun is on a dark day, and when it is night he can tell when it will come daylight. This is because the face of the Father is towards him, and His back is toward us. But after a while the Great Father will quit being mad, and will turn his face towards us. Then our skin will be light.[1]

The obstinacy of Lone Wolf, Kiowa, birth date unknown–1897, at a council held in Ft. Sill, Oklahoma, to the Indian Commissioner:

That piece of paper represents the earth. There is a big water all around the earth. The circular blue paper is the sky. The sun goes around the earth. The sun is our father. All the Red Men in the country, all the buffalo are his. Our Father, the sun, told us that the white men would kill all of them.

When my time comes I intend to die not wait to be killed by white men. I am the man who makes it rain. I talk to the Great Father. If I have any difficulty with anyone and wish them to perish with thirst, I stop the rain, and if I wish them well, I cause it to rain so that the corn can grow.[2]

The questioning of Cochise, Apache, birth date unknown–1874, to a council in Arizona:

Why is it that the Apaches wait to die—that they carry their lives on their fingernails? They roam over the hills and plains and want the heavens to fall on them. Many have been killed in battle. . . . Tell me, if the Virgin Mary has walked throughout all the land, why has she never entered the wigwam of the Apache?[3]

The grief and common sense of Red Jacket, Seneca, 1756–1830, presented to a conference replying to the offers of the whites to bring their religion to the Indians:

Brother! There was a time when our forefathers owned this great island [meaning the continent of North America, a common belief among the Indians]. Their seats extended from the rising to the setting of the sun. The Great Spirit had made it for the use of Indians. He had created the buffalo, the deer, and other animals for food. He made the bear and the deer, and their skins served us for clothing. He had scattered them over the country, and had taught us how to take them. He caused the earth to produce corn for bread. All this he had done for his red children because he loved them. If we had disputes about hunting grounds, they were generally settled without the shedding of much blood. But an evil day came upon us. Your forefathers crossed the great waters and landed on this land. Their numbers were small. They found friends and no enemies. They told us they had fled from their own country for fear of wicked men, and had come here to enjoy their religion. They asked for a small seat. We took pity of them, granted their request and they sat down among us. We gave them corn and meat. They gave us poison (spiritous liquor). The white people now found our country. Tidings were carried back and more came among us. Yet we did not fear them. We took them to be friends. They called us brothers. We believed them and gave them a large seat. At length their numbers were greatly increased. They wanted more land. They wanted our country. Our eyes were opened, and our minds became uneasy. Wars took place. Indians were hired to fight Indians, and many of our people were destroyed. . . .

Brother! You say that you are sent to instruct us how to worship the Great Spirit; and if we do not take hold of the religion which you white people teach we shall be unhappy hereafter. You said that you are right, and we are lost. How do you know this is true? We understand your religion is written in a book. If it was intended for us as well, why has not the Great Spirit given it to us; and not only to us, but why did he not give to our forefathers the knowledge of that book, with the means of understanding it rightly? . . .

Brother! You say there is one way to worship and serve the Great Spirit. If there is but one religion, why do you white people differ so much about it? Why not all agree, as you can all read the book? . . .

Brother! We are told you have been preaching to the white people in this place. These people are our neighbors. We are acquainted with them. We will wait a little while, and see what effect your preaching has upon them. If we find it does them good and makes them honest and less disposed to cheat Indians, we will then consider again what you have said.

Brother! You have now heard our answer to your talk, and this is all we have to say at present. As we are going to part, we will come and take you by the hand, and hope the Great Spirit will protect you on your journey, and return you safe to your friends.[4]

Kicking Bear, Dakota, 1853–1904, to the council of Dakota Indians in 1890:

I bring you word from your father the ghosts, they are now marching to join you, led by the Messiah who came once to live on earth with the white men, but was cast out and killed by them. I have seen the wonders of the spirit-land, and have talked with the ghosts. I travel far and am sent back with a message to tell you to make ready for the coming of the Messiah and return of the ghosts in the spring.[5]

This recognition of the cataclysmic events that lay ahead was brought to a pinnacle in *Black Elk Speaks* by John Neihardt. I wrote about the similarities of things that Black Elk said near Manderson, South Dakota, and John wrote on Patmos in the Book of Revelation, in an essay titled "The Bible and *Black Elk Speaks*,"[6] because it seemed to me that the late nineteenth-century Native American history in *Black Elk Speaks* could be said to parallel the Book of Revelation. It seemed clear to me that among Native people there had been visions of the spirit world and prophecies of a coming doom, and that one of the seers was Black Elk. Like the Book of Revelation's John on Patmos, Black Elk left the earth in a vision. He says, "While I was there I saw more than I can tell and understood more than I saw; for I was seeing in a scared manner the shapes of all things in the spirit."[7]

While in his vision, Black Elk saw a sacred man who was painted red all over his body, and he held a spear as he walked into the center of the people and there he lay down and rolled. And when he got up, it was a fat bison standing there, and where the bison stood a sacred herb sprang up right where the tree had been in the center of the nation's hoop (a symbol of the unity and completeness of the tribe, in much the same way the bald eagle is a symbol for America). Black Elk says, "I know now that this meant, that the bison were the gift of a good spirit and were our strength, but we should lose them, and from the same good spirit we must find another strength."[8] That other strength, of course, to the Christian Indian is Christ. The bison could be seen as the Old Testament, which was replaced by the New, also with cataclysmic events—the death on the cross with the earthquake and darkness on the earth that followed.

John on Patmos had a vision of a red man too: "He was clothed with a vesture dipped in blood; and his name is called The Word of God" (Rev. 19:13 KJV).

In his visions, Black Elk heard someone call: "Then I looked up at the clouds, and two men were coming there, head-first like arrows slanting down and as they came, they sang a sacred song and the thunder was like drumming."[9] Black Elk saw twelve horses in each of the four directions. Then horses dancing without number. The clouds around Black Elk changed into a teepee, and a rainbow stood as its open door. There also was a rainbow around the throne of God in Revelation.

Black Elk Speaks was written by John Neihardt, a white ethnographer and writer, whose daughter, Enid, took notes as Black Elk spoke and shared his story of the close of the Plains Indian history. Two other Indians spoke also. When another Indian sitting with them translated what they said into English, Enid transcribed it. Later, when Neihardt and his daughter returned from South Dakota, Neihardt wrote the story from his daughter's notes.

There is some controversy over what was actually said, whether Black Elk said the hoop of his nation was actually *broken*. But the point is, I suppose, that whatever Black Elk said, it was an amazing story of the vision of one man when he was being told by the grandfather of the air that it was closing time. If ever there has been a reminder of the Book of Revelation, it was this. Maybe it is more meaningful to me because it is a work accomplished between a father and a daughter.

In *Black Elk Speaks*, Black Elk also talks about fights between Indians and cruelties to one another, but mainly there was generosity, a respect of others, a spiritual peace. There is complexity in the Indian character, just as in white. I believe Native literature offers a realistic view of the culture. The Native American is not one-dimensional in these cumulative works. The literature offers a realistic view of history, at least an inclusive view. It adds viewpoints which have been left out of the stories told by Europeans.

The four classics of Native American literature are N. Scott Momaday's *House Made of Dawn,* Leslie Marmon Silko's *Ceremony,* James Welch's *Winter in the Blood,* and Louise Erdrich's *Love Medicine.* These books and their attitudes are mixed, like wheat and tares.

In *House Made of Dawn* by N. Scott Momaday (Harper & Row, New York, and winner of the 1969 Pulitzer Prize), the image set forth in the title, the house made of dawn, was actually from a peyote vision. There is Father Olguin, who must read the old manuscript of Fray Nicolas to find faith to fill the hollows where his own faith should have been but wasn't. There is Angela St. John, a white woman who probably represents Christianity also, who seduces Abel and uses him for her own means. But in the midst of all the voices, points of view, and settings which move back and forth between New Mexico and Los Angeles, somewhere in the Pacific Islands during World War II is a mission with a sign on the door that reads:

LOS ANGELES
HOLINESS PAN-INDIAN RESCUE MISSION
J. B. B. Tosamah, Pastor & Priest of the Sun
Saturday 8:30 P.M.
"The Gospel According to John"
Sunday 8:30 P.M.
"The Way to Rainy Mountain"
Be kind to a white man today.[10]

Here, in this mission, Tosamah preaches a lovely sermon on the Word.

In Principio erat Verbum. Think of Genesis. Think of how it was before the world was made. There was nothing, the Bible says, "And the earth was without form, and void; and darkness was upon the face of the deep." And it was dark, and there was nothing. There were no mountains, no trees, no rocks, no rivers. There was nothing. But there was darkness all around, and in the darkness something happened. *Something happened!*

There was a single sound. Nothing made it, but it was there; and there was no one to hear it, but it was there. It rose up in the darkness, little and still, almost nothing in itself—like a single soft breath, like the wind arising; yes, like the whisper of the wind rising slowly and going out into the early morning. But there was no wind. There was only sound, little and soft. It was almost nothing in itself, but smallest seed of sound—but it took hold of the darkness and there was light; it took hold of the stillness and there was motion forever; it took hold of the silence and there was sound. It was almost nothing in itself, a single sound, a word—a word broken off at the darkest center of the night and let go in the awful void, forever and forever. And it was almost nothing in itself. It scarcely was; but it was, and everything began.[11]

This passage goes on for pages about the word and the importance of language and a warning that we are diluting and duplicating our language until the words lose their strength. "It may be that he [the white man] will perish by the Word."

Notice also the repetition of Momaday's language, which sometimes replicates the rhythms of Old Testament poetry. He does this especially in the passages about the land, and there is much landscape description because the land is a living character and has a voice, a central voice in most Native novels.

In the history, the myth, the story—in the different points of view in *House Made of Dawn,* there is Momaday's own voice, adding, possibly, a creative nonfictional voice, making the book also a mix of genres as well as literary styles:

My grandmother had a reverence for the sun, a certain holy regard which now is all but gone out of mankind. There was a wariness in her, and an ancient awe. She was a Christian in her later years, but she had come a long way about, and she never forgot her birthright. As a child she had been to the sun dances; she had taken part in that annual rite, and by it she had learned the restoration of her people in the presence of Tai-me. She was about seven years old when the last Kiowa sun dance was held in 1887 on the Washita River above Rainy Mountain Creek [Oklahoma]. The buffalo were gone. In order to consummate the ancient sacrifice—to impale the head of a buffalo bull upon the Tai-me tree—a delegation of old men journeyed into Texas, there to beg and barter for an animal from the Goodnight herd. She was ten when the Kiowas came together for the last time as a living sun dance culture. They could find no buffalo; they had to hang an old hide from the sacred tree. That summer was known to my grandmother as Sun Dance When the Forked Poles Were Left Standing, and it is entered in the Kiowa calendar as the figure of a tree standing outside the unfinished framework of a medicine lodge. Before the dance could begin, a company of armed soldiers rode out from Fort Sill under orders to disperse the tribe. Forbidden without cause the essential act of their faith, having seen the wild herds slaughtered and left to rot upon the ground, the Kiowas backed away forever from the tree. That was July 20, 1890, at the great bend of the Washita. My grandmother was there. Without bitterness, and for as long as she lived, she bore a vision of deicide.[12]

I have attended the sun dances and sweat lodge ceremonies. They can be compared to Christ on the cross and in the heat of prayer. But for me, the work of salvation is finished. I don't need to re-create it in ceremony. I have departed from Indian ceremony. Christ is my sufficiency.

The other three novels I consider the classics by Native American writers each offer a possibility by which to re-create meaning in a culture which has been erased. In *House Made of Dawn* the answer is to revive old ceremonies. In Leslie Marmon Silko's *Ceremony,* the suggestion is to create new ceremonies because the old times, during which the ceremonies were created, have disappeared, especially since 1945, when the atomic power of the sun came to earth. According to James Welch, in *Winter in the Blood,* Native culture should simply forget all ceremonies and live with nothing to order life spiritually. And finally, in *Love Medi - cine,* Louise Erdrich appears to offer the possibility of combining old Indian traditions and Christianity, even though, according to Erdrich, none of the deities are functional and, at best, all we have is ourselves and the forgiveness and love which comes from the human heart, unreliable as it is.

This is Lipsha speaking about Christianity and Indian tradition in *Love Medicine:*

God's been going deaf. Since the Old Testament, God's been deafening up on us. . . . Now there's your God in the Old Testament and there is Chippewa Gods as well. Indian Gods, good and bad, like tricky Nanabozho or the water monster, Missepeshu, who lives over in Matchimanito. That water monster was the last God I ever heard to appear. It had a weakness for young girls. . . . Our Gods aren't perfect, is what I'm saying, but at least they come around.[13]

Other Native novels hardly mention Christianity, except with distaste and utter rejection. Often, they blame Christianity for the great suffering of Indian peoples. *Ceremony,* especially, demeans Christianity, and *Winter in the Blood* views it as a hypocrisy and irrelevant.

Today there are many other Native novels, but most repeat one of those four basic messages. Ray A. Young Bear's *Black Eagle Child* and any of Gerald Vizenor's many books are innovative Native literature. There is, today, an abundance of writing: novels, nonfiction, short stories, memoirs of Indian life, much of it torn and irregular, much of it agreeing on little except the tearing, the continuing battle for survival and meaning. The literature is painful, like running your hand along barbed wire.

There's a Christian hymn about the faith of my fathers. Though I never heard my own father speak directly of faith, I saw him live a moral life, even though he was torn with anger and loss and a sense of displacement, by being something he was not. He was a complicated man who took the yoke and plowed the field nonetheless.

That's what civilization is. Maybe Christianity too. We die to the old self. We put on the new Christ life we accepted through acknowledgment of Christ as personal Savior and his death on the cross for our sins. It is a singular, individual act. It can't be done by the tribe or for the whole tribe.

God is an individual seeking the lost. I remember Bible school as a small child—someone showing me Jesus holding a black sheep. That was me in the class of blond children. Maybe because my father loved me, I could believe, yes—Jesus loved even me.

GETTING STARTED
WITH NATIVE AMERICAN LITERATURE

Reading the four classics in the order presented in the essay would be a good start. *Black Elk Speaks* is another important book because of the Native perspective of westward expansion. Besides his numerous visions of the close of the nomadic life of the Plains Indian, Black Elk was present at the 1876 Battle of the Little Big Horn and the 1890 Massacre at Wounded Knee. Black Elk also tells about his trip to England with one of the touring Wild West shows, where he met Queen Victoria.

Anthologies including both historical and contemporary voices are another place to start. *Native American Literature: An Antho - logy* (Lawana Trout, ed.) and *Native American Literature* (Gerald Vizenor, ed.). I also edited an anthology with Mark Nowak titled *Visit Teepee Town: Native American Writings after the Detours* (Minneapolis: Coffee House Press, 1999). A book I have assigned this semester for its historical overview is *Native American Testimony*, Peter Nabakov (Penguin Books).

18

FLANNERY O'CONNOR
Guardian Angel
Harold Fickett

When I was at Brown University in the graduate creative writing program, I worked under the novelist John Hawkes. At one time John Hawkes was said to be on the short list for the Nobel Prize; in the 1970s, certainly, most critics would have named him as one of the best writers in America. Knowing his work mainly by reputation, I went off to graduate school, hoping to learn from him and also impress him with my abilities as a fiction writer.

As a member of Hawkes's fiction workshop I quickly came to understand the nature of his vision. Hawkes follows de Sade and Nietzsche: he believes in a truth "beyond good and evil," which is best expressed in terms of erotic intensities. Reading his novels, I encountered scenes of sadomasochistic sexual initiation: women fitted with horse bridles, chastity

Harold Fickett is a writer and speaker who lives in Santa Rosa, California. His fiction includes *Mrs. Sunday's Problem and Other Stories, The Holy Fool, Daybreak,* and *First Light.* He has also written the critical biography *Flannery O'Connor: Images of Grace.* Most recently, he wrote *The Living Christ: The Extraordinary Lives of Today's Spiritual Heroes.*

belts, and old-fashioned corsets drawn tight enough to induce a heady suffocation. Yet, whatever one might want to say about the monstrous aspects of Hawkes's vision, the lyric power of his work cannot be denied. As a craftsman, he is a genius.

I also came to know Hawkes's scorn for that religion of slaves—as Nietzsche called it—Christianity. Jack (as his students were permitted to call him) told us once of having attended the funeral of a friend; he left early because he could not bear the eulogy the priest had been delivering. Christianity is *so awful,* he said.

As a young fiction writer I was also beginning to understand that for my work to be any good, I would have to write about the world I had grown up in and knew best, the fundamentalist Protestant world. And I would be doing so with some sympathy, for, while my practice as a Christian had changed somewhat—I had joined the Episcopal Church—the basic doctrines I embraced remained those of my first community. I wondered with great trepidation how my stories of fundamentalists were going to be received in that fiction workshop.

One day we were talking about contemporary writers and the name of the novelist and short story writer Flannery O'Connor came up. The members of the class knew O'Connor as the author of two novels, *Wise Blood*[1] and *The Violent Bear It Away,*[2] and two outstanding collections of short stories, *A Good Man Is Hard to Find*[3] and *Everything That Rises Must Converge.*[4] They were aware that O'Connor's fictional rendering of a South populated by backwoods prophets, Bible salesmen, psychotic killers, and almost equally violent rural families constituted some of the very best post–World War II fiction in America. Reading Flannery O'Connor was *de rigueur* for aspiring young writers.

In that discussion I was startled to hear Jack, in speaking of O'Connor, say, "Of course, she believed that Jesus Christ was the Son of God and died for the sins of the world."

A pause followed Jack's statement, a silence in which the group looked to him for the expected ironic smile. In that cynical workshop statements of religious belief were never made except as jokes. Yet, we could see that he wasn't joking. Evidently, O'Connor believed such a statement in as matter-of-fact a way as he had put it. Our teacher valued honesty. And he wanted his students to confront honestly the mystery of a contemporary writer taking seriously the whole appalling business of Jesus Christ crucified.

I was already a Flannery O'Connor reader. I loved her work. But that day O'Connor became to me a guardian angel. Jack had Nietzsche, the radical lesbian feminists had Sappho and Adrienne Rich, the metafictionists had Barth and Barthelme. I had Flannery O'Connor. Her presence as a renowned contemporary writer gave hope that one could be a believer and a writer of serious fiction.

※

O'Connor has played many roles in my life—not only guardian angel. My thoughts about her are bound up with my own attitudes toward art and religion, and these spool out from my sense of self. I feel so close to her that often when I start out thinking about O'Connor I end up examining my own ideas and my own history.

I grew up in fundamentalist circles. I also grew up in the 1960s in Los Angeles. The religious world I knew and the secular one were radically at odds. While the religious world dominated my intellectual and emotional life, the secular world it inhabited reigned supreme for the surrounding culture. We thought of ourselves as the pearl within the oyster. The secular world looked at us as a fungal infection.

These conditions helped bring about an identity crisis in me, one that I think typical of most thoughtful Christians, not only in my time, but in every place and time since the Enlightenment. Whether it be among the encyclopedists in eighteenth-century France, the Fabians in nineteenth-century Britain, the Marxists everywhere in the first half of this century, or the counterculture in Los Angeles in the 1960s, most Christian intellectuals have lived their lives in the midst of competing and, for the most part, triumphant secular ideologies. This makes for personal insecurity and doubt.

My fundamentalist world believed that we could overcome the pagan world around us through argumentation. We could out-think people: they would see the error of their ways—and return to God. The way fundamentalists and evangelicals pursue this strategy often supposes that they stand outside or apart from their culture.

I could never wholly trust this sense of apartness. I knew I was a citizen of both countries, a fan of the Grateful Dead as well as a student of St. Augustine's *Confessions*. This double allegiance made me an alien in both countries as well. Somehow, I needed a way of moving on in my spiritual pilgrimage that did not compromise the truth of my times or my desire to be true to the timelessness of God.

When I started to read the stories and novels of Flannery O'Connor, I sensed immediately that hers was a genuinely contemporary voice: ironic, cold, ruthless, and very funny. These may not be tonal qualities that please everyone, but they color the music I hear in our world of divorce clinics and dial-a-porn. There is a lot that needs laughing at today. The humor in O'Connor's fiction comes not by way of standing outside the contemporary situation and poking fun from a lordly distance; the situations she depicts break open and, like pomegranates, reveal the savory seeds of which they are made. They taste of the experience, the life, they propagate. They are the fruit of an *entering into* the creative force that gives the contemporary situation its shape.

In O'Connor's letters I found corroboration of the author's identification with her times. She wrote: "If you live today you breathe in nihilism. In or out of the Church, it's the gas you breathe."[5] And also, "I am a Catholic peculiarly possessed of the modern consciousness, that thing Jung describes as unhistorical, solitary, and guilty. To possess this within the Church is to bear a burden, the necessary burden for the conscious Catholic. It's to feel the contemporary situation at the ultimate level."[6]

At whatever depth I experience this—feeling the contemporary situation at the ultimate level—I find it, indeed, "necessary," in the sense of inescapable; it is part of my experience. Whether I like it or not, I am immersed in my times. I feel that if I am to create anything of lasting value, it must come out of a radical acceptance of my world.

It struck me that perhaps this is the secret of why O'Connor appeals to Christians and non-Christians alike. Her work is at the opposite remove from escapism. It is all about penetration, finding in a particular place and time the source of being.

If one of my peers had asked what I thought I was doing in John Hawkes's workshop—what it meant for me as a Christian to write serious fiction—I'm not sure what I would have answered. I think Hawkes understood, though, by virtue of O'Connor's example. And I think his gracious treatment of me had much to do with his friendship with O'Connor.

As it happened, Jack once visited Flannery in Milledgeville, Georgia, where she lived with her mother as a semi-invalid on a farm called Andalusia. The author suffered from a disease called lupus erythematosus, in which the immune system begins attacking healthy tissues.

Jack and Flannery carried on a significant correspondence thereafter. Hawkes, like so many literary people, misunderstood Flannery's work at first. He thought her treatment of backwoods prophets entirely ironic; he did not realize that she thought her characters' inability to shake the elusive figure—Christ—who shadowed their lives their chief virtue. Try as they might, they could not rid themselves of the suspicion that God was mysteriously present.

Flannery's letters to Jack clarified many of her views. In them she articulated what must be the fundamental reason any Christian chooses to write serious fiction in the late twentieth century. "It's hard to believe always," she wrote, "but more so in the world we live in now. There are some of us who have to pay for our faith every step of the way and who have to work out dramatically what it would be like without it and if being without it would be ultimately possible or not."[7] O'Connor was not out to proselytize. In her fiction she was trying to win her own way to a genuine vision. That was an approach that Hawkes could respect, for it was his own.

Writers work in a variety of ways, but serious fiction writers most often approach their work as a form of thinking. O'Connor said, "I have to write to discover what I'm doing. Like the old lady, I don't know so well what I think until I see what I say; then I have to say it over again. . . ."[8] In this down-home way O'Connor captures how the action of writing helped clarify her thinking. She worked out *dramatically* the possibility of belief. In creating her fictions she proceeded with her own investigation of the great questions.

I think this view of fiction as a means of *thinking* is crucial, for it helps us to see why fiction cannot be "used" to convey messages. If setting, character, plot, time sequences, etc., are to the fiction writer what syllogisms are to the philosopher, then the play of these terms must be determined solely by the logic of the narrative; if the elements of fiction are the terms of a particular species of thinking, then they dictate the narrative's conclusions. They should not be manipulated to a preconceived end any more than a scientific experiment should be rigged to yield certain data. The difference between serious fiction in this regard and propagandistic or moralizing work is like the difference between astronomy and astrology: the first is a science, the second a sham.

The means of verifying the "thinking" in O'Connor's fiction is always the drama itself. The typical O'Connor short story ends with an "epiphany," a moment of insight or revelation, which the whole story has prepared for. Yet when this revelation comes, it catches us off guard.

> I often ask myself [she writes] what makes a story work . . . and I have decided that it is probably some action, some gesture of a character that is unlike any other in the story, one which indicates where the real heart of the story lies. This would have to be an action or a gesture which was both totally right and totally unexpected; it would have to be one that was both in character and beyond character; it would have to suggest both the world and eternity.[9]

The unexpected gesture and its ability to suggest both the world and eternity come from O'Connor's strict attention to the fictional process itself. She was a genius whose reasoning imagination worked in a way analogous to the reasoning imaginations of scientists. There is that moment in any true process of discovery, whether in literature or mathematics, in which the solution to a problem suddenly crystallizes: the solution is entirely consistent with the available information, and yet because we have not seen the pattern before, it brings with it a tingle of delight.

O'Connor is peculiarly accepted by non-Christians, I think, because her methods as a thinker and a craftsman are unassailable. Secular people often start with the presumption that Christianity is patently false; thus a Christian cannot take the risk of engaging in an open investigation, for if the Christian were to look at the world honestly, he would lose his faith. O'Connor not only shows this to be false, but she makes the nonbeliever question whether *he* has really plumbed the depths of experience. "The artist," she writes, "penetrates the concrete world in order to find at its depths the image of its source, the image of ultimate reality."[10]

It was as an artist that O'Connor first attracted me, too. I went to study with Hawkes because I already understood that the world of art is one—there is no such thing as Christian art or Christian writing any more than there is Christian physics. The task of art and its methodology are something that Christians and non-Christians share by means of common grace. O'Connor understood this and acted on it.

When as an undergraduate I started to write, I looked for writers like O'Connor, whose subject matter resembled what I felt would be my own. I had a sense of what I wanted to do, and I could feel it and hear it and almost smell it in the work of the writers from whom I learned the most.

Again, this had much to do with my dual passport, as a citizen of Zion and Los Angeles. I wanted the knowledge that has come to us in this century to inform my work—what depth psychology has taught us about our irrationally destructive natures, for example. And the history of our times—which has often seemed a horrifying working out of these Freudian perceptions, with its Battle of the Marne, Holocaust, Hiroshima, and Gulag—I wanted that history to be there, too. I wanted to show how our culture's reasoned defenses against the worst in humankind have succumbed to an increasing skepticism. And how this results, especially in the Western world, in people living as if they were cartoon characters—people express something, however unconsciously, when they wear Mickey Mouse on their T-shirts.

I also wanted my own stubbornly Christ-haunted interior life to shape my work. I wanted belief to be the issue, and to make it so by recording what the life of faith might be like. I hoped that I could make the question of belief as real as it was to me, as real as the times' weight of darkness.

And finally, I wanted to incorporate something of the life of the evangelical world as a subculture—seen with a cold eye—into fiction.

With these ambitions, I could certainly have discovered no one better to learn from than O'Connor. For she had accomplished just this and much more. I suppose O'Connor's achievement might have intimidated me into absolute silence had she not worked in a context—the deep South—sufficiently removed from mine.

O'Connor, too, felt she belonged to several worlds. She was a Southerner and a Roman Catholic—nearly as odd a combination as being an evangelical in Los Angeles. Her concerns were never parochial, however. She also made the world of *belles-lettres* her home, and through writing about her region examined the larger world beyond. "It is the peculiar burden of the fiction writer," she writes, "that he has to make one country do for all and that he has to evoke that one country through the concrete particulars of a life that he can make believable."[11]

The characters we meet within Flannery O'Connor's fiction are certainly modern people, no matter how backwoods their origins. The prophet figures from O'Connor's novels spring to most readers' minds when they first think of representative O'Connor characters. Much more of her work, though, has to do with middle-class people who live in small towns or rural settings.

The most repeated pattern in O'Connor's fiction presents us with a family (often with the father or mother missing) living on a farm. The people in these families are not exactly typical bucolics, one with nature, at peace with the world and themselves. Rather, they seek to dominate one another. They are caught up in rivalries, the intensity of which they are often unaware until cruel and sometimes deadly actions ensue. In "A View of the Woods," Mr. Fortune smashes the skull of his favorite granddaughter. In "The Comforts of Home," Thomas shoots his mother, and in "Everything That Rises Must Converge," Julian precipitates the heart attack that kills his mother. Mr. Head denies he even knows his grandson, Nelson, in "The Artificial Nigger," and Hulga obviously despises everything about her maternal parent in "Good Country People." Although O'Connor was no Freudian, her view of human nature was deepened by Freud, and she was able to catch how love when it proceeds out of need can become the most destructive of forces.

O'Connor also showed how the human will to power—and the pride that becomes the personality of this will—extends its deadly consequences into social and even international affairs. In "The Displaced Person," Mr. Guizac and his family, Polish refugees, come to America to escape persecution. Many allusions are made to the boxcars containing Jews on their way to the death camps, and other aspects of the social chaos produced by World War II that have displaced the Guizacs from their homeland. They take up residence on Mrs. McIntyre's farm.

Mr. Guizac, hardworking, clever, and forthright, proves a great addition to the farm. But then his very blamelessness threatens the guilty ways of the other help and finally the possessiveness of the owner, Mrs. McIntyre, herself. At the end of the story Mrs. McIntyre, her foreman

Mr. Shortly, and a black farmhand named Sulk enter into a silent conspiracy that results in Mr. Guizac's death in a preventable tractor accident. O'Connor shows us that the will that led the Nazis to kill six million Jews is the same will that leads people everywhere to persecute the innocent. Life in the twentieth century on the Oconee differs very little from life on the Rhine.

In her fiction O'Connor has a way of turning abstruse ideas of contemporary thought into comic scenes. That anyone could make use of the philosophic position known as logical positivism to flesh out the life of a Tennessee drifter seems incredible. And yet here is Hazel Motes, from *Wise Blood,* summing up his beliefs to a gas station attendant.

> He [Hazel] said nobody with a good car needed to worry about anything, and he asked the boy if he understood that . . . .He said it was not right to believe anything you couldn't see or hold in your hands or test with your teeth. He said he had only a few days ago believed in blasphemy as the way to salvation, but that you couldn't believe in that because then you were believing in something to blaspheme. As for the Jesus who was reported to have been born at Bethlehem and crucified on Calvary for man's sins, Hazel said, He was too fool a notion for a sane person to carry in his head, and he picked up the boy's water bucket and bammed it on the concrete pavement to emphasize what he was saying.[12]

In terms of the history of philosophy, Hazel Motes has emerged out of late Romanticism, with its emphasis on rebellion, into the latter day empiricism of linguistic analysis (or logical positivism) in which only those statements that can be verified through sensory data—"test with your teeth"—are meaningful. This is only the most obvious example of how O'Connor placed present concerns in a supposedly backward locale. She had the same expressionistic gift Kafka had to make exterior in dramatic action interior values, feelings, and ideas.

A story like "The River" brings home how the most important things in life can be misplaced by virtue of the materialism of our times. Bevel is what is known today as a latchkey child. The first scene shows us that his parents spend their lives in socializing and heavy drinking, while Bevel is left to his own devices, or to baby-sitters.

Bevel's life is already so lonely and inhuman that when his baby-sitter takes him to an outdoor revival meeting and he hears of the wonderful life that can be attained through the waters of baptism, he makes up his mind to return to the river.

There, alone, he pushes off and struggles his way down to the icy currents that he expects will take him to this new life.

The story is one of spiritual victory, the prizing of eternal life, in which O'Connor forces us through violent means to consider what we value.

Flannery O'Connor

Bevel's mistaken literalism is not nearly so bad, we feel (it will probably even be divinely rewarded), as his parents' materialism.

Fictions are distinguished in the end by what's at stake in them. O'Connor always put the mystery of God's creative action in our lives at the heart of her fiction. Her characters' response to that action determines everything. She makes belief the issue. What is at stake in her fiction is nothing less than eternal destiny. She writes

> The novelist tries to give you, within the form of the book, a total experience of human nature at any time. For this reason the greatest dramas naturally involve the salvation or loss of the soul. The Christian novelist is distinguished from his pagan colleagues by recognizing sin as sin. According to his heritage he sees it not as sickness or an accident of environment, but as a responsible choice of offense against God which involves his eternal future. Either one is serious about salvation or one is not.[13]

Of course it's one thing for the novelist himself or herself to be serious about salvation and another thing to make the reader serious about it.

I can only suggest here how Flannery O'Connor accomplishes this feat. Earlier in this essay I alluded to the parable-like structure of her work, and that's probably the handiest reference to what she does. Reading O'Connor, we encounter stories that on the surface are all about the "real world." Yet the stories contain dilemmas that have no solutions within a purely naturalistic context. They call for their characters, and the reader after them, to enlarge their views of reality to include the transcendent, in order to grasp a higher logic by which the situation might be resolved.

For example, O. E. Parker, in "Parker's Back," experiences a craving of the spirit that only a tattoo will satisfy—at first. Then his general dissatisfaction mixes with his desire to please his religious wife. He decides to put a tattoo of a "religious subject" on his back, satisfying, he thinks, both his own desires and his wife's demands. And yet within the "all-demanding" eyes of the Byzantine Christ whose image he chooses to have tattooed on his back, he finds at last the source of his craving and its ultimate satisfaction.

Because we *experience* the need for God in O'Connor's work, since she locates that need in unexpected contexts that yet elicit our sympathy, we find ourselves opening up to the possibility of God's presence. This is true for Christians and non-Christians alike. I think John Hawkes paid Flannery O'Connor the highest compliment that any writer who is a Christian can receive. Personally antagonistic toward the faith though he was, Jack said that for the space of reading O'Connor he *was* a Christian; he knew what it felt like to be one.

Opening up spiritual experience for the reader in this way has always been my highest ambition as a writer. This way of putting it, though, is too outward, messianic. I am sure it has much more to do with working out my own salvation through convincing my secular self of my religious self's point of view. It has to do with working out the possibility of faith dramatically. For any post-Enlightenment writer—or at least for this post-Enlightenment writer—art must address the cleavage of the self that the Romantics first experienced. The medieval consensus of faith collapsing in the West made us all heirs to a divided self. I am trying to cope with that in just the same way as my secular peers. It would be nice to think—many have tried—that Christianity restores fragmented sensibilities with its first advent in the individual's life. But for me—and evidently for O'Connor as well—sanctification doesn't work this way.

I think, however, that the writing of fiction can be a means—as all legitimate work can be—through which God can re-create us. I am sure I will meet with skeptics in this. Since most writers have been such scoundrels, after all, can we possibly imagine that the craft of fiction might be the vessel in which someone sails to Jerusalem? I think this *was* true for O'Connor. She has become for me the kind of figure who enlarges my own particular appreciation of how to follow Christ: a saint.

I have said very little about her life other than alluding to its affliction, lupus. After her early twenties, O'Connor lived in circumstances that would drive most writers crazy. Because of her poor health, as I've said, she spent her time in virtual seclusion—a literary contemplative—on the family farm, Andalusia, in Milledgeville, Georgia. She found such meaning and enjoyment in her work that she rarely represented her life as being one of hardship. But it was not the life she had wanted. She had tried, before the onset of her illness, to live as a writer in cultured circles in the North. Lupus forced her to return home.

O'Connor, by accepting the deprivation of her illness as if from God's hands, found in her life another logic, the logic of grace. This logic transformed that life—just as her characters are transformed by their new reading of experience. Rather than be resentful and angry at God for the circumstances in which she found herself, O'Connor used her isolation as a source of creative power. Her example in this has a particular poignancy for me. For as I have lived, life has confronted me with the unacceptable that must somehow be accepted. Acceptance seems to make way for redemption.

Thus I would finally recommend O'Connor's work and the example of her life not so much on intellectual or technical grounds but on the basis of what she has come to mean to me personally. I believe that in reading O'Connor I have experienced something of the communion of the saints through which Christ nurtures the life of his church. I once read Flannery O'Connor to find out how to write, but in the end she gave me much more than that: she showed me how to live.

GETTING STARTED WITH O'CONNOR

Because of Flannery O'Connor's early death (she was only thirty-nine), her major works comprise just a few volumes. Vintage Paperbacks publishes a complete collection of her short stories, probably the best place to start. The two most famous longer works, *Wise Blood* and *The Violent Bear It Away*, are available in the Signet paperback, *Three by Flannery O'Connor*. To truly understand O'Connor's approach, though, it is best to sample her own commentary on her faith and writing: *The Habit of Being* and *Mystery and Manners* contain wonderful letters and essays. The Library of America has also published *Flannery O'Connor: The Collected Works* in an elegant, pricey edition.

19

ALEKSANDR SOLZHENITSYN
A Moral Vision

Karen Burton Mains

I n the twenty-second year of my life and fourth year of my marriage, despite the rapid arrival of children (two already birthed and two more to come), having no college education and saddled with the wifely responsibilities of an inner-city pastorate, I nevertheless felt faint, undisciplined yearnings to write, and thus I embarked on a program of self-education.

In the most unregimented fashion, I began my "Russian period." Coiling backward and outward from the Bolshevik Revolution of 1917, I surveyed philosophies, histories, war chronicles, and accounts of the hemophiliac genealogies of royal European bloodlines. With that background, I went on to study the prophetic literary voices: Tolstoy, Dostoevsky, Turgenev, Chekhov, Pasternak. Finally, I came to Solzhenitsyn.

Karen Burton Mains has worked in several communication media: as cohost with her husband, David, of the national radio program *The Chapel of the Air* and a syndicated television show, as a conference lecturer, and as a writer. Her numerous books include *Open Heart, Open Home; Karen, Karen; The Fragile Curtain;* and *Child Sexual Abuse: A Hope for Healing.*

Aleksandr Solzhenitsyn

One Day in the Life of Ivan Denisovich captivated me. Although I know why Solzhenitsyn's writing moves me now, I don't understand why it moved me in my early twenties. I was then instinctively positive; to me, the world was good and beautiful, as were all the people in it. My compassion was sentimental and naive. In contrast, Solzhenitsyn had felt the crushing heel of injustice, the bruising misuse of human power, the obstinacy of systemic evil. He was formed, hard, and canny; I was unformed, soft, and American. Perhaps I intuitively sensed the great wisdom such a writer could give me: that I would never be complete or useful until I apprehended suffering.

At any rate, the understated short tale about one day in the life of a *zek,* a prisoner in Stalin's Gulag—with the lift at the end so surprising but so typically Solzhenitsyn ("Nothing had spoiled the day and he [Sukhov] was almost happy .. .")[1]—slipped through the crack during the Khrushchev thaw and somehow found its way to me. I have read almost everything Solzhenitsyn has written since, and I have watched much of his life from afar, glancing sideways, trying not to be too hopeful. I am confident his foothold is firm. He is rare: one of the few who informs not only my profession as a writer but also my private self. More, he aids me in the struggle to integrate my Christian faith with both.

Solzhenitsyn's dedication to the task at hand, despite seemingly insurmountable distractions, chastens me, as a writer often at dalliance with my work. Who wouldn't be snapped to reality by this hard knock taken from Solzhenitsyn's writing memoirs:

In retrospect, almost all my life since the day I was first arrested had been the same: just for that particular week, that month, that season, that year, there had always been some reason for not writing—it was inconvenient or dangerous or I was too busy—always some need to postpone it. If I had given in to common sense, once, twice, ten times, my achievement as a writer would have been incomparably smaller. But I had gone on writing—as a bricklayer, in overcrowded prison huts, in transit jails without so much as a pencil, when I was dying of cancer, in an exile's hovel after a double teaching shift. I had let nothing—dangers, hindrances, the need for rest—interrupt my writing, and only because of that could I say at fifty-five that I now had no more than twenty years of work to get through, and had put the rest behind me.

My petty interferences—people, children, housework, public demands (but most of all, my own native undisciplined self)—bump against such reality. I continue to pound my balled fist against my own soft soul and to insist, No Excuses! No Excuses!

On a grander scale, Solzhenitsyn has become for me a rare exemplar of the truly heroic life. His inward moral vision, unshakable, has shaped his outward public acts as well as his art. Not only did he survive the pressures of a regime responsible for the destruction of millions, but he emerged uncowed, with a new voice of eloquent rage to jar the percep- tions of the West and to stir the swirling eddies of freedom in the USSR. His example enables ordinary mortals, like me, to consider that our own small dreams might be attainable.

"Who are your heroes?" my husband, David, frequently asks dinner guests, new acquaintances, the unsuspecting friends of our children. Fre- quently, people respond, "Well, I guess I don't really have any heroes." That common answer has made me pause and consider the topic. Opin- ion polls inform us that we most admire celebrities (Oprah Winfrey for instance, or the late John Lennon, or Michael Jordan). When, some time ago, Brooklyn high school students were asked in a questionnaire, "What would you like to be?" two-thirds of them responded, "A celebrity." But the lives of celebrities usually have little to do with the traditional qual- ities of heroism: moral integrity, the perseverance to surmount obsta- cles, self-sacrifice for the sake of others.

My husband's stock question has made me duly consider my own answer, and I have heard myself baldly announcing that I don't have a hero, at least none living. I am wary, perhaps even antihero. Politicians consistently let us down. The "great" works of modern writers sink toward moral and spiritual lassitude. And the leaders of evangelicalism, that bastion of doctrinal purity in which I was spiritually nurtured, have taught me by example that we are all sinners on a long, slow pilgrim- age toward perfection. I still hurt when a spiritual leader I admire admits to adultery.

Out of such resignation and disillusionment, why, then, do I keep casting my eyes about, glancing furtively, hoping nobody notices? At last I admit, though not loudly: *I need a hero.* I need someone at least faintly heroic, not to idolize, or worship, but rather to cannibalize (though mea- gerly, a bite here, a bite there); someone who can nourish me when my own strength seems devoured by doubt and disillusionment. I need a human who stands morally obdurate somewhere within my history, a person to lean my palm against slightly, only slightly, to steady or right myself.

"Does society need heroes?" Bill Moyers asked Joseph Campbell, the mythologist, in the PBS series, *The Power of Myth.*

Campbell: "Yes. It has to have constellating images to pull together all these tendencies to separation, to pull them together into some intention."

Precisely—I need a constellating image. I need to be reminded of and stirred toward idealism, by seeing a living romance based on selfless- ness rather than selfishness. Moreover, I suspect that heroism hides in each soul, and if so, perhaps one genuinely heroic deed can unleash an unsuspected hero lurking within me. Campbell delineates some of the characteristics of heroism. The hero feels there is something lacking in the normal experiences available or permitted to members of society. The hero undergoes trials and tests and ordeals and thereby experiences a transformation of consciousness. He loses himself for the sake of a higher end, undergoing a form of death and resurrection.

In these ways, specifically, Solzhenitsyn has been a hero for our time. His transformation of consciousness took place in the ordeal of what he came to call "The Gulag Archipelago." "Gulag" (more accurately GULag) is the acronym for the Chief Administration of Corrective Labor Camps, a string of separate camps (islands) scattered over the Russian subcontinent. Solzhenitsyn estimates that between 1918 and 1959, sixty-six million prisoners died in the camps, roughly eleven times the number which perished in Nazi death camps. (Historical estimates of Stalin's victims vary widely; the most widely accepted total is twenty million.) As a record of his experience in the camps, Solzhenitsyn wrote three massive volumes, a martyrology dedicated to those who gave their lives.[2] Throughout its length, the book sustains a tone of outraged sarcasm and unrelieved hostility toward the Soviet regime: "Hitler was a mere disciple, but he had all the luck: his murder camps have made him famous, whereas no one has any interest in ours at all."[3]

The writing began in the camps themselves, where Solzhenitsyn was serving an eight-year term at hard labor for criticizing Stalin in a private letter to friends. There, working entirely from memory, he sought to organize an oral history of the camps. He interviewed surreptitiously. From the accounts of 227 witnesses, along with documents and other bits of revelation, he pieced together the whole. Ultimately, he came to believe that the horrors could not be dismissed as Stalin's aberrations; they traced back to Lenin and the Marxist system itself.

After Solzhenitsyn's release from prison into exile, he committed chunks of the work to paper, which he stuffed into hiding places. At no time did he have the entire body of the manuscript in front of him. This Herculean effort went on even as he taught school and produced his major fictional works. Solzhenitsyn saw himself as on a sacred mission to complete and deliver this work as a memorial to the victims.

It is exceedingly difficult to find a literary signature for *The Gulag Archipelago*. The work is an epic, and much else besides: autobiography, martyrology, oral history, revisionist history, spiritual confession, investigative reporting, a morality dialogue, a philosophical treatise on evil and suffering. In truth, there is not another piece of literature like it in the world. It has shaken the world, and it is shaking it still. Gulag has entered the world's vocabulary—and its way of thinking.

"And the simple step of a simple courageous man is not to partake in falsehood, not to support false actions!" declared Solzhenitsyn in his Nobel Prize lecture. "Let THAT enter the world, let it even reign in the world—but not with my help. But writers and artists can achieve more: they can CONQUER FALSEHOOD! In the struggle with falsehood art always did win and it always does win! Openly, irrefutably for everyone! Falsehood can hold out against much in this world, but not against art."[4] In short, *The Gulag Archipelago* is nearly two thousand pages of truth.

Solzhenitsyn intended the volumes as a last will and testament, to be published posthumously. He especially wished to avoid any recriminations against those still living who had served as informants. In a supreme irony, *Gulag* was catapulted to publication by the very regime against which it was directed. In September, 1973, the KGB detained Elizaveta Voronyanskaya, the manuscript's typist and guardian of one safe copy. Her interrogation lasted for five sleepless days and nights, during which she broke and revealed the hiding place. The copy was confiscated, and Elizaveta committed suicide.

The discovery set into motion the irrevocable. Soviet powers had already been warned that if Solzhenitsyn was imprisoned or killed, works would be released for publication in the West that would be of great embarrassment to the regime. Now that members of the Soviet Centralist Committee were reading the history of the labor camps, Solzhenitsyn's hand was forced and he sent word to the outside to proceed with publication. In December of 1973 the first parts of *Gulag* appeared in Russian. Finally, on February 12, 1974, the author was whisked away to the Lefortovo Prison in Moscow to be deported the next day to the West.

Deportation ended Solzhenitsyn's long internal struggle with the Soviet powers. Like a calf butting its head against a great oak tree (his analogy), he had resisted the bureaucracy and its attempts to control him. He had pressed for publication of his works, had openly challenged (earning an expulsion from) the Union of Soviet Writers, and had leaked information to the West, all the while using his international reputation to confound his opponents.

While still in Russia, Solzhenitsyn had helped to organize dissident Russians, bringing them together in a book of essays, *From under the Rubble.* That collection clarified his spiritual views: it became increasingly clear that Solzhenitsyn saw true spiritual renaissance as Western civilization's only hope. A few years later, he went even further with the essay, *Letter to the Soviet Leaders,* an open letter of criticism directed to church and government authorities. The church had accommodated to the state, he said. And to those aging leaders of the state, he proclaimed: "You will not allow power to slip out of your hands. That is why you will not willingly tolerate a two-party or a multi-party parliamentary system in our country, you will not tolerate *real* elections, at which people might not vote you in. And on the basis of realism one must admit that this will be within your power for a long time."[5]

A long time—but not forever.

He continued, speaking boldly to this atheistic hierarchy, "I myself see Christianity today as the only living spiritual force capable of undertaking the spiritual healing of Russia. But I request and propose no special privileges for it, simply that it should be treated fairly and not suppressed."[6]

In such encounters Solzhenitsyn was employing the cunning skills—courage, tenacity, feint, and counterfeint, facing down the bully—honed through eight years in the labor camps. Ultimately, Solzhenitsyn derived his strength from a faith that he was not alone, that God himself controlled the events of history. Therefore, despite the distress and anxiety, he worked joyfully, as an instrument:

> But what does it mean to *them*? Is the time, perhaps, at hand when Russia will at last begin to wake up? . . .
>
> Once again, my vision and my calculations are probably faulty. There are many things which I cannot see even at close quarters, many things in which the Hand of the Highest will correct me. But this casts no cloud over my feelings. It makes me happier, more secure, to think that I do not have to plan and manage everything for myself, that I am only a sword made sharp to smite the unclean forces, an enchanted sword to cleave and disperse them.
>
> Grant, O Lord, that I may not break as I strike! Let me not fall from Thy hand![7]

Solzhenitsyn and his wife were prepared to make grave sacrifices for the sake of the higher calling. In *The Oak and the Calf,* his literary memoirs, Solzhenitsyn reveals a list of eventualities the two considered after his manuscripts had been seized by the KGB. Number one reads: "They could take my children hostage—posing as 'gangsters,' of course. (They did not know that we had thought of this and made a superhuman decision: our children were no dearer to us than the memory of the millions done to death, and nothing could make us stop that book.)"

What other writer in our time (and one is tempted to ask in what other time?) more dearly conforms to the mythological type of heroism? One doesn't idolize, of course—one is simply left overwhelmed in the face of such towering strength and intransigence. A giant has left his footprints in our century.

✖

For me, disappointed so often in "Christian leaders," it means much that Solzhenitsyn's powerful voice is essentially spiritual. Awarded the

Nobel Prize for literature in 1970 and unable to leave Russia to receive the award in person, Solzhenitsyn sent his acceptance speech to be read in his absence. In it, he contrasts two kinds of artists: the one who "sees himself as the creator of an independent spiritual world," and a second kind who "recognizing a higher power above, gladly works as a humble apprentice beneath God's heaven."[8] Solzhenitsyn clearly identifies himself as being in the second camp.

Solzhenitsyn cannot be understood outside the context of Russian Christian Orthodoxy (though secular literary critics amazingly attempt this!) to which he converted while a prisoner in a Stalinist prison camp. The Russian Orthodox priest, Alexander Schmemann, writes most perceptively of Solzhenitsyn's specifically Christian vision: "But what do I mean when I speak of Solzhenitsyn or of his art as Christian? . . . I have in mind a deep and all-embracing . . . perception of the world, man, and life, which, historically, was born and grew from Biblical and Christian revelation, and only from it." Schmemann then gives a definition which summarizes Solzhenitsyn and has, in fact, helped form my own literary thinking: "I shall call this perception, for lack of a better term, the triune intuition of creation, fall, and redemption."[9]

This triune intuition is always present in Solzhenitsyn. The priest acknowledges that Solzhenitsyn's writings are almost entirely centered in ugliness, located as they are in the depravity of the labor camp, the despair of the cancer ward, the deceit of the *sharashka;* but he insists:

> Yet, nowhere, never, not once (and let the reader check my assertion) do we find or even sense in all his works that ontological *blasphemy* about the world, man, and life, the poisonous whisper of which can be heard so clearly in so much of "contemporary art." I could cite examples of this, but specific instances, of course, are not proof. The proof, rather, is in the overall tonality of the art, in its inner "music" which eludes formal analysis alone. And in Solzhenitsyn this music, though seemingly spun so entirely from the cries of suffering, mystically admits and reveals that very praise which constitutes the ultimate depth of the Biblical vision of the world.[10]

Cancer Ward, one of the novels, uses the metaphor of terminal disease as an environment in which to examine man's universal spiritual and moral condition; disease corresponds to evil in the individual and malignancy in a culture. In this sense, the work does center on "fallenness," which is where most modern writers are mired. Yet it does not stay there but ascends to redemption. I remember vividly coming to the sequence where Oleg Kostoglotov steps out of the cancer hospital, realizing that a cure has given him the chance of life. The chapter is titled "The First Day of Creation."

This was the morning of Creation! The world was being created anew for this alone, to be given back to Oleg: Go! Live!

[He sees an apricot tree in bloom.] This was his reward for not hurrying. The lesson was—never rush on without looking around first. . . . It was like a fire tree decorated with candles in a room of a northern home ... the tree had buds like candles. When on the point of opening, the petals were pink in color, but once open they were pure white, like apple or cherry blossoms. . . . There were many other joys in store for him today in this newly born world.[11]

Such joy in the midst of gloom illustrates the overall tonality of much of Solzhenitsyn's art, the inner "music" about which the Russian Orthodox priest Schmemann speaks. This is the third part of that "triune intuition": redemption, being rescued from death and made new, being restored to an innocent, prefall condition.

For years I have set aside in a single bookcase a collection of books that have gripped me at a deep personal level. It is an odd assortment of titles, ranging from Doris Betts's *Souls Raised from the Dead,* Jan Karon's Mitford series, and Susan Howatch's Starbridge novels, all works of contemporary fiction, to Paul Johnson's *Modern Times,* a history of the twentieth century. Trollope's *Barchester Chronicles* are there, as are Elizabeth Goudge's *Cathedral Trilogy* and Will Campbell's autobiographical *Brother to a Dragonfly.* The shelves hold diverse and uneven writings. Some are overtly Christian, others subtly spiritual: T. H. White's *A Once and Future King,* Chaim Potok's *The Chosen* and *The Promise,* Bernard Shaw's *Saint Joan.* But all strike a soul-ish satisfaction in me.

I grouped these books together without knowing their common thread—was it a hidden numinosity, a holy shining? Now I realize that the Golden String connecting these works traces back to the sense of "triune intuition" I had met in Solzhenitsyn. I see now that I have always leaned toward writers who intentionally or instinctively display creation, fall, and redemption; they mirror to me the vision of what literature should be.

Moreover, this discovery has allowed me to examine my own writing. What is it I'm attempting as I write? *The Fragile Curtain,* a book about refugees, and *Tales of the Kingdom* and *Tales of the Resistance,* allegorical stories for children about Christ and his kingdom—these demonstrate my own groping toward that "triune intuition." Solzhenitsyn aids me as a writer, by giving me a language for my aspiration. Now middle-aged, I can no longer describe a world as only beautiful, for it is not—indeed, for most, it is desperate. But in the midst of desecration, I can strive to be a writer sacramental.

In details, the myths of ancient cultures vary; but their overall themes show an overwhelming similarity. According to mythologists Joseph Campbell and Mircea Eliade, there is really only one story, translated in the traditions and circumstances of myriad peoples: the myth of a lost idyllic Time of Beginnings and of a hero's journey to restore the world to its pristine state of paradisal splendor. In *Memories and Visions of Paradise,* Richard Heinberg asks, "Doesn't this universal statement indicate a common collective memory of a paradisal time that did exist in actuality?"[12] Isn't there truth in a story told so many times?

Rarely, an artist comes along who reminds us of the permanent things. For Solzhenitsyn, countryman Dostoevsky performed such a role; he "was granted to see much, a man of fantastic illumination,"[13] according to Solzhenitsyn. In every generation some people are given to us to shout out the vision of the past wondrous time and of its loss and of its restoration. Without them, society perishes; it reconciles itself to dictators and correction camps and genocide. And shouldn't we then cherish those rare few who can help us recover the buried memory, both individual and collective?

Solzhenitsyn is rare in that he has maintained his integrity in face of publicity and world renown, two corrupting influences that few endure unscathed. He is rare in that he is a writer whose personal life has maintained authentic integrity. He is rare in that he is a Christian whose art is informed by that ethos.

The true artist has learned to recognize and to render what James Joyce called "the radiance" of all things. By showing forth the truth, he or she provides an opportunity for epiphany, and that in itself is a redemptive work: those who care to be made better are informed by this vision, this sight. A better world can exist; we can strive for it. We can hope. There is potentiality, and a promise of restoration. Solzhenitsyn has been, for me, a man wondrously filled with light.

❈

Without being overly adulatory, I am certain that the fall of communism in the former Soviet Union has flowed, in part,from the hot underground springs of many dissidents, chief among them, Solzhenitsyn. History may one day judge that disillusionment with the Marxist system crossed a turning point with the publication of his three shattering volumes about Russian prison camps.

Not everyone, of course, views Solzhenitsyn's life as heroic. As one Russian critic put it, "The works of Solzhenitsyn are more dangerous to us than those of Pasternak: Pasternak was a man divorced from life, while Solzhenitsyn, with his animated, militant, ideological temperament, is a man of principle."[14]

Neither does Solzhenitsyn toady to the West, even though it has given him shelter and income, even though its attention preserved his existence, making it necessary for the regime to charge him with treason and deport him, rather than sending a bullet to his brain. He feels that the West is in decline due to the loss of a sense of the distinction between good and evil: "I am a critic of the weakness of the West. I am a critic of a fact which we can't comprehend: how can one lose one's spiritual strength, one's will power and, possessing freedom, not value it, not be willing to make sacrifices for it?"[15]

He has undergone trials and tests and ordeals and thereby experienced a transformation of consciousness: "A convinced Marxist, a Leninist, in prison I saw that my convictions did not have a solid basis, could not stand up in dispute, and I had to renounce them . . . in those circumstances human nature becomes very much more visible. I was very lucky to have been in the camps—and especially to have survived." He has also undergone a kind of a death and resurrection: "The fact that I was dying [of cancer] also shook me profoundly. At age 34 I was told I could not be saved, and then I returned to life. These kinds of upheavals always have an impact on a person's convictions."

Siberia settled for Solzhenitsyn the primary riddle of existence:

What about the main thing in life, all its riddles? I'll spell it out for you right now. Do not pursue what is illusory—property and position: all that is gained at the expense of your nerves decade after decade, and is confiscated in one fell night. Live with a steady superiority over life—don't be afraid of misfortune. . . . It is enough if you don't freeze in the cold and if thirst and hunger don't claw at your insides . . . and prize above all else in the world those who love you and wish you well. Do not hurt them or scold them, and never part from any of them in anger; after all, you simply do not know: it might be your last act before your arrest, and that will be how you are imprinted on their memory.

From 1976 until 1994, Cavendish, Vermont, was the place of exile within exile for Solzhenitsyn, his wife, Natalya, and their four sons. There he maintained a self-imposed silence, assisted by the fierce loyalty of his Yankee neighbors. There was a sign in the general store: NO REST ROOMS. NO BARE FEET. NO DIRECTIONS TO THE SOLZHENITSYNS. In isolation, racing against approaching age, the writer continued to work, as he has in the several years that have passed since his return to his homeland.

Time's David Aikman quotes the assessment of Vadim Borisov, editor of the Moscow literary journal *Novy Mir,* about Solzhenitsyn's place in Russian literature: "If all of Solzhenitsyn's works had been published in their time and not banned, the character of Russian prose today would be different. When his epic historical cycle is read in its entirety, it will have the same significance for Russian literature as Dante's *Divine Com - edy* has for European literature."[16]

Life in the former Soviet Union has changed dramatically but Solzhenitsyn continues to stand firm on his beliefs. In the end, what I like most about Solzhenitsyn is his continued obduracy. Even though he has now spent five years back in his homeland, he has not altered his principles. That gives me strange comfort. Such obdurate heroism simply means to me that when I waver, when I falter, when I doubt myself, I can reach out (from a far distance, but it is enough) to touch that strength. I am made steady in wobbling moments, I am made strong, because one life has been lived well. Thus have the heroes through all time made the world firmer. They give each of us strength to stand firm, in our own small way, for the sake of others who will reach out a trembling hand to us.

GETTING STARTED WITH SOLZHENITSYN

One Day in the Life of Ivan Denisovich is by far the briefest and most accessible of Solzhenitsyn's works, and thus makes a perfect beginning point. From there, try *The Oak and the Calf,* the literary autobiography which tells the behind-the-scenes story of his struggle to write and publish. Many readers find *The Gulag Archipelago* intimidating because of its gloomy subject matter and its length; start with volume 3, which tells of thrilling escape attempts. Then, you can read the earlier volumes, or sample his longer fiction, either *Cancer Ward* or *First Circle.* Michael Scammel's *Solzhenitsyn* is the most comprehensive biography to date; *Solzhenitsyn: The Moral Vision* by Edward Ericson Jr. gives further insight into Solzhenitsyn's religious views.

20

RAY BRADBURY
Hope in a Doubtful Age

Calvin Miller

When told, "The world is coming to an end!" Mark Twain reportedly said, "Good, we can get along without it." In just this way, exuberant positivism chases out naive pessimism. And, ironically, it was the fertile imagination of a science fiction writer, Ray Bradbury, that gave root to my maturing understanding of how to get along without the burdensome world at hand. For, getting along without this present world is precisely the theme of both Christianity and *The Martian Chronicles*. While they answer the issue in different ways, both exist to say with joy, "The visible world is less important than we have supposed."[1]

Sometime in seminary Bradbury first fell into my world (or perhaps I fell into his). The scholarly tedium of learning how to be "truly spiritual" can coat all things bright and beautiful with dullness, and somewhere

---

Calvin Miller pastored Westside Baptist Church in Omaha for twenty-six years and is currently professor of preaching and pastoral studies at Beeson Divinity School, Birmingham, Alabama. He is the author of over thirty books, the most recent being *Snow*. Ray Bradbury's influence can be seen in his trilogy of fantasy novels called *The Singreale Chronicles* as well as the ever popular *Singer Trilogy*.

between hermeneutics and apologetics I needed something to wake my imagination to wonder. I had previously told myself that Bradbury was not for me, assuming that all his work would focus on Yorgs galactically skimming about in astroconvected starships. I was too far "in" ever to enjoy a writer so "far out." But after two semesters of trying to find joy in the Pentateuch, I needed to get as far from all things seminary as possible. So, nearly brain-dead from high infusions of Calvinism, I decided at last to risk Bradbury's Yorgs.

What a surprise! There were no Yorgs! His more gentle science fiction dealt only casually with the world of tomorrow and spent its energy analyzing and challenging the reader in the world at hand. I thus discovered Bradbury not on Mars but on Earth, my own address. Yet Bradbury's Earth was not the one I thought I knew. Nor was this science fiction writer at all like the one I had imagined.

Fahrenheit 451 was the first Bradbury novel I read. It tells of totalitarian censorship and of how bibliophiles fight to save Shakespeare, Milton, and the Bible, which, along with other great literary works, are perishing in state bonfires. *Fahrenheit 451* is the combustion temperature of paper, and, like burning glory, my own temperature rose enthusiastically as Bradbury penetrated into my theologically encrusted world. Hooked was I.

I immediately read *The Martian Chronicles*. Once again the ray guns, interplanetary wars, and glass-domed demons tracking Flash and Dale through the Asteroids of Amzar were absent; I found instead real people and circumstances which, while only mildly scientific, soared far above what I expected from "science fiction." To be sure, Bradbury is a prime mover in the science fiction genre, as many of his short stories and at least one of his novels suggest. But he offers so much more. An enthralling sense of cosmic mystery pervades his science fiction, suggesting that reality is always more than meets the eye. In this sense his works are "mystical." Bradbury seems to attest that all things of worth and meaning are "things of the spirit." He plunges us into the delightful world of a reality unbound by merely natural phenomena.

His web of "spiritual" intrigue pulled me forward from book to book. As a reader, I have always stalked the entire imagination of those writers I enjoy, to the point of reading all their works. Fortunately, I have always been able to find Bradbury's works (which remain almost entirely in print), and nearly always in paperback (which makes them cheap).

For me, sweltering under a terminal case of seminary burnout, Bradbury made our initial encounter sweet with ecstasies that only writers and readers locked in print can ever understand. Why has Bradbury contributed so much to my own way of seeing life? Perhaps because he satisfies my basic reasons for reading fiction. Those reasons are four.

I'm not sure all people read to celebrate art, but I do, and that's my first reason for reading. Maybe it is because I am a watercolorist that I see art, or the lack of it, everywhere I look. Light, form, color, perspective, image—these snag my errant eyes and bid them see what might otherwise elude their nervous flitting. Further, an artist in one field—if he or she has paid any price of discipline for art—cannot fail to respect the disciplined artist in any other field. So the cellist admires the painter; the dancer, the actor; the writer, the sculptor.

Bradbury once sat and listened to Bernard Berenson, the writer and sculptor, explain how Michelangelo had created David. The Renaissance master, said Berenson, had designed an eighteen-inch wax model of the projected sculpture, which he submerged in twenty inches of ink. Inch-markings on the towering column of marble corresponded to minute calibrations on the sides of the glass container. Each day Michelangelo drew a small amount of ink from the jar, exposing an eighth of an inch more of the scaled-down wax model. He then worked the marble column, duplicating the newly exposed section with his carvings on the Carrara stone. The Renaissance thrift of such a technique fascinated Bradbury.[2]

There are other parallels between various fields of art. All artists—painter, sculptor, and writer—must deal with two torments, if their work is to bear lasting value: the persecuted psyche is caught between the created world and the world where they pay rent. As a painter, I have often been caught between these worlds. When I spend myself on my artistic focus (for creativity is the most draining of pastimes), I despise the stress and wish I was doing something else. But when I do anything else, I long to be back at my art.

Storytellers experience a peculiar variation of this torment: the act of creating other worlds often moves them far away from the world at hand. Earth must be a mundane home for anyone whose imagination can dome Mars with glass, for instance. And Bradbury must surely speak for himself when his rocket man, who often finds himself homeless in every world, testifies: "Don't ever be a rocket man . . . because when you're out there you want to be here, and when you're here you want to be out there. . . . Don't let it get hold of you."[3]

Mars is an edgy place, to be sure, and a long way from Bradbury's California. But on Mars, Bradbury (and all the rest of us) do not have to deal with light bills and lawsuits. Art presents a way out, an escape from the boring world where the rent is due.

Some years ago I too created a planet, called Estermann, to serve as the milieu of three novels. As this "Mars" of my own came alive, I often caught myself despising the world I lived in. I would enter my study in Nebraska, but soon fly away with Raccomann Dakktare in the bright skies of Estermann. While writing *The Estermann Chronicles,* I often felt angry when the "earth-phone" in my study would ring and I would have to leave the wonderful world I was creating for the annoying one where I was a minister.

The writer begins by creating an artificial world, one which he controls completely. But the writer must live as both the hunter and the hunted. Once the story begins to take form, it—with life of its own—tracks the storyteller. The teller becomes the spoor of his own art. Many a midnight I have been driven to my typewriter by some demanding half-tale that wanted to finish itself whether or not my groggy mind was up to the job. Bradbury depicted such sufferings by making himself (and every storyteller) into a tangible metaphor he called "The Illustrated Man."[4]

Poor and to be pitied is Bradbury's illustrated man. His body was a mass of color, form, and lines.[5] Everywhere he looked was a story. More than tattoos, these colorful and ever-changing illustrations played freely on his skin.[6] He had but to look at his hand and see a short narrative.[7] To take off his shirt was to open the floodgates of untold tales that soon drenched his tortured mind. The illustrated man wept his pain: "I keep my collar buttoned. ... Everyone wants to see the pictures ... yet nobody wants to see them."[8]

My own storytelling has so often left me feeling like the illustrated man. I write stories to souls who may never want to read them—my elusive fans who live in silence—all the while trying to convince myself I really do have readers out there. My books sell, but I never see the buyers. And what of those reviewers who overlook my latest and most stunning work of genius? I would like to shed my stories and live straight, without my torment, but I cannot, alas. "I'd like to burn them off! I've tried sandpaper, acid, and a knife!" says the illustrated man.[9] Still, on and on the stories come and they must be written down! Is writing a gift? If so, is God to be blessed or cursed for such a gift?

Yet from such torment, we who tell stories find out who we are and why we are born. I keep reading Bradbury because for twenty years he has helped me understand this process. Bradbury quotes Gerard Manley Hopkins in citing his reason for being in this world: "What I do is me, for that I came." When people ask me where I get my imagination, I simply lament, "God, here and there, makes madness a calling."

※

A second reason we all read is to broaden our understanding. From several sources I have heard the tale, perhaps apocryphal, of the octogenarian who had just begun a detailed study of Plato. When a young man asked why a man so old should begin to study Plato, he replied, "Why, to improve my mind, of course." I am always looking for those writers who, like Bradbury, are mind expanders. There are many steps in this mind-expanding process.

Sometimes the mind broadens in a flash. Such a breakthrough to a new level of consciousness suddenly indicts older views of reality as inadequate. This kind of instant broadening amounts to a *conversion*. As an evangelical Christian, I have always viewed that word theologically; but Bradbury has helped me to see that any experiential impact that instantly causes us to see ourselves in a new way and open new worlds rather amounts to a conversion.[10]

The Dill Brothers Combined Traveling Shows brought their seedy traveling carnival to Waukegan, Illinois, several times in the late 1920s. Each time, the little Bradbury boy was there to watch the sideshow assistant throw the switch and proclaim, "Here go ten million volts of pure fire, ten million bolts of electricity into the flesh of Mr. Electrico!" At the surge of current, Mr. Electrico's hair flew, his eyes blazed, and a white haze swirled about his flesh. And then he would take his glowing sword and touch the shoulder of a mystified child—inevitably, young Bradbury. As a skittering current lit the boy's system, Mr. Electrico said simply, grandly, "Live forever!" It was heady stuff for a tinselman to bequeath to an imaginative child, especially since Mr. Electrico's gifts came the same year as his (Bradbury's) parents gave him a toy typewriter. Together, the two gifts were fodder for a fancy that would astound his times.

I know no "Mr. Electrico," but my first pastor was Sister Rose, who headed our small Pentecostal Assembly. My Christian conversion at age nine had changed my life. Sister Rose might just as easily have been "Sister Electrico." She spoke of hell and demons and high-flying archangels. She tracked the denizen through the Book of Jonah, and made us quake with her apocalyptic description of the "great whore on the great beast." Whores and beasts were both mysteries to me then, but I was "converted" to a world of picturesque thought. I wanted to know more. Because of Sister Electrico, my imagination grew, my world broadened (the Hebrew word *yasha,* translated as "salvation," means to create space). Conversion, as Bradbury attests, is glorious and expansive. To be converted even to Christ does not reveal everything religious at once, but it offers a generous first step into a larger, roomier world.[11]

Reading Bradbury exposes the reader to the possibility of sudden, mind-expanding experiences, but not only that. His works are also suffused with his wide learning from the classics, and that love of the classics gradually threaded its way into my own affections, partly because it was so much a part of his affection. Shakespeare surfaces in one of his titles, *Something Wicked This Way Comes,* a line from *Macbeth.* Byron's verse, "We'll go no more a-roving," is a haunting theme of the early voyages to Mars. I first discovered the verse of Sara Teasdale in *The Martian Chronicles.* The title of one of Bradbury's volumes of short stories is based on a Whitman line: *I Sing the Body Electric*. His love for the art of the Renaissance seems to affect his own visual style in much the same way that Hemingway's love of Impressionism colored the way he wrote. Bradbury enriches me by making his learned life part and parcel of my own.

Maybe it's because of his subject (space) or maybe because of his magnanimous spirit, but Bradbury seems to find boundless excitement in learning. He commented enthusiastically on the tenth anniversary of the moon landing, "We have insured our place in the universe. . . . We can move out to the planets . . . to Alpha Centauri . . . our race will go on forever." Bradbury (then fifty-nine years old) does not sound like a man ready to shutter his worldview. And Bradbury, while not often explicit about the content of his faith, professes a glorious, self-declaring confidence in God. I have scarcely heard Pentecostals be more rapturous than was Bradbury's exuberant declaration on that tenth anniversary of the Apollo landing:

> This is the most exciting time in the history of the world. . . . Landing on the moon was our greatest achievement. Now we're touching Mars and flying past Jupiter. . . . God is coming alive in this part of the universe! . . .
>
> We are gifted with miracles we forget to acknowledge or think about. . . . we are the only creatures . . . who have seen the stars and know what we're looking at. God has privileged us with the ability to represent Him in this part of the cosmos and to go out and change things—one hopes—for the better.
>
> Our descendants will circle Alpha Centauri or some other sun. And all the knowledge that we have developed in the past 15,000 to 20,000 years will go on with us. Shakespeare will survive and live with us in space. Christ will be there in space.[12]

My own concept of God can never remain static after coming into contact with the fictional output of a man driven by such near-spiritual forces, a writer with such a dynamic view of the God who leads man toward scientific maturity. Bradbury, at his best, is not only a prophet for a depressed people; he is a kind of deliverer, awakening our sensibilities.

A third major reason that I read is to escape the heaviness of the moment. With a writer like Bradbury I can, paradoxically, have my mind stretched and expanded even as my spirit grows tighter.

The past invites reflection; the future, speculation. But now is where we must live, and now is therefore the heavy time. All the tonnage of life presses down in present tense. Through the Christian disciplines (prayer, Bible reading, and meditation) I can wriggle out from beneath the awesome heaviness, and in my best sermons I enthusiastically claim to soar. But when I am honest, I confess that my heaviness knows one other great Sabbath: fiction. I lay aside my burdensome world and run off with Bradbury to see what is going on at this late hour on Mars or whatever world he beckons me to enter.

The truth is that most of us, as T.S. Eliot said, can only bear so much reality. If Bradbury accented the two words "science fiction," his accent would fall on the last word—for this reason I have found him a major prop in my worldview. We cannot live without some *mystery*. Bradbury doesn't answer every question he raises, because mystery saves us by its very unanswerableness. Although scientifically aware, Bradbury acknowledges that great meaning rarely issues from science alone. As Hamlet replied to Horatio on the walls of Elsinore, "There are more things in heaven and earth than are dreamed of in your philosophy."

In one Bradbury story, a rocket ship heads for Mars, filled with logical men on a mission to stamp out the last vestiges of fiction. On the red planet lives a colony of the damned—literary greats like Shakespeare and Dickens—who are making a last stand for mystery. Now the very last of their books are being burned—purged from the human conscience. (Most of their books had already suffered that fate, the same year that "Halloween was outlawed and Christmas was banned.")

In Bradbury's story, Edgar Allen Poe is the protagonist who advances the cause of mystery as the living heart of literature. As he sees fiction and imaginative worlds coming to an end, Poe wants the classic writers to move on from Mars and colonize a planet farther away from the destructive and scientific literalists. Poe laments the passing of imagination from the fiction-deadened world: "'What must it be on earth' wondered Poe, 'without Christmas? No hot chestnuts, no tree, no ornaments or drums or candles—nothing, nothing but the snow and wind and the lonely factual people.'"[13]

Bradbury warns us away from any science that leaves no room for imagination; I find a similar danger at work in some Christian circles. The gospel itself may be made harsh by precepts void of warm narrative. In spite of the fact that the Bible is filled with parables and stories, our zeal to evangelize and to encounter secular cultures with moral reform has shackled evangelicals to deadening presuppositions. These presuppositions do not kill because they are false (they are indeed true) but because they strip away mystery and process—the very ingredients of a good story. In their evangelistic intensity some Christians see fiction (classic and otherwise) as a waste of time in a lost society where so many are "perishing in hell."

For me, Bradbury has made a plea for balance that fits both secular science and a hyperearnest evangelicalism. His narratives call for an openness to the meaning hidden in the mysterious issues his stories address. Life can bear only so much reality; we need the mysteries to live. In every message that I preach, I call men, not to a scientifically reasonable faith, but to a faith which gains its power through stories— stories of God invading history through a virgin's womb and then shattering death (in defiance of more reasonable, and powerless, definitions of death).[14]

I yearn for Mars when life gets too heavy on earth. But Bradbury's Mars is not just a planet. Mars is anywhere the world unfolds greater meaning. The elusive Martians who stand at the center of *The Martian Chronicles* are a curative myth. In pursuing them, I am healed of the excessive heaviness of earth.

※

Finally, I read, and reread Bradbury, because I need to believe in a better world. Since we all must inherit the future, we need the future to be there, and to be a place of goodness and hope. Bradbury's stories offer that prospect of both goodness and hope.

Throughout, Bradbury's work expresses a hungering after morality. Goodness is a fearsome but all important business. Charles Holloway hears this account of it all in *Something Wicked This Way Comes:* "Sometimes the man who looks happiest in town . . . is the one carrying the biggest load of sin. There are smiles and there are smiles: learn to tell the dark variety from the light . . . and men do love sin well, how they love it, never doubt in all shapes, sizes, colors and smells. . . . For being good is a fearful occupation: men strain at it and sometimes break in two."[15]

But hope is the real stuff of Bradbury. A Christian positivism pervades his works and that quality, more than anything, marks his work as distinctively Christian in tone. In the glorious finale to *Something Wicked This Way Comes,* Jim Nightshade is brought back to life by a father and son dancing and singing "Camptown Races." Joy is the only cure for every monstrous evil work.

Hope may be Bradbury's greatest contribution to our age of despair. To my knowledge, no other contemporary writer sees the world so full of possibility. Bradbury's latest offering, *The Toynbee Convector,* is perhaps his most buoyant celebration of hope. Craig Bennett Stiles, 130 years of age, is the inventor of and sole traveler in the Toynbee Convector, a time machine he had last used in 1984. The year is now 2084, and the time traveler, who has lived in silence for one hundred years, at last agrees to make his exploits public. He will be interviewed at that precise moment in 2084 when his marvelous time machine from 1984 appears in the southern California sky: thus Stiles will be the only man from two eras to appear in the same place at the same time.

World excitement over this unique event runs high. The earth in 2084 is a mature and optimistic world, due in no small part to Stiles himself. It was Stiles who, a century earlier, on his journey to the future, brought to the world of 1984 this glorious and transforming news: The world will survive! He had seen that the Earth in the next century had made a glorious planet of itself. Thus Stiles's predictions about the future had, in a sense, helped create that future.

"We made it!" he said. "We did it! The future is ours. We rebuilt the cities, freshened the small towns, cleaned the lakes and rivers, washed the air, saved the dolphins, increased the whales, stopped the wars, tossed the solar stations across space to light the world, colonized the moon, moved on to Mars, then Alpha Centauri. We cured cancer and stopped death. We did it—Oh Lord, much thanks—we did it! Oh future's bright and beauteous spires arise!"[16]

But the world of 2084 waits in vain for Stiles's appearance from 1984. The earlier Stiles never shows. He is forced to confess that he has lied. The Toynbee Convector had in fact never flown, and the wonderful photos of 2084 (shown to the world of 1984) were contrived. The older world had been redeemed by a lie—Stiles's lie. Why had he lied?

Because I was born and raised in a time, in the sixties, seventies, and eighties, when people had stopped believing in themselves . . . reason . . . no longer gave itself reason to survive. . . . Everywhere was professional despair, intellectual ennui, political cynicism . . . incipient nihilism.

You name it, we had it. The economy was a snail. The world was a cesspool. . . . Melancholy was the attitude . . . bombarded by dark chaff and no bright seed, what sort of harvest was there for man in the latter part of the incredible 20th century?[17]

As a Messiah symbol, Stiles is ambiguous, for he has used a wondrous and magnificent lie to save. Still, the story is blatantly, overwhelmingly positive about the future. It offers hope. As a symbol of his confidence in the future of the earth, Bradbury dedicates this latest, joyous volume to his four granddaughters, who one day may live to discover the world of the Toynbee Convector.

John of Patmos (not totally unlike Bradbury) once rocketed forward in time to bring God's final joyous image to despairing Christians in the age of Nero. John saw a "Toynbee-ized" or rather "Bradbury-ized" setting of the New Jerusalem:

He who was seated on the throne said, "I am making everything new!" . . .
"Come, I will show you the bride, the wife of the Lamb." And he carried

me . . . to a mountain great and high, and showed me the Holy City, Jerusalem, coming down out of heaven from God. It shone with the glory of God. . . . laid out like a square. . . . 12,000 *stadia* in length. . . . made of jasper . . . of pure gold, as pure as glass. . . . The city does not need the sun . . . for the glory of God gives it light. . . . The nations will walk by its light, and the kings of the earth will bring their splendor into it. On no day will its gates ever be shut. . . . Now the dwelling of God is with men, and he will live with them. They will be his people. . . . He will wipe every tear from their eyes. There will be no more death or mourning or crying or pain, for the old order of things has passed away. . . . The river of the water of life, as clear as crystal, [is] flowing from the throne of God.

REVELATION 21:5–26; 21:3–4; 22:1

How wondrously parallel are these two pictures of human redemption, Bradbury's and John's. Vance Havner once quipped that all Christians should view history optimistically—we have, after all, read the last chapter.

Bradley directed his optimism toward his home country when in 1979 he pointed out

As Jean-Francois Revel has written, the only true and lasting revolutionary country in the world is America. We have the only revolution that works. . . . We've made it possible for people to reach the age of 80 and say. "What have I always wanted to be? I'll do it now." That is why I think America's future is exciting.

I'd like to come back every 50 years to check us out. I'm that certain about our future.[18]

Optimism is not only Bradbury's great gift to a despairing culture but his great gift to me personally. I was first awakened to the possibilities of God in my life in the rural, fiery Pentecostalism of Enid, Oklahoma. The only eschatology I ever heard was definitely "Henny Penny." Our utterly safe, red-shaled county needed something to fear, so we listened to the evangelists whose breath, hot as hell, billowed the sides of their gospel tents. Jesus was coming again. The sky really was falling.

In turn, we branded each in a succession of world leaders as the infamous Antichrist. This demiurge would put his charcoal "mark of the beast" on everybody's head in Garfield County (like the Catholics did on Ash Wednesday), and then the fire would fall. First Hitler was the Antichrist, said the roaring Pentecostal prophets. At Hitler's death the baton went to Stalin, at whose passing it fell to Khrushchev, at whose passing I can't recall to whom.

Ultimately Henry Kissinger inherited the Antichrist title, though now I can't remember why. About this time I gave up my Henny Penny theology. I couldn't visualize Henry Kissinger, a gentle and brilliant statesman, coming to Garfield County to label all non-Pentecostals as fuel for the fires of hell. I must confess I have since lost all interest in who the Antichrist may be. For Bradbury, sixteen years older than I, has fast-forwarded my confidence, and now I see so much farther than I used to. Age has a way of brightening our certainties, even while it shores up our honesty.

The Toynbee Convector got its name from Arnold Toynbee, who once said that those who do not run to seize the future are doomed to live in the past. Skeptics have long said the future is always like the past, once you get there. Not true! Not true! In the first place, we never "get to" the future—it beckons us, never to receive us. But it is always there and it is a place of hope! Such is the insight we need in order to get up in the morning. This insight, which I sucked from the very marrow of Bradbury's bones, is also the ultimate promise of Christ. Christ is alive—his Living Being is the transforming Easter news! But Jerusalem—made new—is descending: this living vision is the hope that guarantees our future.

GETTING STARTED WITH BRADBURY

A writer so immensely popular offers a cafeteria of options for beginning. But take note: Bradbury needs to be read, so don't allow yourself to be siphoned off into any of his many video movies or Bradbury Theater segments. *The Martian Chronicles* may be the easiest, most typically Bradburian beginning point. Then in order, I would recommend *Dandelion Wine,* or *Something Wicked This Way Comes.* These charming tales, seen through a child's eyes, are as enchanting in image as they are intriguing in plot. Finally, Bradbury's short stories (*I Sing the Body Electric!, R Is for Rocket,* and *The Toynbee Convector* are his best-known short-story collections) must be read, for this indeed is the genre which is "Bradbury." Also, it is both legitimate and delightful to enjoy Bradbury by listening to him read his own works (as in the popular audio tape, *The Toynbee Convector*).

21

ALICE MUNRO
A Quiet Grace
Jeanne Murray Walker

I
t was one of those clear, cool mornings early in September when sunlight falling through trees turns everything transcendent green. It might have been the morning of the world. I was just thirty, still exultant over the fact that I had passed my Ph.D. exams in literature. Days before I had convinced my husband that we should buy and lay down a shaggy grass-green carpet in the fourth bedroom of our brick townhouse. Here I planned to hole up for ten months and write a four-hundred-page dissertation on Edmund Spenser; and if things went my way, by summer I would be called *Doctor*. That title would give me the right to find the job of my heart's desire, teaching Spenser's *Faerie Queene* and the great Shakespeare plays to students in a university.

Jeanne Murray Walker is a poet and playwright. Her books of poetry include *Nailing Up the Home Sweet Home, Coming into History,* and *Gaining Time.* Her plays have been produced in Boston, Washington, Chicago, and London. She reads and gives workshops at writers' conferences and universities across the nation and is the recipient of many awards including a National Endowment for the Arts and a Pew Foundation Fellowship.

He left for work at 8:30 A.M., his black wingtips turning the corner, his feet patting the steps, the front door closing. A momentous quiet settled in the house. I sat down at my worktable and picked up a pencil and a legal pad (because this was eleven years before we had a computer in the house) and then in the nursery next door, the baby turned over. It was not the sound of her turning over in her sleep. She was awake. I knew that. I knew things about her even when I didn't want to. It was as if I were wired into her network. Like an Eskimo with dozens of words for *snow,* I could distinguish, even from another room, a dozen different ways she turned over. There was her startled bird-motion of fear at finding herself out of the womb and alone, for example. Then there was her leisurely, ruminative way of turning, as if she were about to discover a profound idea. And her swimming motion, her way of shifting for the sheer pleasure of exercise. Suddenly I heard her whimper. I could see her brilliant blue eyes. They would be turned toward the door where she expected me to be standing. I could feel her loneliness in my hands and arms.

It was not as if I didn't realize that I had a choice. I knew I could either go to her or stay and write the first sentence on the blank yellow legal pad. I stared at my hand holding the pencil. It looked like the claw of some creature I didn't recognize. I couldn't remember what I wanted to say about *The Faerie Queene.* It had been written a long time ago in a quaint language (Spenser wrote in Antique English on purpose) which could make me feel distant from it. I couldn't, honestly, think of anyone who would want to read what I was about to write, even my advisers at the university. I knew that getting down four hundred pages of serviceable prose was all that stood between me and a Ph.D. But considering there were no tenured women faculty in my department, I didn't entirely buy the fact that I, a woman, could be a Ph.D. anyway. As if it were a neighborhood where, I was coming to realize, we couldn't afford to live, I was starting to wonder if a doctorate might not be beyond me.

I went to pick up the kid. I took her to the park.

Around that time a neighbor told me that I should read Alice Munro. Of course, I, who had been madly spinning through Chaucer and Shakespeare and Thomas Carlyle for the last seven years and hanging out in the graduate seminar room with other driven graduate students, had never heard of Alice Munro. Or many other contemporary authors. I studied the English Renaissance, eighteenth century, and Victorian periods in part because I wasn't going to have anyone teaching me the culture of my own times. But we had just moved, and the woman who came over with cookies while I was unpacking dishes turned out to be an endless source of good titles and gentle, healing advice of every kind. Munro became a writer of great importance to me.

In those days, I was mad with the need to Do Something Important. Not that I was sure of what to do. It was the early seventies. The seams of the world had already split open. Many of us had protested about civil rights. Then came the assassinations. Between them, we strode with banners down the wide avenues of Chicago protesting the Vietnam War. We stopped traffic and made obscene gestures at the police. We huddled in rallies and gave press conferences about how we were going to dump Lyndon Johnson. And we won at least part of what we wanted. But underneath all the action, I felt a profound skepticism. A lot of our behavior felt shallow to me. Our moralisms against the older generation often sounded like self-righteous cant. Calamity threw its shadows all around us and it was not easy to figure out what to do. My confusion made me feel that it was all the more urgent to do something fast.

The Baptist church where I was reared (all day Sunday and Wednesday night for prayer meeting as well as other days for special services) had pounded into me the fleeting nature of time. *Work for the night is coming,* thrummed in my brain no matter what I was doing, like a heavy beat under a melody. *Work for the night is coming!*

The brevity and seriousness of life was underscored by the death of my father when I was thirteen. He had suffered for years with a serious heart problem. Specialists had given him the option: he might live for as long as three years or he could elect to have surgery to correct the problem, but he had a fifty-percent chance of dying on the table.

The pressure for a choice, the high stakes, the bad odds, and above all, my inability to do anything to fix it, made me wild. He decided not to have surgery. He wanted to be with us kids as long as he could. He grew sicker. Both my mother and father acted with great courage. They set about getting my mother ready to support the family.

I learned the value of action. I learned that women had better find some way of supporting themselves and their children. Since I had already experienced success as a writer, I skewed off to graduate school to earn a Ph.D. in English. I had felt the power of words and books. I believed they could change the world.

Around the time I began writing my dissertation, I was just beginning to realize that I would be peeling a lot of potatoes for the rest of my days. I didn't understand this until so late because, since emerging into adulthood, I had been living the sheltered life of a student. Ideas reign supreme in universities and the cafeteria makes the meals.

By contrast, I was drowning in details. Everything we owned, every single spoon and paper clip, had just passed through my hands twice—I had packed and unpacked it to move. And then there was the dailiness of taking care of another human being, the diapers, the stroller, the playpen, the bottles, the special implements for washing the bottles, the lamby she couldn't do without, and on and on. I was beginning to realize that, by marrying and becoming a mother, I had emerged as the Keeper of Things. I was overwhelmed by all the stuff and bereft of words to explain its meaning. Uneventful as my life must have seemed to others, every day I awoke to a crisis. I didn't complain much; I felt it would have been childish to grouse about details. After all, someone has to wash the dishes (although it certainly seemed odd that I was washing dishes every time I turned around). I was grimly determined to become efficient, to learn how to get the details over with quickly and then move on to Something Important.

The first time I opened a book of Munro's stories, I was assaulted by the difference between her and the writers I had been studying in graduate school. In Munro's fiction I found a vast wealth of smells and sights and sounds I knew. The stories were not only set in familiar places like skating rinks and school book rooms, but they were filled with the smell of disinfectant, the taste of root beer, the touch of a slippery fish sliding out of the boat and splashing into the water. It dawned on me that a world so robust with particulars must have been called into place by meticulous attention and care. I remembered Richard Wilbur's poem, "Love calls us to the things of this world."

Indeed, Munro's stories insisted on the importance of details. Within the borders of her fiction, a tea strainer meant something. I soon understood that she saw significance, not only in a rose (which we are supposed to know is a symbol of Love or something like that) but in everything. It's not that she assigns objects symbolic meanings. It's more that in her fiction nothing is accidental. It is a question of having her eye upon the sparrow.

Here she is, describing a woman after a long car trip in the story, *Miles City, Montana:*

> I was thirsty, and got out of the car to look for a concession stand, or perhaps a soft-drink machine, somewhere in the park. I was wearing shorts, and the backs of my legs were slick with sweat. I saw a drinking fountain at the other side of the park and was walking toward it in a roundabout way, keeping to the shade of the trees. No place became real until you got out of the car. Dazed with the heat, with the sun on the blistered houses, the pavement, the burned grass, I walked slowly. I paid attention to a squashed leaf, ground a Popsicle stick under the heel of my sandal, squinted at a trash can strapped to a tree. This is the way you look at the poorest details of the world resurfaced, after you've been driving for a long time—you feel their singleness and precise location and the forlorn coincidence of your being there to see them.[1]

Sitting here as I write this now, twenty-five years later, it is hard to describe the joy I felt when I first read passages like this. Someone had already hacked a path through my wilderness. As Robert Browning pointed out, we frequently don't see in life what we haven't seen first in art. And much of the literature I had read in graduate school (though not all) had performed the service of showing me my own life. But no writer I knew had catalogued this particular remote terrain. Without Munro's stories, I believe I would have endured those days silently, rather like an animal, and then forgotten them, since I had no words to catalogue or remember them by. In short, her stories showed me the acts of my own strange and solitary life in a way that gave those acts meaning.

I began to think of Munro's stories as a means of grace.

Every day I dragged myself like a mule to the legal pad in the room with the green rug. Frankly, I got very little pleasure out of it. I was becoming less sure that I could finish. No one from my class had yet. In fact, a number had been flunked out and some had quit. But I gritted my teeth and hunkered down to work because I couldn't think of any other way into a world of power and ideas outside that study.

My even-tempered child grew and developed with the miraculous speed of all normal children. Soon she was crawling beside me on the floor and playing with her toys. Because she watched me every day and mimicked what she saw, she could hold a pencil properly by the age of nine months. By then she was talking, too.

My husband and I began to take her with us wherever we went. In restaurants, after she was done eating we could let her down from her high chair and she would toddle from table to table, enchanting people. We had her pegged as a diplomat. We were scandalously proud of her. From time to time I would look at her and think with astonishment that if I ever got done with the book, this child would have a doctor for a mother. What a strange household for her to grow up in! That's how I found it easiest to imagine my own improbable future, through the prism of my child, who seemed contented to be used in that way. She was already a little character. Already we could predict what she would be like: talkative, straightforward, sensible, in short, ready to do anything to accommodate our plans.

At night, after I tucked my child in bed, I read Alice Munro's stories compulsively. They were about people like me. Munro passes over people who are already in the club. She doesn't seem interested in big money—though she's fascinated by what money does to those who don't have it. She doesn't give a hoot about people with power. They appear sometimes, but only as giant lifeless figures of the backdrop on a stage where the focus is on what the little people in the story will do next. Munro writes about an old man who is in despair over the fact that he will never see his brother again, a high school music teacher pinned in place by gossip, neighbors in a housing tract who are dissecting one another with knives of jealousy. They're people of straitened means from small Canadian towns, people who are in some kind of minor trouble.

At some point along the line, I realized that Alice Munro thinks incarnationally. In the body. That's what Jesus did. He lived a daily life. Like a jeweler focusing her light on the fault in a stone, she searched out minute, commonplace, and apparently unremarkable relationships between those people. In the best sense it was like gossip. It supplied wonderful companionship.

In the story, "Jesse and Maribeth," for example, I found myself reading about the love relationship between two preadolescent girls. I don't mean anything sexual, which is what we tend to reserve the word "love" for. I'm talking about that sweet, intense, life-changing attraction between girls that makes them say they're "best friends." This experience had been crucial to me, too, at one time, but I had never read about it in fiction.

And I think I've read very little about it since, though I know more contemporary fiction now than I did then. I suppose the idea of "best friends" has been dismissed by most writers as too small. Or maybe it doesn't even rise to consciousness; it's not in the running when the subjects are picked. But surely it is significant. Like an early turn in a long journey, a relationship like that can change where a person comes out in the end.

The story, *Jesse and Maribeth,* begins this way:

> In high school, I had a tender, loyal, boring friendship with a girl named MaryBeth Crocker. I gave myself up to it, as I did to the warm, shallow, rather murky waters of the Maitland River in summer, when I lay on my back, and just fluttered my hands and feet, and was carried downstream.
> This began one day in Music period, when there were not enough songbooks to go around and we were told to double up—boys with boys, of course, and girls with girls. . . .[2]

And Munro is off and running, describing the smoldering, edgy competition and condescension between Jesse and Maribeth which erupts in name-calling and then self-sacrifice. I loved it. Stories like this one could cast light backwards through years of my life and make me see things I had never before understood. That's part of why they seemed to me bearers of grace. And there was another thing. Reading them didn't

merely assuage my impatience at not being out in the world, doing something—it also made me consider (and sometimes appreciate) the jewel-like value of the small life I was leading.

My child was sitting on the same green carpet every day, getting sick of watching me draw tiny marks on a yellow pad. But until I got a job, I knew we would have no money for day care. And I couldn't find a job until I had a Ph.D. We were trapped in what Joseph Heller had recently nicknamed a "catch-22." With frenzy that made me shut out almost everything else, I plowed forward to bring the dissertation to an end before I buckled under the financial pressure and went out to find some other work.

I would sit on the floor alternating between writing about Spenser and showing my daughter how to stack her fat, bright-colored doughnuts on their Playskool spike. While she tried it, I would jot a sentence. We developed ritualized conversations about characters in her books or on Sesame Street. I could actually talk to her while taking notes on the *Faerie Queene*. Sometimes I was frantic, but I tried not to show it.

✦

I have said that Alice Munro's brash, realistic stories flooded a rather bleak period of my life with grace. Indeed, I have no idea what Munro's politics or religious confession would be if it were possible to get her to talk about those things. In fact, much later I tried to recruit her to give a reading at the university where I teach. She turned us down politely. She wrote that she doesn't leave her hometown often. She seems not to talk much about her work, either. In the current literary world of raucous press agents and brokered deals, she is unusually reticent.

I'd better confess right now that there is never any overt moralism in Munro's writing. In fact, there is very little explanation at all about the meaning of her characters' actions. Munro doesn't use theological language or make biblical allusions. Indeed, I suspect some readers may be surprised to find Alice Munro showing up in a book of essays about spiritual sources and vision. She can sound very snippy about the church and preachers and all the paraphernalia of religion. But that's part of why I like her. Munro writes about the same eternal truth Jesus spoke of, and, like Jesus, she subverts the religious establishment.

Don't be fooled. Her stories are about grace and forgiveness. Her characters might drink too much or have affairs, or hate organized religion, but when all is said and done, they fall into one of two categories. Either they can forgive and love others or they can't. If they can, they can be reached. They can experience grace. If they can't, they are lost.

In "Accident," for example, the music teacher, Frances, meets Ted, the history teacher, whenever she can for breathless sex in the empty church. Frances feels contempt for the women who sing in her choir. They've set their sights pretty low, she thinks; they're perfectly satisfied with Jesus. "Smell of corsets, sickening revelations. Sacrificial looks they would get in the choir. It was all a dreary sort of sex. *He walks with me and he talks with me and he tells me I am his own.*"[3] For most of the women in town, who are not as audacious or chic as she is, she feels contempt. When Ted's son is struck by a car and lies in the hospital within hours of death, he talks to Frances about whether they can make a bargain with God. If he can bring himself to give up Frances, Ted postulates, perhaps God will keep his son from dying. But he doubts it. In fact, how could he? There is no god. Ted is an atheist of a particularly defiant, rigid, angry kind. Later, Frances's friend, Adelaide, suggests again that Ted's son died because "God was paying him back" for the two of them having an affair. They have defined God, not as someone who showers all things with life, but as a sort of meter maid who gives tickets for bad deeds.

By the end of the story, after marrying Ted and living for many years with him, the sexual connection for which Frances gave up everything has come to ashes. "'What difference,' thinks Frances." And she realizes that though "she's had her love, her scandal, her man, her children, . . . inside she's ticking away, all by herself, the same Frances who was there before any of it."[4] She imagines herself slipping into a hideously predictable old age. It isn't her affair that damns her, it's her inability to experience grace. She can't accept God's grace because of the petty way she's defined him. And she won't accept grace from anyone else; she's never seen anyone else's point of view. She can't learn and change. She feels no joy.

The truth of the matter is that as I read this story, I fumed with Frances over the wimpy women in town. I adored her verve. I sympathized with her boredom. The end came as a shock to me. It took a while before I realized how accurate it is. Without love and forgiveness we are without grace. And without grace we're trapped in ourselves forever. The awful tyranny of the self! What used to be called Pride. What medieval theologians claimed was the be-all and end-all of evil. That's the only thing Munro finds damning. Sins of the flesh are forgivable. They're external. They graze the surface. But pride goes deep and blocks every chance for joy or insight.

By contrast, in the story "Labor Day Dinner," Roberta and George, who are lovers caught in a seemingly endless grudge, manage, by the end, to spring free. All evening they tear at one another with mean, petty insults. They think about one another in cold, strategic ways. At one point, Roberta feels the awful "lightness, the freedom, the great tactical advantage of being the one to whom the wrong has been done, the bleak challenge offered, the unforgivable thing said."[5] But after all the small recriminations of the evening, as they are driving home, George offers an apology.

"A gibbous moon."
It was Roberta who told George what a gibbous moon was, and so his saying this is always an offering. It is an offering now, as they drive between the black cornfields.
"So there is."

She accepts his offering that simply. Minutes later grace comes to this couple in the form of a black car that flashes before them, swimming up from the cornfields with no headlights, traveling at between eighty and ninety miles an hour. It crosses the road in front of them too fast for George to see it or hit the brakes. Yet by a miracle they emerge unscathed. Munro writes, "What they feel is not terror or thanksgiving, not yet. What they feel is strangeness. They feel as strange, as flattened out and borne aloft, as unconnected with previous and future events as the ghost car was."[6] It is the strangeness of grace.

✖

I have come to believe that the way Munro frames the neglected and forgotten is not an accident of where she was born or a matter of her casual preference. Like all good writers, she moves to where the energy is. In the crosshairs of a story, she locates a person who can change. The character can change because she has suffered and as a result, has opened her heart. Aware of her need for grace, she has chosen to be its recipient. That is why troubled and minor people are preferable as subjects, because they don't have the finances or the power to keep themselves safe. They are vulnerable. They live under awful pressures.

I began to detect an irony here. It is the irony Erasmus pointed out in his brilliant *In Praise of Folly,* which I had studied in graduate school. I began to see that if I wanted to Do Something Important, I'd better watch out. Important people, because of their money and power, don't get into the kingdom of heaven. It's easier for a camel to go through the eye of a needle. It was because of Munro's fiction that, after knowing it all my life, I finally understood this and took it to heart. It's not that one shouldn't Do Something Important, but in a major sense, one has to be a fool. One has to peel potatoes and take care of children. One has to get *joy* out of those things. One has to enter this kind of detailed life of service in a spirit of love and forgiveness. This is a great paradox. I saw it as a threat to my future plans. It threatened everything I was working for.

271

The parable of the prodigal son really drills the paradox home. The dutiful older child, who has spent his years as a partner with his father in the family business, can't believe his eyes. Out in the courtyard his father is throwing a party for his younger brother, the kid who has blown his inheritance. He is the guest of honor. The older son no doubt knows full well his kid brother came back because he likely ran out of food—he had no real choice. The savage injustice of his father throwing a party for this irresponsible son! The older brother pitches a fit.

Maybe that's petty. Or evil. But I don't think that was Jesus' point. Surely the point is that the older brother is only worth writing about once he's been catapulted out of his dutiful rut. Once he feels hurt and abandoned, he has some prayer of getting insight. That's when something is going to change. That is when grace becomes a possibility.

I plowed on, come hell or high water, with my dissertation that spring.

One Monday morning in March when I opened the door to her room, my daughter, who was by now a toddler, hung back. I told her I would take her out for a walk soon. We went into my study and sat down on the floor. All night I had been feverishly working out an idea for the last chapter of my dissertation. She waited courteously for a few minutes as I scribbled, then tugged on my jeans to go. I turned to her with what must have been a vacant stare. She tugged again. "Okay," I said, but I didn't get up. A thought was forming and I was wooing it, hoping it would distill itself into an English sentence. She must have recognized the look in my eyes. I had done this before. In fact, I was capable of wooing an English sentence for hours.

With volcanic force she erupted, an eruption that seemed more terrible because she had always been so even tempered. She deliberately turned her back to me and braced her chubby hands against the wall and twitched up her face and screamed.

I leapt up. It was like a natural catastrophe. She wouldn't stop crying. I felt her for fever. I changed her clothes, which I thought might be itchy or too tight. She screamed with incredible fury. I think it was the first time it really dawned on me—as I have had to realize over and over again—that she wasn't an extension of me.

I understood. I had made impossible demands on her. I felt prostrate with terror, lest by these demands I had already destroyed her. God had trusted me with a child and after only a year, look what I had done! I had locked her in a dungeon with a cell mate—me, who was, most of the time, abstracted and silent. I was aware, even then, that I was slightly hysterical in thinking this way. But there you are. It's a thought I've had more than once since—that one of my children might not survive some ghastly circumstance, often caused by some adult, frequently by one of us parents.

There is something funny about this scene and my guilt, now that I know from experience how children bounce back, how they tend to take whatever is given to them and make the best of it. I think now that the health of young things is a kind of mercy. But it shouldn't be presumed upon. And that day I felt childlike, gauche, awful remorse.

I apologized and took her out. The sky was one foaming broth of clouds when we started walking toward the park. Before we arrived back home, the sun had come out, and I felt dazzled by a quiet grace. The walk had given me some perspective. Miraculously, it was what I needed. My child was happy and I was able to write. In less than a month I finished the dissertation.

Carrying on any kind of long, close human relationship is like housework. It requires a lot of finely calibrated small moves. The ones between a child and her mother are a good example. To get one child to the age of eighteen requires six thousand, five hundred seventy-some days filled with diapers and carpooling, hurts, and repercussions, grudges, strategizing on both sides, frustration, scolding, rebellion, and forgiveness. And also joy and grace.

When my child was a year old, I hadn't yet read Munro's story, "Miles City, Montana"; it hadn't been published. But I felt a pang of familiarity when, later, I read these words:

So we went on, with the two in the back seat trusting us, because of no choice, and we ourselves trusting to be forgiven, in time, for everything that had first to be seen and condemned by those children: whatever was flippant, arbitrary, careless, callous—all our natural, and particular, mistakes.[7]

GETTING STARTED WITH MUNRO

Because Munro is still writing fiction, it is possible to read her stories as they are published. They come out in periodicals such as *The New Yorker*, *Grand Street*, and *The Paris Review*. There is something heady about reading an author's work right after it's been written, but maybe, because Munro's current stories can be rather difficult, it's best not to start there. To get a taste of Munro at a simpler stage, I'd pick up her middle books first—either *The Moons of Jupiter* or *The Progress of Love*. Then I'd move backward to her earlier collections, *Dance of the Happy Shades, Something I've Been Meaning to Tell You*, and *The Beggar Maid*, all available in Penguin paperbacks. Finally on to *Open Secrets* and then to the new work.

NOTES

Introduction

1. Annie Dillard, *Encounters with Chi - nese Writers* (Hanover, N.H.: University Press of New England, 1985), quoted in *Harvard Magazine,* July/August 1983, 44.

2. John Updike, *Bech at Bay* (New York: Random House, 1998), quoted in Walter Kirn, "Updike at Ease," *New York,* 19 October 1998.

3. Alexander Solzhenitsyn, *The Gulag Archipelago,* vol. 2 (New York: Harper and Row, 1975), 615.

4. Frederick Buechner, speech, Wheaton College, Wheaton, Ill. (n.d.).

5. J. R. R. Tolkien, *The Tolkien Reader* (New York: Ballantine, 1996), 68–69.

6. James E. Flecker, "Biographical Sketches," *Modern British Poetry,* ed. Louis Untermeyer (New York: Harcourt, Brace & Howe, 1920).

7. D. M. Thomas, *Biography of Solzhen - itsyn* (New York: St. Martin's, 1999).

Chapter 1: The Devotional Masters

1. Dietrich Bonhoeffer, *The Cost of Dis - cipleship* (New York: Macmillan, 1963), 99.

2. Ibid., 47.

3. Ibid.

4. Dietrich Bonhoeffer, *Life Together* (New York: Harper & Row, 1976), 99.

5. Dietrich Bonhoeffer, *Letters and Papers from Prison* (London: SCM Press, 1953), 14.

6. Ibid., 45–46.

7. *The Confessions of Saint Augustine,* trans. E. M. Blaiklock (Nashville: Thomas Nelson, 1983), 15.

8. *The Confessions of Saint Augustine,* trans. Rex Warner (New York: New American Library, 1963), 183.

9. Ibid., 41.

10. Ibid., 51.

11. Julian of Norwich, *Enfolded in Love* (New York: Seabury, 1980), 1.

12. Ibid.

13. Ibid., 6.

14. Ibid.

15. Julian of Norwich, *Showings,* trans. Edmund Colledge and James Walsh, *The Classics of Western Spirituality Series* (New York: Paulist, 1978), 199.

16. Julian of Norwich, *Enfolded,* 33.

17. Paul Sabatier, *The Little Flowers of Saint Francis: The Acts of Saint Francis and His Companions* (Ann Arbor, Mich.: Servant, 1985).

18. Ibid.

19. Brother Ugolino di Monte Santa Maria, *The Little Flowers of St. Francis* (New York: Doubleday/Image, 1958), 67–68.

20. Ibid., 79–83.

Notes

21. Blaise Pascal, *The Mind on Fire:An Anthology of the Writings of Blaise Pascal* (Portland, Ore.: Multnomah, 1989), 15.

22. *The Journal of John Woolman and a Plea for the Poor* (Secaucus, N.J.: Citadel, 1972), 22.

23. Ibid., 8.
24. Ibid., 41.
25. Ibid.
26. Ibid., 230.

27. Jean-Pierre de Caussade, *The Sacra-ment of the Present Moment* (San Francisco: Harper & Row, 1982), 54.

28. Ibid., xix.
29. Ibid., 79.
30. Ibid., 59.
31. Ibid., 100.
32. Ibid., 3, 52.

33. George Fox, "Exhortation to Friends in the Ministry," *The Journal of George Fox,* ed. John L. Nickalls (Richmond, Ind.: Friends United, 1952), 263.

Chapter 2: Søren Kierkegaard

1. Søren Kierkegaard, *The Journals of Kierkegaard,* trans. Alexander Dru (New York: Harper and Row, 1959), 53.

2. Ibid., 58.
3. Ibid., 244–45.

4. Søren Kierkegaard, *The Point of View of My Work As an Author*, trans. Arthur Lowrie (New York: Harper & Row, 1962), 89.

5. Ibid., 87–88.
6. Ibid., 88.

7. Søren Kierkegaard, *Fear and Trem-bling and the Sickness unto Death*, trans. Walter Lowrie (Princeton: Princeton University Press, 1954), 44.

8. Ibid., 48.
9. Ibid., 45–46.
10. Ibid., 46.
11. Ibid., 51.

Chapter 3: Thomas Merton

1. Thomas Merton, *The Seven Storey Mountain* (New York: Harcourt Brace, 1948), 412.

2. Charles Williams, *The Figure of Be-atrice* (New York: Octagon Books, 1972), 128–29.

3. Merton, *Seven Storey Mountain,* 410.

4. Ibid., 400.
5. Thomas Merton, *No Man Is an Island.*
6. Edward Rice, *The Man in the Sycamore Tree: An Entertainment* (New York: Doubleday, 1971), 25.

7. Thomas Merton, *The Secular Journal of Thomas Merton* (New York: Dell, 1960), 222.

8. Thomas Merton, *The Sign of Jonas* (New York: Harcourt Brace, 1953), 97–98.
9. Ibid., 228.

10. Thomas Merton, *Conjectures of a Guilty Bystander* (New York: Image, 1968), 208.

Chapter 4: Henri Nouwen

1. Henri Nouwen, *The Genesee Diary: Report from a Trappist Monastery* (Garden City, N.Y.: Image, 1981), 36.

2. Ibid., 56–57.
3. Ibid., 57.
4. Ibid., 56.

5. Henri Nouwen, *In the Name of Jesus: Reflections on Christian Leadership* (New York: Crossroad, 1989), 45.

6. Henri Nouwen, "Reflections on Theological Education," *Seeds of Hope: A Henri Nouwen Reader* (New York: Bantam, 1989), 28.

7. Nouwen, *In the Name of Jesus*, 38–39.
8. Nouwen, *The Genesee Diary,* 45.
9. Ibid., 9.
10. Nouwen, *In the Name of Jesus,* 58.

11. Eugene Peterson, *The Message* (Colorado Springs: NavPress, 1995).

12. Richard Wilbur, "Two Voices in a Meadow," *New and Collected Poems* (San Diego: Harcourt Brace, 1988).

13. Nouwen, *The Genesee Diary,* 76.
14. Nouwen, *In the Name of Jesus,* 44.
15. Ibid., 58–59.
16. Ibid., 61–62.

Chapter 5: Paul Tournier

1. Paul Tournier, *The Meaning of Per-sons* (San Francisco: Harper & Row, 1957), 198ff.

2. Paul Tournier, *A Place for You* (New York: Harper & Row, 1968), 162–63.

3. Tournier, *The Meaning of Persons,* 159ff.

Chapter 6: Musings

1. "Canterbury Tales," *Chaucer's Poetry: An Anthology for the Modern Reader*, ed. E. T. Donaldson, 2d ed. (New York: John Wiley & Sons, 1975), lines 1925–26.
2. Julian of Norwich, *A Book of Showings*, ed. Edmund Colledge and James Walsh (Toronto: Pontifical Institute of Mediaeval Studies, 1978).
3. Andrew Marvell, "To His Coy Mistress."
4. "Canterbury Tales."
5. William Butler Yeats, "Bald Heads," lines 2–5.
6. Personal Conversation with W. H. Auden, Dartmouth College, 1969.
7. *Faerie Queen* 1.10.600–601.
8. William Wordsworth, "Elegiac Stanzas," lines 15–16.
9. Wordsworth, "Ode: Intimations of Immortality," lines 56–57.
10. Henry Vaughan, "The Night: John 3.2," lines 49–54.
11. Andrew Marvell, "The Garden," lines 45–48.
12. John Keats, "Ode to a Nightingale," lines 65–67.
13. Ibid., lines 69–70.
14. *Paradise Lost* 9.354.
15. Gerard Manley Hopkins, "God's Grandeur," lines 1–2.
16. Gerard Manley Hopkins, "The Golden Echo," line 35.
17. Gerard Manley Hopkins, "Pied Beauty," lines 3–4, 8–11.
18. T. S. Eliot, *The Four Quartets*, "East Coker," canto 4, lines 1–4.
19. T. S. Eliot, *The Four Quartets*, "Little Gidding," canto 5, lines 27–46.

Chapter 7: John Milton

1. John Milton, Sonnet 19, lines 1–2.
2. *Paradise Lost* 1.254–55.
3. *Paradise Lost* 5.266–72, 275–85.
4. "Lycidas," lines 70–72.
5. John Milton, Sonnet 7, lines 1–4.
6. Ibid., lines 9–14.
7. John Milton, Sonnet 19.
8. John Milton, *Areopagitica*.
9. Ibid.
10. Ibid.

11. William Wordsworth, "London, 1802," line 1.
12. Ibid., lines 6–7.
13. Ibid., lines 9–14.

Chapter 8: William Shakespeare

1. *The Merchant of Venice* 5.1.54–59.
2. *As You Like It* 2.7.139–42.
3. *A Midsummer Night's Dream* 2.1.175.
4. *Henry V* 1.1.175.
5. *Macbeth* 2.3.18–9.
6. C. S. Lewis, "Hamlet: The Prince of the Poem?" *Selected Literary Essays* (London: Cambridge University Press, 1969), 104.
7. *Love's Labour's Lost* 5.2.578–80.
8. Caroline F. E. Spurgeon, *Shakespeare's Imagery and What It Tells Us* (Cambridge: The University Press, 1958), 202–3.
9. Ibid., 204.
10. *The Merchant of Venice* 4.2.182–84.
11. *King Lear* 1.4.287–88.
12. Jean Daniélou, *Le saints "paiens" de l'Ancien Testament* (Paris: Editions du Seuil, 1956).

Chapter 9: John Donne

1. John Donne, "Expostulation IV," *Devotions upon Emergent Occasions* (Ann Arbor: University of Michigan Press, 1959), 25.
2. Personal conversation with Dr. Paul Brand, 12 March 1980.
3. John Donne, "Expostulation II," *Devotions upon Emergent Occasions* (Ann Arbor: University of Michigan Press, 1959), 15.
4. John Donne, "Expostulation VI," *Devotions upon Emergent Occasions* (Ann Arbor: University of Michigan Press, 1959), 38.
5. Ibid., 41.
6. Ibid., 40.
7. C. S. Lewis, *The Problem of Pain* (New York: Macmillan, 1962), 93.
8. John Donne, "Expostulation XXI," *Devotions upon Emergent Occasions* (Ann Arbor: University of Michigan Press, 1959), 141.
9. Izaak Walton, "The Life of Dr. John Donne," introduction to *Devotions upon Emergent Occasions* (Ann Arbor: University of Michigan Press, 1959), xxii.

10. John Donne, "Expostulation XVIII," *Devotions upon Emergent Occasions* (Ann Arbor: University of Michigan Press, 1959), 118.

11. Walton, xlii.

12. Walton, xliii–xliv.

13. Sermon preached at St. Paul's Cross, 22 November 1629, <http://user.fundy.net/msgr/john_donne_sermon_21b.htm>.

Chapter 10: Hans Christian Andersen

1. Bruno Bettelheim, *The Uses of Enchantment* (New York: Alfred A. Knopf, 1976).

2. Ibid., 10.

3. Ibid., 8–10.

Chapter 11: George MacDonald

1. C. S. Lewis, preface to *George Mac-Donald: An Anthology* (New York: Macmillan, 1978), xxxi.

2. George MacDonald, *The Princess and Curdie*, chap. 8, <http://www.pagebypagebooks.com/George_MacDonald/The_Princess_and_Curdie/Curdies_Mission_pl.html> (February 2002).

3. George MacDonald, *Sir Gibbie* (London: J. M. Dent, 1914), 152.

4. George MacDonald, *At the Back of the North Wind*, <http://people.redhat.com/johnsonm/northwind/northwind.html> (February 2002).

5. George MacDonald, *Weighed and Wanting* (London: Sampson Low, Marston, Searle & Riverton, 1882).

6. George MacDonald, *Robert Falconer,* chap. 12, <http://www.ccel.org/m/macdonald/rfalconer/htm/ii.xii.htm> (February 2002).

7. George MacDonald, "The Consuming Fire," *Unspoken Sermons,* Series 1, <http://www.ccel.org/m/macdonald/unspoken1/htm/iii.htm#iii> (May 2002).

8. Ibid.

9. George MacDonald, *The Princess and the Goblin,* <http://www.pagebypagebooks.com/George_MacDonald/The_Princess_and_the_Goblin/The_Old_Ladys_Bedroom_p4.html> (February 2002).

10. Lucy Maud Montgomery, *Emily of New Moon* (New York: Yearling Books, 1999).

11. George MacDonald, "August 1855," *An Expression of Character: The Letters of George MacDonald*, ed. Glenn Edward Sadler (Grand Rapids: Eerdmans, 1994).

12. George MacDonald, *A Book of Strife in the Form of a Diary of Old Soul,* January 15 (London, 1880), <http://www.bookrags.com/books/doaos/PART3.htm> (May 2002).

13. George MacDonald, "The Consuming Fire," *Unspoken Sermons,* Series 1, <http://www.ccel.org/m/macdonald/unspoken1/htm/iii.htm#iii> (May 2002).

14. MacDonald, *At the Back of the North Wind,* <http://people.redhat.com/johnsonm/northwind/northwind.html> (February 2002).

15. George MacDonald, "The Cause of Spiritual Stupidity," *Unspoken Sermons,* Series 2, <http://www.ccel.org/m/macdonald/unspoken2/htm/iv.htm#iv> (May 2002).

16. George MacDonald, quoted in Greville MacDonald, *George MacDonald and His Wife* (n.p.: Johannesen, 1989), 373.

Chapter 12: J. R. R. Tolkien

1. Humphrey Carpenter, *The Letters of J. R. R. Tolkien* (New York: Houghton Mifflin, 1981).

2. J. R. R. Tolkien, "On Fairy Stories," *Essays Presented to Charles Williams,* ed. C. S. Lewis (Grand Rapids: Eerdmans, 1966), 75–76.

3. C. S. Lewis, "On Three Ways of Writing for Children," *Of Other Worlds* (London: Geoffrey Bless, 1966), 27.

4. Carpenter, *Letters,* 135–36.

Chapter 13: Fyodor Dostoevsky

1. Fyodor Dostoevsky, *The Idiot* (Baltimore: Penguin, 1955), 575.

2. Fyodor Dostoevsky, quoted in Joseph Frank, *Dostoevsky: The Years of Ordeal, 1850–59* (Princeton: Princeton University Press, 1986), 73.

3. Dostoevsky, *The Idiot,* 595.

4. Fyodor Dostoevsky, quoted in Nicholas Berdyaev, *Dostoevsky* (New York: Living Age, 1957), 53.

5. Fyodor Dostoevsky, *Letters from the Underworld* (New York: E. Dutton, 1957), 36.

6. Fyodor Dostoevsky, quoted in Nicholas Berdyaev, *Dostoevsky* (New York: Living Age, 1957), 53.

7. Ibid., 54.

8. Ernest Becker, *The Denial of Death* (New York: Free, 1973), 241.

9. Ibid., 244.

10. Dostoevsky, *The Idiot,* 500.

11. Karl Barth, *The Epistle to the Romans* (London: Oxford University Press, 1960), 122.

12. *Spiritual Quests,* ed. William Zinsser (Boston: Houghton Mifflin, 1988), 122.

13. Fyodor Dostoevsky, *The Brothers Karamazov* (New York: Heritage, 1949), 279.

14. Ibid., 245.

Chapter 14: Charles Dickens

1. Charles Dickens, *Bleak House,* in *The Works of Charles Dickens in Thirty Volumes* (New York: P. F. Collier & Son, n.d.), 1.

2. Charles Dickens, *Pickwick Papers,* in *The Works of Charles Dickens in Thirty Volumes* (New York: P. F. Collier & Son, n.d.), 614.

3. Charles Dickens, *The Old Curiosity Shop,* in *The Works of Charles Dickens in Thirty Volumes* (New York: P. F. Collier & Son, n.d.), 508–9.

4. Ibid., 77.

5. Charles Dickens, *David Copperfield,* in *The Works of Charles Dickens in Thirty Volumes* (New York: P. F. Collier & Son, n.d.), 52.

6. Ibid., 53.

7. Ibid., 25–26.

8. Ibid., 50.

Chapter 15: Evelyn Waugh

1. Martin Stannard, *Evelyn Waugh: The Early Years, 1903–1939* (London: J. M. Dent, 1986), 1.

2. Ibid., 2.

3. Christopher Sykes, *Evelyn Waugh: A Biography* (Hammondsworth, England: Penguin, 1977), 181.

4. Evelyn Waugh, quoted in Martin Stannard, *Evelyn Waugh: The Early Years, 1903–1939* (London: J. M. Dent, 1986), 3.

5. Evelyn Waugh, *The Essays, Articles, and Reviews of Evelyn Waugh,* ed. Donat Gallagher (Boston: Little, Brown, 1983), 161–62.

6. Ibid., 206.

7. Evelyn Waugh, *A Handful of Dust* (Boston: Little, Brown, 1934), 38.

8. Ibid., 79.

9. Ibid., 287–88.

10. T. S. Eliot, *The Complete Poems and Plays,* 1909–1950 (New York: Harcourt Brace, 1971), 143.

11. Evelyn Waugh, *Brideshead Revisited* (Boston: Little, Brown, 1945), from a preface that was suppressed in later editions.

12. Waugh, *Essays, Articles, and Reviews,* 304.

13. Waugh, *Brideshead Revisited,* 89.

14. Ibid.

15. Thomas Howard, speech, (n.d.).

16. Waugh, *Brideshead Revisited* (Boston: Little, Brown, 1945), 309.

17. Ibid., 133.

18. Evelyn Waugh, *Brideshead Revisited* (Boston: Little, Brown, 1945), from a preface that was suppressed in later editions.

Chapter 16: Sherwood Anderson

1. Sherwood Anderson, *Winesburg, Ohio* (New York: Penguin Classics, 1987), 58.

2. Ibid., 163.

3. Ibid., 164–65.

4. Ibid., 228.

5. Ibid., 36.

6. Ibid.

7. Ibid., 30.

8. Ibid., 31.

9. Ibid., 60.

10. Ibid., 62.

11. Ibid., 121.

12. Ibid., 123.

13. Ibid., 122.

14. Ibid., 127.

15. Ibid., 172.

16. Ibid., 175.

17. Ibid., 231.

18. Ibid., 232.

19. Ibid., 241.

20. Ibid., 247.

Chapter 17: Native Perspectives on the Written Word

1. *Indian Oratory: Famous Speeches by Noted Indian Chieftains,* comp. W. C. Van-

derwerth (Norman, Okla.: University of Oklahoma Press, 1971), 127.

2. Ibid., 148.

3. Ibid., 153.

4. Ibid., 44–47.

5. Ibid., 244.

6. Diane Glancy, "The Bible and *Black Elk Speaks*," *The Cold-and-Hunger Dance* (Lincoln: University of Nebraska Press, 1998), 37–48.

7. Ibid., 43.

8. Ibid., 39.

9. Ibid., 22.

10. N. Scott Momaday, *House Made of Dawn* (New York: Harper & Row, 1968), 89–90.

11. Ibid., 91.

12. Ibid., 132–33.

13. Louis Erdrich, *Love Medicine* (New York: Harper Perennial, 1993), 236.

Chapter 18: Flannery O'Connor

1. Flannery O'Connor, *Wise Blood* (New York: Farrar, Straus & Giroux, 2000).

2. Flannery O'Connor, *The Violent Bear It Away* (New York: Farrar, Straus & Giroux, 1987).

3. Flannery O'Connor, *A Good Man Is Hard to Find* (New York: Harcourt Brace, 1992).

4. Flannery O'Connor, *Everything That Rises Must Converge* (New York: Farrar, Straus & Giroux, 1965).

5. Flannery O'Connor, *The Habit of Being*, ed. Sally Fitzgerald (New York: Farrar, Straus & Giroux, 1979), 97.

6. Ibid., 90.

7. Ibid., 15.

8. Ibid., 5.

9. Flannery O'Connor, *Mystery and Manners* (New York: Farrar, Straus & Giroux, 1979), 111.

10. Ibid., 157.

11. Ibid., 27.

12. O'Connor, *Wise Blood,* 206.

13. O'Connor, *Mystery and Manners,* 167–68.

Chapter 19: Aleksandr Solzhenitsyn

1. Aleksandr Solzhenitsyn, *One Day in the Life of Ivan Denisovich* (New York: Bantam, 1981), 203.

2. Edward Ericson, *Solzhenitsyn: The Moral Vision* (Grand Rapids: Eerdmans, 1980), 147.

3. Aleksandr Solzhenitsyn, *Gulag Archipelago,* vol. III (New York: Harper & Row, 1974), 359.

4. Aleksandr Solzhenitsyn, "Aleksandr Isaevich Solzhenitsyn—Nobel Lecture," *Nobel e-Museum* <http://www.nobel.se/literature/laureates/1970/solzhenitsyn-lecture.html#not_2> (May 2002).

5. Aleksandr Solzhenitsyn, *Letter to the Soviet Leaders* (New York: Harper & Row, 1974), 49–50.

6. Solzhenitsyn, *Letter to the Soviet Leaders,* 57.

7. Aleksandr Solzhenitsyn, *The Oak and the Calf* (New York: Harper & Row, 1980), 379.

8. Solzhenitsyn, "Nobel Lecture."

9. Alexander Schmemann, "On Solzhenitsyn," *Aleksandr Solzhenitsyn: Critical Essays and Documentary Materials,* ed. John B. Dunlop, Richard Haugh, and Alexis Klimoff, 2d ed. (New York: Collier Books, 1975), 39.

10. Ibid., 40.

11. Aleksandr Solzhenitsyn, *Cancer Ward* (New York: Bantam, 1969), 485.

12. Richard Heinberg, *Memories and Visions of Paradise* (Wheaton, Ill.: Theosophical, 1995).

13. Solzhenitsyn, "Nobel Lecture."

14. Appendix to Aleksandr Solzhenitsyn, *Cancer Ward* (New York: Bantam, 1969), 550. Also in appendix to Aleksandr Solzhenitsyn, *The Oak and the Calf* (New York: Harper & Row, 1980), 473.

15. Aleksandr Solzhenitsyn, *Warning to the West* (New York: Farrar, Straus, & Giroux, 1976), 106.

16. David Aikman, quoted in Paul Gray, "Russia's Prophet in Exile," *Time,* 24 July 1989, 56.

Chapter 20: Ray Bradbury

1. Ray Bradbury, "The Renaissance Prince and the Baptist Martian," *Horizon* (July 1979): 65.
2. Ibid., 64.
3. Ray Bradbury, "The Rocket Man," *R Is for Rocket* (New York: Doubleday, 1962), 45–46.
4. Ray Bradbury, "Prologue," *The Illustrated Man* (New York: Doubleday, 1951), 2.
5. Ibid., 3.
6. Ibid., 2.
7. Ibid., 3.
8. Ibid.
9. Ibid., 4.
10. Bradbury, "Renaissance Prince and the Baptist Martian," 66.
11. Ray Bradbury, "It Changed My Life," *Reader's Digest* (June 1983): 13–16.
12. Ray Bradbury, "God Is Alive in This Part of the Universe," *U.S. News & World Report* (25 June 1979): 56.
13. Ray Bradbury, "There Is Life on Mars," *Reader's Digest* (November 1981): 107.
14. Ray Bradbury, *Dandelion Wine* (New York: Doubleday, 1957), 177–78.
15. Ray Bradbury, *Something Wicked This Way Comes* (New York: Simon & Schuster, 1962), 98.
16. Ray Bradbury, *The Toynbee Convector* (New York: Alfred A. Knopf, 1988), 2.
17. Ibid., 7–9.
18. Bradbury, "God Is Alive in This Part of the Universe," 56.

Chapter 21: Alice Munro

1. Alice Munro, "Miles City, Montana," *The Progress of Love* (New York: Viking Penguin, 1986), 99.
2. Alice Munro, "Jesse and Meribeth," *The Progress of Love* (New York: Viking Penguin, 1986), 162.
3. Alice Munro, "Accident," *The Moons of Jupiter* (New York: Viking Penguin, 1986), 78.
4. Ibid., 109.
5. Alice Munro, "Labor Day Dinner," *The Moons of Jupiter* (New York: Viking Penguin, 1986), 158.
6. Ibid., 159.
7. Munro, "Miles City, Montana," 105.

Philip Yancey earned graduate degrees in communications and English from Wheaton College Graduate School and the University of Chicago. He joined the staff of *Campus Life* magazine in 1971 and worked there as an editor for eight years. A freelance writer, more than six hundred of his articles have appeared in eighty different publications, including *Reader's Digest, Publishers Weekly, National Wildlife, Saturday Evening Post, Christian Century,* and *The Reformed Journal.* He writes articles and a monthly column for *Christianity Today* magazine, which he serves as editor-at-large. He also serves as cochair on the editorial board for *Books and Culture.* His books include *Soul Survivor, Where Is God When It Hurts, The Student Bible,* and *Disappointment with God.* He is the recipient of twelve Gold Medallion Awards, and his books have sold more than five million copies. The Yanceys live in Colorado.

James Calvin Schaap earned graduate degrees in English from Arizona State University and the University of Wisconsin-Milwaukee. A former high school teacher, he has been a professor of English at his undergraduate alma mater, Dordt College, in Sioux Center, Iowa, since 1976. His many works include essays, feature articles, plays, short stories, and novels, the most recent of his novels being *Things Hoped For, Things Not Seen; Paternity; Romey's Place;* and *The Secrets of Barneveld Calvary.* He is the recipient of numerous awards including several from the Associated Church Press Association and the Evangelical Press Association. The father of two adult children, he and his wife, Barbara Van Gelder, live in Iowa.